THE

SYRIAN CHURCH IN INDIA

D1871158

THE
SYRIAN CHURCH IN INDIA

GEORGE MILNE RAE, M.A.

GYAN

Published by

GYAN

Gyan Publishing House
5, Ansari Road
Daryaganj, New Delhi-110002
Phone: 011-47034999, 9811692060
E-mail: books@gyanbooks.com

Distribution Network
gyanbooks.com
India, USA, Canada, UK, Australia, France

© Publisher

All rights reserved. No part of this work may be reproduced, stored, adapted, or transmitted in any form or by any means, electronic, mechanical, photocopying, micro-filming, recording or otherwise, or translated in any language, without the prior written permission of the copyright owner and the publisher.

ISBN : 978-81-212-9166-8 (PB)
First Published, 1892

2nd Impression 2023

Printed at: Gyan Press, Delhi.

The book is sold subject to the condition that it shall not, by way of trade or otherwise, be lent, resold, hired out, or otherwise circulated without the prior publisher's written consent.

THE SYRIAN CHURCH IN INDIA
Author: GEORGE MILNE RAE

THE

SYRIAN CHURCH IN INDIA

PERSIAN CROSS IN OLD CHURCH AT COTTAYAM.

About Tenth Century.

Frontispiece.

THE SYRIAN CHURCH IN INDIA

BY

GEORGE MILNE RAE, M.A.

FELLOW OF THE UNIVERSITY OF MADRAS; LATE PROFESSOR
IN THE MADRAS CHRISTIAN COLLEGE

WILLIAM BLACKWOOD AND SONS
EDINBURGH AND LONDON
MDCCCXCII

TO

MY WIFE

PREFACE.

The Syrian Church in India, which is sometimes called the Church of the Christians of St Thomas, has hitherto been but little known in the West. The first of the European nations that held intercourse with it was the Portuguese, and it was from the records of the ecclesiastical relations between the Portuguese and the Syrians that Michael Geddes compiled his 'History of the Church of Malabar' (1694), which was the first work in English on the subject, and is still of considerable value. Gibbon, who approached it by a different route, introduced into a memorable chapter of the 'Decline and Fall' a notice of the ancient Church which for comprehensiveness of grasp and general accuracy has not been surpassed. But it was reserved for Claudius Buchanan, whose aims were of a distinctly practical character, to habilitate in this country a knowledge of the Syrian Christians.

Buchanan, however, did not write history but only an account of his own travels and observations; and, in so far as he touched on Syrian history or Syrian doctrine, his information was imperfect and in many cases misleading. He depended for light largely on the talk of the Syrians themselves. Still, his 'Christian Researches in Asia,' which seldom failed to communicate a gleam of his own enthusiasm to his followers, became the chief guide of a band of writers, who, it must be added, never moved out of traditional grooves.

When some twenty-four years ago I went as a missionary to Madras in the service of the Free Church of Scotland, I came, like Buchanan, into direct touch with the Syrians. I found that there were always representatives of the Syrian community among my students in the Christian College. During the midsummer vacation in 1870, I paid a visit to the Malabar coast, where the Church had existed from a date earlier than the coming of St Augustine and his monks to Canterbury. From time to time I examined the holy places sacred to St Thomas in the neighbourhood of Madras, where a sister Syrian Church had existed for the better part of a thousand years, and ceased to be only about the time when Luther was becoming a power in Europe. But satisfactory historical knowledge seemed hard to acquire, and something more was demanded than Geddes, or Gibbon, or Buchanan and his following, or the Syrians themselves could supply.

At length I was led into more fruitful fields of inquiry. I explored the primitive traditions concerning St Thomas, with a view to ascertain the origin and value of the local tradition. I studied the history of Christianity in other parts of Asia, with a view to discover the true kinship of the Syrian Church. I became acquainted with the results of archæological research and of Dravidian scholarship relevant to my subject. I tracked the footsteps of travellers in India in the middle ages, and followed the political relations of European peoples to the dwellers on the Malabar coast. Finally, I acquired possession of copies of the documents, the evidence of witnesses, and the decisions of the judges in a case of disputed succession in the bishopric of the Syrian Church, which ran the gauntlet of the civil courts of Travancore, and which remained for ten years, 1879-89, on their files. Of my obligations to these classes of authorities, and to others, specific acknowledgments are made in an appendix of notes.

Certain of the following chapters appeared in such Indian periodicals as the 'Madras Christian College Magazine,' the 'Indian Evangelical Review,' and the 'Harvest Field.' I was anxious to offer facilities for criticism to educated members of the Syrian community, from whose views on the origin of their Church I strongly differed. My challenge, if I may call it such, was promptly taken up by a Syrian graduate of the Madras University. From others, suggestions of value were received. Many of the chapters therefore have been entirely recast; and the work, which has been prepared in the midst of a busy missionary life, is now submitted to the kindly consideration of scholars and the public, as a contribution to the history of Christianity in India.

G. M. R.

CONTENTS.

INTRODUCTION.

THE NESTORIAN PERIOD.

THE ROMAN PERIOD.

THE JACOBITE PERIOD.

ILLUSTRATIONS.

INTRODUCTION

*** *The reference figures in this volume apply to Notes collected in the Appendix.*

THE SYRIAN CHURCH IN INDIA.

CHAPTER I.

THE HOME OF THE SYRIANS.

THE SYRIAN CHURCH of Southern India is the oldest of all the Indian Churches. It has seen the lapse of nearly fourteen centuries of time, and it still lives as a community more than 400,000 strong on the mountain-slopes and in the valleys of the Malabar coast.

Malankarai, which is the official designation of the Syrian diocese, falls within two native States allied for the last hundred years as feudatories to the British Government. It includes the whole of Cochin and the northern or Malayalam-speaking portion of Travancore, as far south as Trivandrum, the capital.

The largest number, and probably the most enlightened of the Syrians, dwell to-day in Travancore.

This land in which the Syrians live is possessed of extraordinary riches in respect to both its fauna and its flora.[1] On his recent visit to Southern India, one of the entertainments arranged for his Royal Highness the late Duke of Clarence and Avondale was a run into the hunting-grounds of Travancore after such big game as elephants and bison, tigers and black panthers; while the export of pepper and cardamoms, together with the fibre and other products of the palm-tree, enrich the markets alike of the Old World and the New. Its ever green undulations of surface form a striking contrast to the often parched plains on the eastern side of the Ghauts.

The most outstanding feature of the landscape is the great water-way which runs from end to end of Malankarai. It consists of a series of lakes, connected with one another, and separated from the sea by a belt of land. Sometimes this back-water expands to a breadth of many miles, sometimes contracts to quite narrow channels. The banks are clothed with cocoanut-palms and studded with villages. All traffic is by water, and vessels of many sorts and sizes are seen gliding in all directions, giving life and animation to the foreground of a picture which is rendered still more impressive by a background of lofty mountains. Along this route the voyager may travel, if he avoids the monsoon, with much enjoyment. In one of the commodious cabin-boats, manned by some fifteen lusty brown rowers, whose indefatigable labours are accompanied with songs or responsive chants in ringing metallic notes, he is borne along at the rate of from four to five miles an hour, with a wealth of tropical vegetation mirrored in the bright blue waters by day, and the flitting light of myriads of fire-flies at night, so that at every turn he is almost constrained to fancy himself in fairy-land. The Brahmans have invented the legend that all this region west of the Ghauts was rescued from the sea by Parasurama, an incarnation of Vishnu; and, if it was so, the feat was worthy of his mace.

The civil government of these two native States has long been remarkably successful. The members of the royal families have in some cases been accomplished men, a series of able native dewans have been at the head of the administration, and the whole has been in a manner controlled by a British Political Resident.

The Rajahs are Sudras, not Brahmans—an illustration of the fact that, when the Brahmans first came to Southern India, they sometimes found the government in the hands of native princes, whom they had the best of all reasons for not attempting to replace. In the division of Sudras to which the Rajahs belong, commonly called Nayars, a peculiar law of inheritance obtains. Succession runs in the female line. With us the king is succeeded by his son or his son's son, but there he is succeeded by his sister's son or his sister's daughter's son. Normally the nephew is the heir. If the king's sister has several sons, the eldest may be succeeded by the second, and the second by the third, and so on. In the event of sisters or sisters' daughters failing, recourse must be had to adoption of women from other families, who thus, according to law and custom, become the sisters of the princes of the blood-royal. The Rajah's own children usually receive some private property in the lifetime of their father, but have no claim on the throne or royal honours; and their descendants in course of time sink to the level of ordinary Sudras. Nor is this peculiar law of inheritance [2] confined to the royal families. The sons of any woman of that caste inherit the property and heritable honours, not of the father, but of their mother's brother.

They are their uncle's nearest heirs, and he is their legal guardian. A man's sister's son and a woman's own son, as their respective nearest blood relatives, perform (if their age permits) the funeral rites on their decease.

The sovereigns of Travancore have to pass through a singular experience. They are, as we have seen, not Brahmans, but Sudras; and, although the law of the Brahman is the same as that of the poet — he is born, not made — yet the Maharajah of Travancore is an exception of the kind which proves the rule. He is made a Brahman, and the ceremony by which this transformation is effected is curious.[3] His Highness is first weighed against gold taken from his own treasury, which is then melted and worked into the form of a hollow cow. Into this hollow cow the Maharajah is laid, and then removed, and thus born again—the cow being a peculiarly sacred animal in Hindu symbolism, and possessing a sort of sacramental virtue. But this old-fashioned method of exhibiting the pagan idea of regeneration has been superseded within recent memory by another, perhaps less undignified. The gold in this case is worked into the form of a hollow cylinder, surmounted by a lotus-shaped cover adorned with precious stones — the lotus among flowers being considered peculiarly sacred. The entrance of the king into this cylinder, and his exit from it — preceded, accompanied, and followed by worshipful acts of an idolatrous character—are supposed to produce the desired effect; one indispensable condition to be fulfilled by the royal neophyte being that, whatever form the golden matrix may have taken, the cow or lotus-crowned cylinder, having served its purpose, shall be converted into coins and distributed among the Brahmans, in return for the doubtful privilege, which the now twice-born Maharajah thenceforward enjoys, of being no longer able to eat food with the members of his own family.

This weighing ceremony is not in general performed immediately on the accession of a sovereign; and it has been suggested that it is put off to allow his Highness time to increase in stoutness and weight, and so the more to fatten the Brahmans. Indeed there are darker rumours, to the effect that the days of the Maharajah are sometimes shortened by means not sanctioned in the moral law, on the unacknowledged plea that the oftener such an enriching ceremonial is repeated the better. However this may be, when the weighing ceremony was performed in 1870, the quantity of gold placed in the scale opposite to the Maharajah, weighted with his sword and shield, was 204 lb. avoirdupois. But this was only a small part of the expenses attending all the ceremonies connected with the materialistic exhibition of the idea of regeneration. If Travancore were not naturally rich, and well administered financially, it would be unable to stand such drains, in this and other forms, as are made on its revenue in the name of the gods.

With Brahmans, Nayars, and other Hindu castes, with agrestic slaves and others who have no caste at all, the Syrian Christians share the picturesque territory of Malankarai; and they have from time immemorial claimed to be, in point of social precedence, next to the Nayars. In daily contact with pagan life and isolated as they were for centuries from the rest of Christendom, it is not wonderful that the habits of thought, the forms of worship, and the life-practices of the Syrians have been found to differ from those of other Christian communities and to have become deteriorated. Nevertheless their adhesion to the worship of the one living God; their adoration of Father, Son, and Holy Spirit; their preservation and use of the Holy Scriptures in the *Peschito* version; their maintaining houses of prayer, and not forsaking the assembling of themselves together on the weekly Day of Rest; their administration of the Christian sacraments; their observance of the festivals of the Christian year; and the comparative respect and liberty accorded to their women;—all these things seem to entitle them to one of the many mansions in the visible Church.

They of course hold these doctrines and follow these practices in their own oriental way; and much ignorance and many errors no doubt mingle with them. Few weak communities, however, have suffered so much at the hands of stronger ones, on account of their being misunderstood and unsympathetically regarded. It seems always difficult for the ecclesiastical mind, of whatever school, to meet members of remote Churches on the broad platform of humanity, to deal with them in the first place as men bearing the image of God, and to be helpful to them apart altogether from considerations of proselytism. The Syrian Christians have suffered not only at the hands of non-Christian princes, but also at the hands of ecclesiastics, both European and Asiatic, more especially the Portuguese, so that in their isolation and distress they have been sometimes compared to the Waldenses. The valleys of Malabar have awakened memories of the valleys of Piedmont. The Syrians will still tell you, as they told Claudius Buchanan at the beginning of the century, how as a people they had seen better days, and how they had been harried not only by the pagan, but by folk from the West whom they had reason to expect to be their friends. The advent of the British to power on that coast delivered them from at least the coarser forms of persecution.

The Syrian churches are prominent objects in the landscape, being so much larger than the houses in the villages where they are built. Towers and spires are rare, and there is little show of architectural elegance. Unadorned structures of brick and plaster, roofed with tiles and dimly lighted, receive the Syrian worshippers. No seats are provided, and the idea of pews has not yet reached Malabar. At the western end of the church is a gallery, part of which is divided into rooms for the accommodation of the bishop on the occasion of his visits. Part of the nave immediately in front of the chancel is railed off, and is used as a place for the interment of priests;

and over this space hangs a brass lamp which is kept burning night and day, and from which oil is said to be sometimes taken for use in the baptismal service, and sometimes for medical purposes. In one of the side walls, and remote from the chancel, is the baptismal font, which consists of a hemispherical basin of hewn stone, large enough for the baptism of infants by immersion. Attached to or surrounding the central edifice are open sheds, cook-houses, and other buildings for the accommodation of the people on festive occasions.

Public worship is conducted chiefly in Syriac, and the Liturgy of St James, which has been made accessible to English readers,[4] is that which is now used in the diocese. Additions, apparently authorised, are sometimes made to the Order of St James. Claudius Buchanan, for example, describes an act which pleased him much at the close of a service which he witnessed one Sunday. "The priest (or bishop if he be present)," he says, "comes forward, and all the people pass by him as they go out, receiving his benediction individually. If any man has been guilty of any immorality, he does not receive the blessing; and this, in their primitive and patriarchal state, is accounted a severe punishment." "Instruction by preaching," he adds, "is little used among them now."

Again, the Rev. S. Mateer, who has been for many years a missionary in Travancore, and who was present one Sunday at public worship in a Syrian church, describes a ceremony called 'giving the peace,' "which," he says, "was performed before the consecration of the elements. The deacon who carried the censer took from it a double handful of the smoke, which he smelled, and then appeared to hand it to the priest, who received it with both hands. Going to the people, he gave it into the hands of two or three of the nearest, who put it to their faces, and then pretended to pass it on to the others, till it went round the whole congregation. One of the good people came up to me where I was standing, and said, 'Do you want this peace, sir? This is the sign of peace.' 'Yes,' I replied, and gave my hand, which he took in both his and slightly stroked."

As a rule, marriages are celebrated on Sundays, and forbidden on fast-days; and the bride and bridegroom must attend public worship before being married, else a fine is imposed.

The local head of the church is the bishop or metran (*i.e.*, metropolitan), with priests (*cattanars*) and deacons under him. In old times the metran not only was the spiritual ruler of his people, but also had, within certain limits, jurisdiction over them in civil and criminal affairs. Even still he retains some tokens of a departed glory. When he makes a visit of ceremony, his state palanquin, the red umbrellas of his attendants, the white dresses of the priests, and the flutter of a little crowd of hangers-on, form a picturesque group in procession. On such an occasion he wears a cassock of figured lawn over crimson satin, and a tippet of embroidered cloth stiff with gold; a mitre of red and green velvet, with gold ornamentation; a golden cross studded with rubies on his breast; an ornamental bag in his hand; while a silver crosier is carried behind him by an attendant priest.[5]

The metran's position might still be one of great and beneficent influence over a peaceful, industrious, and fairly prosperous section of the people of the Malabar coast. But we can hardly be in a position to understand the divided condition of the diocese and other causes of its present weakness, or to attempt to forecast its future, until after we have traced the evolutions of its history from the beginning down to the present time.

CHAPTER II.

THE MIGRATION OF A TRADITION.

THE SYRIAN CHURCH of Southern India is a most interesting monument of the permanence of the fruit of missionary effort. It is a heretical branch of the Oriental Church, and its history must be viewed in relation to the history of Christianity in other parts of Asia.

Unfortunately its history has been overgrown by a mass of local tradition. The local tradition postulates the personal advent of St Thomas, the apostle, to peninsular India. The story goes that St Thomas, having landed at Malankara, an island in the lagoon near Cranganore, preached to the natives and baptised many that believed; that, having planted seven churches[1] on the Malabar coast like the seven churches of the Apocalypse, he ordained two priests over them and departed; that he went to Mailapore on the Coromandel coast and converted the king and all the people; that he extended his journey to China with like results; and that, returning to Mailapore, he excited by his successes the jealousy of the Brahmans, who stirred up the people to stone him, after which one of them thrust him through with a lance.

For these last scenes in the career of St Thomas, fitting localities have been invented. There are three such places in the neighbourhood of Madras. They are marked respectively by a grave, a cross, and a cave; at each a church has been built; and they are all under the jurisdiction of the Roman Catholic Bishop of Mailapore, who is subject to the Archbishop of Goa.

The first of these holy places is Mailapore, or, as the Portuguese named it, San Thomé, three miles south of Fort St George. Attached to the Roman Catholic cathedral is a little chapel, in the floor of which a trap-door gives access to what is popularly regarded as the grave of St Thomas. From this dark underground chamber many a handful of dust is, as in the days of Marco Polo, carried off by the faithful to cure diseases. Over the altar is a quaint old *scrinium*, with a cruciform reliquary, made of brass, and adorned with precious

RELIQUARY IN CHAPEL, MAILAPORE CATHEDRAL.

Said to contain the Relics of St Thomas.

stones, in which are deposited some of the ashes and bones of the apostle, together with fragments of the spear by which he won the crown of martyrdom.

The discovery of these relics has all the interest of a little romance. It appears that in 1517 certain Portuguese adventurers visited the Coromandel coast in company with an Armenian merchant who was well acquainted with that part of India. They landed at Pulicat, and went thence to Mailapore, where they saw many ruined buildings and stones of divers colours, still retaining traces of ancient grandeur; whilst in the midst of these ruins was a chapel, entire, of mean appearance, on the inside and outside of which many crosses of a peculiar form were carved. It would seem that the Christian population of Mailapore had by that time become extinct[2]; but a Musalman who resided there, perceiving the strangers examining the locality, came up and told them that the church, of which only a small part was then standing, was the place where St Thomas and some of his first converts lay buried. No further action, however, seems to have been taken on this discovery until 1522, when Duarte Menezes, viceroy of Goa, in pursuance of orders from John III. of Portugal, appointed a commission to visit Mailapore and search for the body of St Thomas. The labours of this commission resulted in their unearthing, from beneath the ruins of the ancient church, what they believed to be the bones of the apostle, together with those of the king whom he converted. It was easy for them, they thought, to distinguish the apostle's bones on account of their superior whiteness, and to identify the head of the fatal lance, found at the same time. The relics thus discovered were transported to Goa, and received into the city with great rejoicings, and deposited in a shrine enriched with silver, in the church named after St Thomas. It must be presumed that a portion of the relics was left at Mailapore.

The second of the holy places is St Thomas's Mount, about eight miles south-west of Fort St George. There, in 1547, while the foundations of a chapel or hermitage were being dug, there was found a slab of dark granite, two feet by one and a half, which may have been cut from the rocks near Sadras and Mahabalipuram. One face of it was adorned with a bas-relief cross of the Greek type, with floreated ornamentation at all the ends. At the top of the upright shaft is figured a bird like a dove, with its wings expanded, "as the Holy

Ghost is usually represented when descending on our Lord at His baptism, or on our Lady at her Annunciation." It has an inscription upon it which was then wholly unintelligible. But this symbol of Christianity, with its mysterious words, was at once connected with St Thomas; and the unintelligible inscription had not long to wait for an interpreter. An unscrupulous Brahman, knowing what was wanted or expected, volunteered to apply his learned mind to the solution of the difficult problem. He represented that the characters were hieroglyphs, and explained that the inscription set forth the story of the incarnation and of the spread of Christianity in the world through the agency of the twelve apostles; how one of the apostles came to Mailapore "with a pilgrim's staff in his hand;" and how "the time came when St Thomas died at the hands of a Brahman, and his blood formed a cross."[3] Assurance about the correctness of this rendering was made doubly sure when "another learned person from a distant part of the country was sent for, and, without having any communication with the first, or knowing his interpretation, gave one to the same effect."[3]

Looking back across the generations, and having a scientific rendering of the brief inscription before us,[4] we may regard this double hoax with some degree of amusement. But it is not so easy to treat with equanimity the pious frauds practised by certain Portuguese ecclesiastics who invested the cross with the power of working periodical miracles of the sweating kind, after the manner of St Januarius at Naples; while Menezes, Archbishop of Goa, instituted (1599) a festival of the Church, to be observed annually on the 18th of December, "being the day whereon the holy cross of St Thomas did sweat." [5]

The third holy place is the Little Mount, six miles south-west of Fort St George. It is situated on the right bank of the Adyar, at the end of the Marmalong bridge, and near the gate of Guindy Park, the suburban residence of the Governor of Madras. It is a bare scalp of rock, of insignificant height. In the rock there is a cave, where it is asserted that St Thomas took refuge from his pursuers. On the top of the rock there is a cleft, miraculously made by the apostle, into which he introduced a supply of living water to refresh him during the period of his concealment in the cave. The apostle's footprints here and there on the surface of the rock are also shown, to the admiration of the credulous. Over the cave a church has been built, whose walls are adorned with a slab bearing in relief a bust of St Thomas, with an inscription in Portuguese which attests the fact that the church was built by Antonio Gonsalvez de Taide at his own expense in 1612. This figure represents St Thomas as raising his right hand in the attitude of benediction, and holding in his left hand a carpenter's square.

To the Portuguese Roman Catholics we owe the preservation and embellishment of the local tradition. Had they not, for reasons of their own, tried by means of ecclesiastical festivals and other special devices to keep the memory of it alive, it would have probably perished, on the Coromandel coast at least, when that branch of the Syrian Church, which lingered there for the better part of a thousand years, vanished from history. Yet it is curious that, though the Portuguese Roman Catholics hold fast by every jot and tittle of the Thomas tradition, the authorities[6] of the Irish Roman Catholic Mission in Madras reject the whole *corpus* of local tradition about the apostle. On the other hand, not only the Syrians of the Malabar coast, but even some Protestants, hold by the substance of the local tradition, believing that thus an orthodox origin is secured for Christianity in India.

But, though we think it impossible to treat this local tradition as literal history, it is only fair to consider what those have to say who hold a different opinion. Writers who are inclined to favour the local tradition and to believe that "there is something in it," have usually pointed to certain landmarks in history, with a brief introductory dissertation on the probabilities of the case. It is not improbable, they allege, that one of the apostles should have found his way to India, seeing that from earliest times there was a great deal of coming and going between the West and the East. It is admitted on all hands, for instance, that there was a very active commerce between Southern India and the marts of the Roman Empire. Gems and spices, ivory and ebony and steel, silks and muslins, poured into the Roman market. Moreover, Southern India is full of Roman money to this day. Coins of copper, of silver, and of gold—sometimes in hundreds together—have been found in many districts of the Madras Presidency, in Nellore, Coimbatore, Salem, Madura, and Malabar. In the collection of coins found in Southern India, and lodged in the Madras Government Museum, all the emperors from Augustus to Hadrian, and not a few of later date, are represented.[7] From facts like these it is contended that it would be strange indeed if, while merchants were thus finding their way to the heathen Orient, no missionaries of the Cross should have attempted to follow in their wake. All the probabilities, it is maintained, are in favour of the supposition that at least some Christians must have penetrated thus far into the East, and that a South Indian Church therefore may have existed from apostolic times. But such reasoning is based rather on modern missionary ideas than on ancient Church history. Moreover, the question is one of fact, and not one of mere probability.

Still, it is argued, there is a series of passages in Church history which distinctly refer to the existence of a Church in India in early times; and, though none of these are within the first century, yet they form, as it were, a dotted line which may be held to be continuous at least between the extreme points, and may easily be supposed to run back into the apostolic age.

It will be found on examination, however, that the argument of every one of those passages turns upon a double meaning of the name India. In writings belonging to the early Christian centuries, as well as in writings much more ancient, the name India is often found in a sense altogether different from modern usage; so that we must, in every case where it occurs, determine from the context and such collateral evidence as may be available, in what precise acceptation it is employed. Thus the several passages in Church history which have been often applied to the history of the Church in Southern India, can be proved to have no connection with it whatever. They apply, as we shall show at a later stage, to other localities known likewise in those days by the name India. In short, we look in vain among the writings and monuments of the first five centuries for any attestation of the existence of a South Indian Church. No historical evidence, we submit, can be produced to show that such a Church was planted until the beginning of the sixth century. This being so, the notion that the local tradition can be regarded as literal history is absolutely discredited.

The view which seems on the whole most consistent with all the facts of the case is, that the local or South Indian tradition concerning St Thomas is an example of that curious phenomenon commonly described under the name of the migration of traditions. Not St Thomas, but only the tradition, migrated to Southern India.

To make good this position, it will be needful to

go back to the stories of the sub-apostolic age and to examine the post-canonical literature concerning St Thomas. More especially we shall have to examine the primitive traditions which represent him, now as the apostle of the Parthians, and now as the apostle of the Indians. Besides finding in these, and especially in the former, a foundation for that view of apostolic succession which runs through the whole history of the Syrian Church, we shall find proof that St Thomas is described as giving his services to the cause of Gospel propagation in a locality far removed from Southern India, and that he lived and laboured, died and was buried, in that remote locality, so that not only is no opportunity left for a visit to Southern India, but the possibility of it is excluded.

Not the least important result of examining the primitive tradition is, that it is seen to be the parent of the local tradition. The latter is but a clumsy reproduction of the former, both in what is personal and in what relates to the localities. Though so much is made now-a-days of the local tradition, the fact is that it was never heard of until a late date in the middle ages. There seems to be no definite reference to it in literature, so far as research has gone, earlier than the book of

Ser Marco Polo,[8] who visited Mailapore in 1292; although there is some reason to suppose that it may have been developed by the tenth century.

In the remaining chapters of this section we shall introduce the reader to the two primitive traditions concerning St Thomas as the apostle of the Parthians and as the apostle of the Indians, and shall submit a critical examination of those passages in Church history which have been used to uphold the local tradition, or at least to support for the South Indian Church a date of origin earlier than history, rightly interpreted, seems to warrant. In a subsequent section[9] we hope to describe the causes and the process of the development of the local tradition, and thus still further to show that it is an example of migration.

CHAPTER III.

ST THOMAS, THE APOSTLE OF THE PARTHIANS.

THE legends of the sub-apostolic age describe a past that never was present, and yet they are full of instruction to the historian. If they do not always describe facts, they at least record opinions; if they do not trace the evolutions of actual history, they at least exhibit the interpretation of facts adopted by ecclesiastical authority, and accepted by the generations following as a basis of belief; and acts founded on the belief of such traditions can be understood only through some acquaintance with the traditions themselves.

Some of these legends have arisen in connection with the allotment of fields of labour for the apostles. The principle accepted by the ecclesiastical mind of the period was, that, wherever

Christianity might be found in any particular country, it must have been originally planted there by an apostle; indeed this was perhaps needful as a foundation whereon to build a theory of apostolic succession. Accordingly it was held that, soon after the ascension of our Lord, fields of labour were assigned to the apostles by lot. Some obtained one region, and others another; but ecclesiastical authorities have never been quite agreed as to the delimitation of the fields originally assigned; and in some cases additions were made long afterwards to the original allotment. Thus St Thomas was, according to some authorities, made the apostle of the Parthians; while, according to others, he became the apostle of the Indians. But, as a matter of fact, he was in later times recognised as the apostle of the whole East, the apostle of all the regions east of the Euphrates in which Christianity had found a footing, including Southern India, Northern China, and Eastern Tartary; and there have been times when the Church of St Thomas had at least as many members as that of St Peter.

It is not easy to discover the *rationale* of the favour accorded by the oriental mind to St Thomas, and yet it may have proceeded from a true instinct. The supremacy of St Peter in the Church of the West is largely due to particular interpretations of our Lord's words in connection with the confession made by the 'man of rock' at Cæsarea Philippi; and may not the high place accorded to St Thomas in the East be similarly based on his noble confession, when he exclaimed in the presence of his brethren, "My Lord and my God"?

But whatever may be the true explanation of the extraordinary favour with which the Orient accepted St Thomas as its apostle, it is tolerably clear that the doctrine embodied in St Thomas's confession as a *datum* of experience was, especially in the earlier generations and in the martyr age, a prominent factor in the life of the Church of Edessa, which is the source of all our post-canonical information concerning St Thomas.

Beautiful for situation was the city of Edessa. On the banks of the Daisan, which feeds the Belik, a left-hand tributary of the upper Euphrates, it is famous for its fountains of living water, from which it acquired the epithet Callirhoë, the City of the Fair Streams. It was the capital of the little kingdom of Osrohene, in the higher latitudes of Mesopotamia, between Mount Masius and the river Chaboras on the east, and the great bend of the Euphrates below Samosata on the west. It was ruled by a series of elective monarchs, who each bore the title of Abgar, just as the kings of Egypt were called Pharaohs, the Roman emperors Cæsars, and the kings of Syria Antiochi.

The Abgars were tributary vassals of the great Parthian empire, which was the second power in the world for three hundred years, and formed a counterpoise to Rome. Its territories extended from the Indus to the Euphrates, and from the Indian Ocean to the Caspian Sea and the Hindu Kush. Over this vast area the Parthian kings—the Arsacids, as they were patronymically called, after Arsaces, the founder of the dynasty—exercised dominion on a well-recognised plan, not unlike in some respects to the feudal system in Europe. They established in the various countries either viceroys holding office for life, or sometimes dependent dynasties of kings. In either case the rulers, so long as they paid tribute regularly to the Parthian monarchs and aided them in their wars, were allowed to govern the people beneath their sway at their pleasure. The viceroys were fourteen or fifteen in number; and among monarchs, besides the King of Osrohene, were those of Persia, Elimais, Adiabene, and of Armenia and Atropatene, when they formed, as they sometimes did, portions of the Parthian empire.[1] Thus the Abgars were dependent monarchs; and Edessa came to be known, in her own native literature, as 'Edessa of the Parthians.'

The precise date at which Christianity was introduced into Edessa cannot be ascertained; but several converging lines of evidence, which we cannot here trace out, lead to the conclusion that it must have been well established early in the second century, from which time the City of the Fair Streams became a centre of light for generations to the regions beyond. Edessa became famous for its schools of learning; many of its learned men were employed on the translation of the Scriptures into the Syriac language; and, according to some of our best scholars, the translation of the New Testament into Syriac was first made at Edessa itself; so that for reasons like these it has been called the 'Athens of Syria.' The strength of its spiritual life may be indicated by the number of its citizens who thought the truth of more value than life and sacrificed themselves as martyrs, and by the hosts of missionaries who went forth from it spreading far and near the good tidings of salvation.

But, as the noblest trees may have their vitality sapped by parasites, so the spiritual life of Edessa became tainted by sacerdotalism and a love of relics, and more especially the relics of St Thomas; and hence it was led to invent stories to bolster up its fantastic notions on these subjects.

Of all the documents which connect St Thomas directly or indirectly with Edessa, probably the earliest is one which Eusebius[2] discovered among the public records of that city; and, whatever may be thought of the historian's opinion of its authenticity, his report of its contents has been curiously confirmed by its reappearance within our own day. For among the manuscripts acquired by the British Museum in 1841, 1843, and 1847, from the Nitrian Monastery in Lower Egypt, Dr Cureton tells us that he found a considerable portion of the Aramaic document which Eusebius cites as preserved in the archives of Edessa.[3] This document contains two letters which purport to have been written in the fifteenth year of the Roman Emperor Tiberius. The writer of the first letter was Abgar Uchomo, or Abgar the Black. It appears that Abgar had occasion to send messengers to Phœnicia, who there heard of the works of marvellous beneficence that were being done by Jesus Christ at Jerusalem. Thither accordingly they extended their journey to verify the strange intelligence. Like the Queen of Sheba, they found that the half had not been told them; and, on their return to Edessa, they related at Abgar's court all they had seen and heard. It came to pass soon afterwards that Abgar fell sick of a grievous disease, and he despatched Anan, his *tabularius*, who had brought the tidings from Jerusalem, with a letter to Jesus, begging Him to come and cure him, promising at the same time to share his kingdom with "the excellent Saviour," and to protect Him from the Jews. The same document contains the reply which Abgar Uchomo is said to have received, to the effect that Jesus had work in Jerusalem which He might not leave; but that, after He had been "received up," He would send one of His disciples to cure the king and to give life to those with him. Now it was Judas Thomas—as the apostle seems almost invariably to be called in Edessene literature—who, according to the legend, acted as Christ's amanuensis in writing this reply, and it was Judas Thomas who "by a divine impulse" sent Thaddæus,[4] after the ascension, to Edessa, where he not only restored the king's health, but spread the Christian faith throughout his dominions. He built churches in Edessa and the villages far and near, and finished and adorned them, and appointed in them deacons and elders, and instructed those who should read the Scriptures, and taught the ordinances of the ministry "within and without." After all these things he fell ill of the sickness of which he departed from this world. And he called for Aggæus[5] before the whole assembly of the Church, and bade him draw near, and made him "guide and ruler" in his stead. And Palut, who was a deacon, he made elder; and Abshelama, who was a scribe, he made deacon. And so Thaddæus left a name and an example which lived long in Edessa.

As the master had done, so did the disciple. Aggæus too, with the same ordination which he had received, made "priests and guides" in the whole of Mesopotamia, including Persia, the Assyrians, the Armenians, and the countries round about Babylon as far as the borders of the Indians.

Now Aggæus was, before he entered into the service of the Church, a maker of silks, and in his day the throne was occupied by one of Abgar Uchomo's wicked sons, who sent word to Aggæus saying, "Make me a head-band of gold, such as those thou usedst to make for my fathers in former times." To such an insolent message there was only one possible reply, with which the king was so enraged that he despatched a second messenger, who brake the legs of Aggæus as he sat in the church expounding; so that the bishop suddenly died, and there was no time for him to lay his hands on Palut, his destined successor. Palut, therefore, went to Antioch and received ordination at the hands of Serapion, the bishop of that see.

Not to dwell on the flagrant anachronism in this story—Serapion being Bishop of Antioch at the end of the second century—the point to be noted is the fact of the dependence of Edessa on the see of Antioch at the time when these stories were invented. But from the beginning it had not been so. These stories were intended to prove that the succession of Edessene bishops was in the last resort traceable to St Thomas.

The same device was repeated, only on a larger scale, in connection with the work of Maris,[6] another disciple of Thaddæus, who went to Ctesiphon, the capital city of the Parthian kings. Ctesiphon was situated on the left bank of the Tigris, just opposite to Seleucia; and the double city—hence called by the Arabs Al Modain—afterwards became the head of the vast Patriarchate of the East. Mar Maris is said to have discipled Doorkhan, Cashgar, the two Iraks, Al Ahwaz, Yemen, and the Island of Socotra, and to have returned to Ctesiphon, where at a good age he died. His disciples, who had diligently inquired of the dying bishop about his successor, and been instructed to "seek him at Jerusalem," sent at once to the Holy City to demand a prelate for the East; and the venerable Simeon sent them Abres, a kinsman of his own, who during an episcopate of sixteen years consecrated a large number of bishops, and was much beloved for his charity. His immediate successors, Abraham and Jacob, both of the same family as Abres, were consecrated at Antioch; and after them an important change was introduced into the administration. When the see of Seleucia-Ctesiphon became vacant after the death of Jacob, his son Achadabues and Jab-Jesus were both sent by the Church to Antioch, with a request that the bishop of that see would consecrate whichever of the two he thought the most worthy of the dignity. They were both, however, arrested by the Roman prefect as Persian spies; and Jab-Jesus with his host was crucified, while Achadabues escaped to Jerusalem and there received consecration. But the incident suggested an arrangement whereby it should be unnecessary for the bishop-elect in future to seek consecration at Antioch. The bishop of this see renounced his right of ordination; and so, when Seleucia-Ctesiphon again fell vacant, a synod of bishops was assembled, and the prelate-elect received consecration at their hands. Thus the link between Seleucia-Ctesiphon and Antioch seems to have been practically severed, and the former became, as it is called, Autocephalus—a change in the external relations of the Parthian Church which was effected not long before the dynasty of the Arsacids was overthrown by the Sassanians in the year 226.

Without insisting on the anachronisms which likewise characterise the lists of the bishops of Seleucia-Ctesiphon, it is to be observed that about the time when these stories were written, Antioch was the metropolitan see, and held the right of ordaining the Parthian bishops. But from the beginning, as the stories were intended to prove, it had not been so. At the beginning the fountain of ecclesiastical orders for Seleucia-Ctesiphon, as well as Edessa, was St Thomas; for Maris, like Aggæus, was ordained by Thaddæus, his deputy. Thus from St

Thomas the first bishop of Seleucia - Ctesiphon derived his ecclesiastical pedigree: thus by him the chief see in the Parthian empire may be said to have been founded.

It is therefore as a question of apostolic succession that we are to view St Thomas's patronage of all the churches in the Parthian empire and the East.

CHAPTER IV.

ST THOMAS, THE APOSTLE OF THE INDIANS.

THE story of St Thomas's Indian apostleship is first told with great fulness of detail in the apocryphal 'Acts of Apostles.' In that collection the 'Acts of Thomas' is one of the best-preserved chapters. The date of it has been approximately determined. Both external testimony and internal evidence seem to agree in assigning it to the end of the second century.[1] It was written by one of the Syrian Gnostics, who was most probably of the city of Edessa. The name of the author is not known, but it has been suggested that the treatise might have been written by Bardesanes.

Bardesanes fulfilled probably all the conditions, save one, requisite for the authorship. He was a Syrian Gnostic and a native of Edessa, having been educated as the companion of Abgar VIII., who was a fervent Christian; he lived from 151 to 223, so that he would have been a man in his prime when the 'Acts' was written; he was interested in Indian affairs, having compiled 'Hypomnemata Indica' from oral information which he received from an Indian embassy passing through Edessa on its way to the court of Rome; he had a patriotic zeal for the honour and glory of Edessa; and he was, according to Renan, "an ardent preacher of Christianity, almost a missionary."[2] Whoever wrote the 'Acts' had undoubtedly such conditions as these to fulfil; but Bardesanes was married, and had a son, Harmonius, who inherited in enhanced richness his father's gift of hymn-writing, and whose hymns became so popular that St Ephrem found no other means to dethrone them and to keep children from their charm than to compose orthodox hymns to the same airs. Now it is morally impossible, as will be seen hereafter, that the author of the 'Acts' could have been himself a married man. But though Bardesanes is thus excluded, the treatise before us may have been written by a disciple of the school of Bardesanes.

The opening scene in the 'Acts of Thomas' is laid in Jerusalem, where the apostles had just portioned out the regions of the world among them;

and "Judas Thomas, also called Didymus," is represented as being ill content with his lot. He professed himself unable, on account of the weakness of the flesh, to go to India, saying, "How can I, being an Hebrew man, go among the Indians to proclaim the truth?" And, though the Saviour appeared to Thomas in the night bidding him be of good courage, and assuring him of the sufficiency of His unfailing grace, the doubting apostle still refused to obey, saying, "Wheresoever Thou wishest to send me, send me elsewhere, for to the Indians I am not going." Meanwhile an Indian merchant of the name of Abbanes, sent by King Gondophares to procure a carpenter to build him a palace, appeared in Jerusalem; and, having met in the slave-market with Jesus, who pointed to Thomas as a fit and proper person for his purpose, bought of Him the apostle-carpenter for three pounds of uncoined silver. Next day Thomas came to the Lord and said, "Thy will be done," whereupon Abbanes and he began to sail away; and they had a fair wind, and sailed fast until they came to Andrapolis, a royal city.

When they arrived there, the marriage-feast of the king's daughter was being celebrated, and Thomas accompanied Abbanes to the feast. And, when he saw them all reclining, he reclined also in the midst. But he would neither eat nor drink; and a flute-girl, a Hebrew by race, stood and played over him a long time, and presently he sang a Hebrew song, setting forth the praises of the bride, which none but the flute-girl understood. Meanwhile a naughty cup-bearer struck the stranger, and Thomas quietly replied that God would forgive him in the world to come, but the hand that had been lifted against His apostle would be dragged along by a dog. And so it came to pass; for the cup-bearer, having gone to the fountain to draw water, met a lion there, and the lion rent him in pieces, and the dogs immediately seized his limbs, among which also one black dog, laying hold of his right hand in his mouth, brought it to the place of the banquet. And when it was proved to be the hand of the cup-bearer who had struck the apostle, the flute-girl broke her flutes in pieces and threw them away, and went and sat down at the feet of Thomas, saying that he was either God or God's apostle. And the king having heard, came and said to him, "Rise up and go with me, and pray for my daughter, for she is my only child, and to-day I give her away." And having prayed and laid his hands on them, he said, "The Lord will be with you," and he left them in the place, and went away.

It is at this point that the author of the 'Acts of Thomas' first unmistakably shows the cloven hoof, painting his hero in colours so strongly condemned by St Paul as characteristic of evil times; making him both "abstain from meats," and also begin his crusade against matrimony.

For when the bridegroom, after the departure of all the guests, lifted the curtain which separated him from his bride, he saw Thomas, as he supposed, conversing with her. Then he asked in surprise, "How canst thou be found here? did I not see thee go out before all?" And the Lord answered, "I am not Judas Thomas, but his brother." And the Lord sat down, and ordered them also to sit down, calling on them to remember all that His brother had said to them against matrimony, and promising that, if they would undo the knot which had been tied that day, they would partake of the true marriage, and enter the bride-chamber full of light and immortality. The young couple obeyed this exhortation, much to the grief of the king, who ordered Thomas to be apprehended; but he and Abbanes were already on their way, and so escaped his hands.

And when they came to the cities of India, Abbanes introduced St Thomas to King Gondophares, who, having shown him a place beyond the gates of the city, well wooded and well watered, where he wished to erect a palace, asked St Thomas if he would undertake the work, and when he would be ready to begin. "I shall begin," said the apostle, "in October and finish in April." And the king wondering, said, "Every building is built in summer; but canst thou build and make a palace in winter itself?" "Thus it must be," replied St Thomas, "and otherwise it is impossible." The king, thinking that the apostle-carpenter was likely to know his own business best, judiciously fell in with this part of his proposal. "And the apostle, having taken a reed, measured the place and marked it out; and he set the doors towards the rising of the sun, to look to the light, and the windows towards its setting, to look to the winds; and he made the bakehouse to be towards the south, and the water-tank, for abundance, towards the north." And the king exclaimed, "Thou art a craftsman indeed, and it is fitting that thou shouldest serve kings." The king then, having "left many things for the apostle," took his departure, sending from time to time "the money that was necessary for the living, both of him and the other workmen." And one day the king sent asking St Thomas to report progress; and the royal messenger was instructed to reply that the palace was finished all but the roof, and that more money was needed. Gold and silver uncoined were therefore despatched, and the wheels of time moved on; but a crisis was near. For "when the king came into the city, he inquired of his friends about the palace which Judas, who also is Thomas, had built;" and they said that he had neither built a palace nor done anything else of what he promised to do, but he went round the cities and districts, giving all he had to the poor, and teaching that there is one God; that he healed the diseased, and cast out demons, and did many extraordinary things, and they thought that he was a magician. "But his acts of compassion and the cures done by him as a free gift, and still more, his single-mindedness, and gentleness, and fidelity, show that he is a just man, or an apostle of the new God whom he preaches; for he continually fasts and prays, and eats only bread with salt, and his drink is water, and he carries one coat, whether in warm weather or in cold, and he takes nothing from any one, but gives to others even what he has."

On hearing this the king was perplexed, and "stroked his face with his hands, shaking his head for a long time." So he sent for St Thomas and Abbanes, and asked whether the palace was finished, and when he might see it. Then St Thomas replied that it was ready, adding, "Now thou canst not see it; but when thou hast departed this life thou shalt see it." And the king was greatly enraged, and put St Thomas in chains, and cast him and Abbanes into prison, resolving to flay them alive and burn them with fire. But his weakly brother Gad was so distressed at the indignity suffered by the king that he suddenly died; and in the other world he saw a palace so beautiful that he begged the angels to let him live in its lowest chambers. But they answered that it could not be, for this was his brother's palace, erected by the Christian. Gad therefore asked and obtained leave from the angels to go back to the world that he might buy the palace from his brother. So when they were putting grave-clothes on the body it returned to life; and Gad at once sought an interview with the king and implored him to sell him the palace. But Gondophares wished to keep it for himself, and assured his brother that St Thomas, who was still alive, would build him a better one. Then King Gondophares and Gad became followers of the apostle, and begged for the seal of baptism; and the apostle sealed them, and they heard the voice of the Lord saying, "Peace to you, brethren." And many others also believed, and were added, and came to the refuge of the Saviour.

Now the great purpose of this apocryphal treatise is to advocate celibacy as a Christian institution; and, in order to give his opinions an authoritative character, the author puts them into the mouth of St Thomas, around whose head all the devices of his cunning art have been insidiously employed to paint a magnificent halo. The more he exalted St Thomas, the more authority he hoped to secure in support of his own opinions; and so he spared no pains to glorify, after his own fashion, the apostolic puppet that his unchastened imagination had created — so different in all respects from the portrait drawn in a few touches by St John. We have already seen that he represented St Thomas as the twin brother of the Lord Jesus Himself, both being so much alike that the one could not be distinguished from the other; and it was doubtless in consequence of this identification that he thought it needful to prefix 'Judas' to the apostle's name.[3]

The author does not hesitate even to suggest the identity of the disciple with the Master. For this identification he skilfully prepares the way. He introduces St Thomas, not as a fisherman, but as a carpenter; a representation which seems to have captivated the imagination of later generations in the Church, so that, wherever the story of St Thomas has been subjected to artistic treatment, the apostle is invariably represented — as, for example, in Raphael's fine picture in Rome, on the Indo-Portuguese coins that bear the apostle's name, and on the slab in the Goanese Roman Catholic Church at the Little Mount, near Madras—with a carpenter's rule in his hand. The purpose of this conception is made abundantly clear by the fact that St Thomas is presently invested with a function peculiar to our Lord—namely, that of preparing mansions in heaven for them that believe. If any further proof of the preconceived tendency of these representations were required, it would be found in the testimony of Friar Jordanus, who certifies that in his day (*circa* 1322) the Christians of St Thomas on the west coast of Southern India held it as an article of belief that their patron saint was no other than the Christ of God.[4] How long before the fourteenth century this tenet was accepted, it is perhaps impossible to trace back, step by step, through the generations; but the fact of its acceptance is a curious example of the influence of the 'Acts,' and an unexpected proof of the direct or indirect connection of the ancient Church in Southern India with the still more ancient Church of Edessa.

When our author has invested his hero with this extraordinary rank and power, it is not wonderful that, in accordance with a notion so popular in his time, he should have yielded to the temptation of multiplying miracles as a means of conversion. The miraculous element runs through the whole treatise; but there are three notable miracles to which vast importance is evidently attached. They are entitled, (1) About the dragon and the young man; (2) About the demon that dwelt in the woman; (3) About the young man who killed the maiden. The narratives of these miracles cannot be pronounced unexceptionably pure, but they do not fail to record that each was productive of a large addition to the membership of the Church of St Thomas.

The Church being thus established on a celibate foundation, it was deemed a fitting thing that its apostolic founder should move on to another region of India, and there carry forward his successful crusade against matrimony until he should achieve even in this doubtful cause the honour of martyrdom. So, when St Thomas left the capital city of Gondophares and passed to that of Misdeus, he converted first Mygdonia,[5] the wife of the chief minister, who in obedience to the apostle's instructions refused to live any longer with Charisius, her husband; and the king had hardly received Charisius's complaint on the subject when he discovered that his own queen, Mygdonia's sister, as well as his son, Juzanes, and others of his household, had become converts to the same doctrine. Then, at the command of this irate Indian king, St Thomas was cast into prison, where he preached the Word to the prisoners, so that all rejoiced at his presence. But one day St Thomas overheard the jailers wrangling and saying, "What wrong have we done to that sorcerer that, availing himself of his magic art, he has opened the door of the prison and wishes to set all the prisoners free?" So they took him, and stripped him, and girded him with a girdle, and thus they stood before the king. "And how," said Misdeus, "hast thou run away and come to this country?" And Thomas said, "I came here that I might save many, and that I might by thy hands depart from this body." Then the king became impatient, and rose, taking Thomas, with a few soldiers under arms, outside the city. And when they had gone forth three stadia, he delivered him to four soldiers and to one of the polemarchs, and ordered them to take him to the mountain and spear him; but he himself returned to the city.

Such being the substance of the life of St Thomas according to the 'Acts,' the question that now falls to be considered is whether any fragment of truth may be extracted from this apocryphal story. It seems not unreasonable to assume that, after eliminating the miraculous elements and doctrinal vagaries, there may remain a few geographical or historical facts on which the author could hang his own opinions. Some light has been cast on the subject by modern research, and archæological experts have been for some time at work on helpful lines. In consequence of the extension of our Indian frontier towards the north-west, and our diplomatic and military relations with Afghanistan, interesting discoveries have been made which tend to show that it is in that region we must look for the realm of Gondophares and the field of St Thomas's labours. Numerous coins bearing Greek legends—certainly not less than thirty thousand in number, and ranging over a period of more than

Gondophares Coins, First Century.

three centuries—have been found in Cabul and the Punjab. The greater number belong to the series of pure Greek princes who ruled over the Indian provinces of Alexander the Great. The remainder belong to their Scythian conquerors and to their Indo-Parthian contemporaries. Among these Indo-Parthian princes is to be reckoned Gondophares.

The inscription on the obverse side of these

Gondophares coins is in Greek characters, on the reverse side in Indian Pali. The Greek form of the name is, on the horseman coins, **ΓΟΝΔΟΦΑΡΟΥ**, on the bust coins, **ΥΝΔΟΦΕΡΡΟΥ**; while the Indian Pali equivalent is *Gudapharasa* or *Gadapharasa.*

The important questions concerning Gondophares are, Where and when did he rule? Both are

Gondophares Coin, First Century.

answered in the following extract from General Cunningham[6]: "The coins of Gondophares are common in Cabul and Candahar, and Sistan, and in the Western and Southern Punjab. All these countries, therefore, must have owned his sway. He was, besides, the head and founder of his family, as no less than three members of it claim relationship with him on their coins—viz., *Orthagnes*, his full brother, *Abdagases*, his nephew, and *Sasa* (or *Sasan*), a more distant relation. The coins of Orthagnes are found in Sistan and Candahar, those of Abdagases and Sasan in the Western Punjab. I presume, therefore, that they were the viceroys of those provinces on the part of the great King Gondophares, who himself resided at Cabul. All the names are those of Parthians, but the language of the coins is Indian Pali. Abdagases is the name of the Parthian chief who headed the successful revolt against Artabanus in A.D. 44. The great power of Gondophares, and the discovery of a coin of Artabanus countermarked with the peculiar monogram [7] of all the Gondopharian dynasty, make it highly probable that the Indo-Parthian Abdagases was the same as the Parthian chief whose revolt is recorded by Tacitus (Annal. xv. 2) and Josephus (Antiqua, xx. iii. 2). This surmise is very much strengthened by the date of the revolt (A.D. 44), which would make Gondophares a contemporary of St Thomas."

Further light regarding the period of Gondophares' government is derived from an inscription on the Taht-i-Bahi [8] stone, now in the Museum at Lahore. Unfortunately for history, this stone was used for many years, perhaps for many centuries, for the grinding of spices, so that all the middle part of the inscription has suffered and become indistinct, and some portions have been obliterated altogether. The whole inscription consisted of six lines of writing. It can be inferred from the concluding part of the inscription, imperfect as it is, that the stone commemorates the building of a *stupa* or a *vihar* by some pious Buddhist, "for his own religious merit and the religious merit of his father and his mother." The first two lines, which contain the name of the king and the date, are translated by Professor Dowson [9] as follows: "In the twenty-sixth year of the great King Gondophares, (and) on the third day of the month Vaisakha, (year) one hundred (100) of the Samvatsara." As the Samvatsara or era of Vikramaditya corresponds to 56 B.C., the date on the stone, according to this reading, would be 44 A.D.

The result of the testimony derived from coins and from the Taht-i-Bahi stone, then, is that an Indo-Parthian king of the name of Gondophares ruled over India in the first century, that the seat of his government was at Cabul, and that his India coincides with the Punjab and Afghanistan, and does not include peninsular India.

It will thus be seen, on review, that the author of the 'Acts,' by two strokes of his pen, brings

St Thomas from Jerusalem to the court of Gondophares. (1.) "They began to sail away, and they had a fair wind, and they came to Andrapolis." (2.) "And when the apostle came into the cities of India, with Abbanes the merchant, Abbanes went away to salute Gondophares, the king, and reported to him about the carpenter whom he had brought." Can we fill up the interspaces? The attempt to do so is at least worth making. From Jerusalem Abbanes and St Thomas would go down to Cæsarea and take ship at that port for Alexandria, from which the route to India in those days was as well defined as the overland route of the P. & O. Company from London to Bombay is in this year of grace 1892. From Alexandria they would go by boat up the Canopic branch of the Nile to Andrapolis or Andropolis[10]; and, after halting there, would pursue their course to Coptos. From Coptos they would go by land to Berenice on the Red Sea shore, almost under the tropic, a distance of 258 Roman miles, where they would again embark. Departing from Berenice, and sailing, according to the ancient mode of navigation, along the Arabian shore, to the promontory Syagrus, they would hold their course along the coast of Persia and Gedrosia (now Beloochistan), directly to Pattala (now Tatta), at the head of the lower delta of the Indus; then up the Indus as far as (say) Attock, whence they would strike to the left up the valley of the Cabul river till they came to Gondophares' capital. Thus St Thomas reached the scene where he was to begin his apostolic labours in foreign parts.

But the India of St Thomas was wider than that of Gondophares. The fact is, that the whole area between the Indus and the eastern frontier of Persia, and between the Indian Ocean and the northern boundary of Afghanistan, was formerly denominated India. In the treaty made between Seleucus Nicator and Chandragapta, the Hindu Kush, with its continuation to the east and west, was to be the boundary between Iran and India,—the latter sovereign having sway "not merely over the Ganges valley in all its extent, and the whole north-west of India, but, in the region of the Indus, at least over a part of what is now Cabul; further, over Arachosia or Afghanistan; presumably also over the waste and arid Gedrosia, the modern Beloochistan, as well as over the Delta and mouths of the Indus."[11] But the agreement referred to did not last long; and when the Parthians rose to power, all India west of the Indus fell into their hands. Pliny informs us that "many indeed do not reckon the Indus to be the western boundary of India, but include in that term also four satrapies on this side of the river," which, in the language of modern geography, correspond to Beloochistan, Candahar, Herat, and Cabul.[12] It may be added that it is in the sense of India west of the Indus that the name is used in the Bible; and it is in this sense that St Thomas's India is to be understood.

When St Thomas left the kingdom of Gondophares, he entered another Indian kingdom or satrapy, and made the acquaintance of another Indian king, at whose court he began work afresh, and at whose hands he was ultimately put to death. Later authorities give the name of the place where St Thomas was dismissed from his sufferings as Calamina, the identification of which is one of the puzzles that still perplex the student of the history of the Church of St Thomas. The earliest mention of this name appears to be by Hippolytus,[13] who died between the years 235 and 239. According to one reading of the text of Hippolytus, the name is Caramene; and, if this reading is allowed, the burial-place of St Thomas is evidently to be identified with Caramana,[14] the modern Kerman, in Eastern Persia; but if not, then we must look for it in Calama, a town mentioned by Nearchus, on the seaboard of Gedrosia. In any case, it is evident that, according to this apocryphal story, which is almost the only post-canonical information we have concerning St Thomas, the apostle died and was buried in that India west of the Indus to which he went on receipt of his commission. In that India he preached, and performed miracles, and established churches. From the date of his arrival in the country to the date of his death he never left it. That and that alone is the India of which he was the apostle. The whole circle of early literature knows no other India thus distinguished. So Calamina[15] must be sought, at all events, within the four corners of India west of the Indus.

But Calamina was not destined to be the final resting-place of St Thomas's bones, for "long afterwards, when one of the king's sons became demoniac, Misdeus opened the apostle's tomb to find a bone wherewith to touch and cure his son. But, behold, no bones were there, for one of the brethren had carried them away to (Edessa in) the region of the west. Wherefore he took some dust from the place where the bones had lain, and touched his son with it, and immediately the devil left him. Then Misdeus met with the brethren under the rule of Syphorus, a presbyter in the mountain, and entreated them to pray for him, that he might obtain mercy through Jesus Christ."

It thus appears that the destination of the relics of St Thomas, which is a point in the post-canonical history of the apostle that has received a vast amount of attention, was something well known at the date of the 'Acts.'[16] In fact the author of the 'Acts' seems to record the speedy removal of the dead apostle to his own worshipful city with an air of triumph, as if St Thomas, who had not been able to visit the Edessenes in person during his lifetime, could yet, being dead, not escape their loving guardianship. It is perhaps not too much to suppose that one of the author's motives for writing the 'Acts' was to put in circulation what might be accepted as an authentic account of the deportation of St Thomas's remains to his beloved Edessa. Anything that would add glory to his beloved city was dear to the heart of the disciple of Bardesanes.

To us not the least interesting aspect of the story lies in the question, which it cannot fail to suggest, Was there really a Church in India west of the Indus during the latter part of the second century? History has little to say in reply. Perhaps the nearest approximation to an answer that history makes will be found in our next chapter. But the position of the author of the 'Acts' in relation to the question before us can hardly be doubtful. He would have answered it with an unhesitating affirmative. His business was to supply a fictitious genesis for a Church of whose existence he was well assured, in such a manner as to make it appear that the Indian Church was but a younger sister of the Church of Edessa, both having sprung directly or indirectly from the apostolic efforts of St Thomas.

CHAPTER V.

THE FIRST INDIAN MISSIONARY.

THE story of the first Indian missionary is bound up with the story of the Indian apostleship of St Bartholomew. It forms an instructive episode in the history of the Church of Alexandria, which seems to have fascinated and perplexed every student of the early propagation of the Gospel in India. It carries us back to a time when the last of the apostles was already full fourscore years in his grave. For, although the origin of Christianity in Alexandria is usually ascribed to St Mark, yet we know little of the history of the Alexandrian Church beyond the names of its bishops, till the fourth quarter of the second century. In the year 179, a notable man ascended the ecclesiastical throne. His name was Demetrius. His origin was so humble, and his episcopate so distinguished for success in administration, that his introduction into office was accounted for in later ages on the hypothesis of miraculous intervention. While Bishop Julian—so runs the Egyptian legend—was on his deathbed, he was informed by an angel that the man who should on the succeeding day bring him a present of grapes, was designed as his successor. On the morrow a countryman, who could neither read nor write, and who was married, made his appearance in the predicted manner, and Julian acknowledged him as the chosen of the Lord. Demetrius was most unwilling to accept the proffered dignity, and he had to be ordained by main force. But from the time of his consecration he became another man. He immediately applied himself to the study of the Scriptures, and proved one of the most learned prelates of his time. His being married rendered his flock unwilling at first to receive him, as it happened that, from St Mark downward, none such had been promoted to the see. This reluctance, however, was shortly removed, and Demetrius entered on his long and successful reign of more than forty-two years—a longer period than the chair of St Mark was ever filled by any one prelate, with the exception of Athanasius.[1]

One of the most remarkable distinctions of the episcopate of Demetrius was the development of the catechetical school of Alexandria to a standard higher than it had previously attained. It was at first a mere preparatory class for the instruction of catechumens in the elements of the Christian faith; but under the presidency of successive distinguished teachers, it grew into a commanding centre of philosophical research and theological learning. The influx of converts of every age and rank, from the midst of a community which had served itself heir to all the science and philosophy of the world, had necessitated on the part of the Church a profound investigation and scientific development of the first principles of her faith, unknown because unneeded in earlier times. To meet this necessity, eminent men were providentially raised up. In the days of Demetrius there were three such masters, who eclipsed all their predecessors. They were Pantænus, Clement, and Origen.

The writings of Clement and Origen survive, and their opinions, character, and influence are well known; but the works of Pantænus have been lost, and the fragments of his history that have come down to us seem to give but a faint idea of his powers. A Hebrew by nation, a Sicilian by birth,

Pantænus was in philosophy an eclectic, drawing his principal dogmas from the Stoic and Pythagorean sects;[2] and having been converted to Christianity, he was placed at the head of the catechetical school of Alexandria. Clement, his convert and pupil, describing his teachers, speaks of Pantænus as the last of them, but the first in power, and continues: "Having tracked him out, concealed in Egypt, I found rest. He, the true, the Sicilian bee, gathering the spoil of the flowers of the prophetic and apostolic meadow, engendered in the souls of his hearers a deathless element of knowledge."[3] About the year 189 or 190 he became the first historical missionary to India. The story of this episode in his life has been told both by Eusebius and Jerome. And since their testimony on this point has frequently been used as helping to prove the existence of a Church in South India in the end of the second century, and so far encouraging the belief in an apostolic origin for that Church, it becomes necessary in this place to discuss the question.

The testimony of the learned Bishop of Cæsarea is to the effect that Pantænus "displayed such ardour, and so zealous a disposition respecting the Divine Word, that he was constituted a herald of the Gospel of Christ to the nations of the East;" that he went as far as India; that he there "found his own arrival anticipated by some who were acquainted with the Gospel of Matthew, to whom Bartholomew, one of the apostles, had preached, and had left them the Gospel of Matthew in the Hebrew, which was also preserved until this time."[4] Jerome's account, which is in entire harmony with that of Eusebius, is, for one or two touches of its own, worthy of separate quotation. "Pantænus," he says, "was a man of such learning, both in the sacred Scriptures and in secular knowledge, that Demetrius, the Bishop of Alexandria, sent him to India at the request of ambassadors from that nation. And there he found that Bartholomew, one of the twelve apostles, had preached the advent of our Lord Jesus Christ according to the Gospel of Matthew written in Hebrew, which he brought away with him on his return to Alexandria."[5]

How long Pantænus laboured in India, or what were the fruits of his labour, is uncertain. It would seem that he had a comparatively short career in the country, and that he had no successor, at least from the Church that sent him. At all events he returned to Alexandria and resumed from Clement, who officiated for him in his absence, his work at the head of its famous school; and it is probable that both Clement and Origen owed some of their knowledge of India and its people to this mission of their admired preceptor. The former, in a well-known passage, speaks of Indian Gymnosophists and 'other barbarian philosophers,' with a minuteness of detail which it is not unnaturally supposed must be due to information supplied him by an eyewitness. "Of these," says Clement, "there are two classes, some of them called Sarmanæ and others Brahmans; and those of the Sarmanæ, who are called Hylobii, neither inhabit cities, nor have roofs over them, but are clothed in the bark of trees, feed on nuts, and drink water in their hands. Like those called Encratites in the present day," he adds, "they know not marriage nor begetting of children."[6] This account was probably taken down from the lips of Pantænus, and Jerome has a passage equally decisive of the class of people that he visited. It runs as follows: "Pantænus, on account of the renown of his excellent learning, was sent by Demetrius into India, that he might preach Christ among the Brahmans and philosophers of that nation."[7] The fact here stated is important as proving that the India to which the mission of Pantænus carried him was part of the India of modern geography—the India, as we shall see, of Alexander the Great; and disposes at once of a difficulty raised by Mosheim,[8] who came to the conclusion that the "Indians instructed in Christianity by Pantænus must have been certain Jews living in Arabia Felix," on the ground, as it would seem, that a book written in a Semitic language would be most unsuitable for the instruction of other than a Semitic people, and that the name 'India,' being loosely employed by early writers, has been known to be applied even to Arabia,[9] or some part thereof. But Jerome was too well informed a writer to people any part of Arabia with Brahmans. Neander,[10] though not without misgivings, suggests Malabar. "The mention of the Hebrew Gospel," he says, "is not at all inconsistent with the supposition that India proper is here meant, if we may assume that the Jews, who now dwell on the coast of Malabar, had already arrived there. The language of Eusebius seems to intimate that he himself had in view a remoter country than Arabia, and rather favours the conjecture that he meant to speak of India proper." But Sir W. W. Hunter,[11] with none of the hesitation of the elder and more cautious historian, holds that a Jewish colony existed on the Malabar coast in the apostolic age; that Christian merchants, "both of Jewish and other race, would in the natural course of trade have reached Malabar within the second century;" that "rumours, apparently brought back by the Red Sea fleet, of a Christian community on the Malabar coast, fired the zeal of Pantænus;" and that "the evidence of the early Christian writers, so far as it goes, tends to connect St Thomas with the India of the ancient world—that is to say, with Persia and Afghanistan—and St Bartholomew with the Christian settlements on the Malabar coast." But why should Mosheim, Neander, and Sir W. W. Hunter assume that the Gospel of Matthew would be any less unacceptable to Jews in the second century than it is to-day; and on what grounds of fact, reason, or testimony does the last-named writer suggest that many, or even a portion of the Syrian Christians were converted Jews? Not to press these points, it is sufficient to remark that, in the second century, there were neither Jews, Christians, nor Brahmans in Malabar.

We are constrained, therefore, to exclude both Arabia and Malabar as in any way satisfying the language of Eusebius and Jerome, and to hold that the India to which Pantænus went was the India of Alexander the Great, the India which the city that he honoured with his own name had known from its foundation, the India with which it traded for centuries after it had become a Roman possession.

But how did it come to pass that Indian Christians should possess a gospel in Hebrew? At first sight it certainly seems anomalous that a Semitic book should have been introduced into a locality presumably occupied by Aryans; and this apparent anomaly has led some writers to question the accuracy of the narrative of Eusebius, and others to shift the scene of Pantænus's labours to latitudes far removed from the India of the Alexandrian teacher. Is there then, after all, so great an anomaly in the few simple facts that Eusebius and Jerome relate?

In the first place, it is generally admitted that St Matthew wrote a gospel in Hebrew, although critics are not agreed as to the relation in which that gospel stands to the canonical gospel in Greek.[12] But it must be kept in mind that St Matthew's Hebrew was Aramaic, the language of the Targums, or translations and paraphrases of the Old Testament, written during the centuries immediately preceding and following the Christian era. It was the language of Babylonia, as transplanted to Palestine, and the dialect spoken by Christ and His disciples. The few authentic words preserved in the New Testament as spoken by our Lord in His own language, such as *talitha kumi*, *ephphatha*, *abba*, are not in Hebrew (strictly so called), but in the Chaldee or Southern Aramaic, as then spoken by the Jews, and which remained the literary language of the Jews till the tenth century.[13]

In the second place, it is to be remembered that a knowledge of the Aramaic language was widely diffused throughout the Parthian empire; and that, at the date in question, the Parthian empire, roughly speaking, extended from the Indus to the Euphrates, and from the Indian Ocean to the Caspian Sea and the Hindu Kush; and embraced therefore, or at least touched, the India of St Bartholomew. In how large a portion of this vast area Aramaic was vernacular will at once occur to every reader. Moreover Ctesiphon, the capital, situated on the Tigris, twelve or thirteen miles below the modern Baghdad, was in the heart of the Aramaic country, and it was the centre of an extensive caravan trade from many parts of Asia.

It is most natural, therefore, to suppose that the vernacular of that region would, in connection with government, trade, and education, spread widely in the empire.

Some would probably be prepared to suggest that a knowledge of Greek rather than Aramaic was prevalent in that quarter at the time of which we are speaking, and there is undoubtedly abundant proof that, wherever Alexander the Great carried his conquests in Asia, the Greek language obtained an extensive footing. Bactria, Afghanistan, and the Punjab were largely hellenised. The coins of Gondophares bore Greek legends, and we know that, when the Parthians carried on negotiations with the Romans, it was the Greek language that was used by both parties. Still the inducement to keep up the knowledge of Greek must have been declining, whereas a knowledge of Aramaic was of increasingly practical value. At all events, there is some reason to believe that a knowledge of Aramaic was as a matter of fact very widely diffused, and probably more so than Greek. For, when Josephus wrote his 'Wars of the Jews,' he wrote the book, as he distinctly informs us in the preface, in Aramaic, for the information not only of "the Babylonians, and the remotest Arabians, and those of our own nation beyond Euphrates, with the Adiabeni," but also "the Parthians"; and that he afterwards translated it into Greek "for the sake of such as live under the government of the Romans." If Josephus could have counted on as large a Greek-reading as an Aramaic-reading constituency in the East, he would most probably have used Greek as the original language of a work to which he himself evidently attached a great deal of importance. The fact of this wide diffusion of the knowledge of Aramaic is perhaps also confirmed by a tradition preserved by Hippolytus to the effect that St Matthew, having published his Aramaic Gospel at Jerusalem, went to Parthia, where he "fell asleep at Hieres."[14] It must further be remembered that the Parthians, while "lax and changeful in their own religious practice, were naturally tolerant of a variety of creeds among their subjects."[15] So that both Jews and Christians enjoyed an easy toleration under the Arsacian monarchs.

Whether, therefore, Aramaic was to those Christians, whose later representatives Pantænus found in the valley of the Indus, their mother tongue or an acquired speech, it may be easily imagined that Christians able to use the Aramaic scriptures for instruction in righteousness would readily find their way, in the interest of trade, agriculture, or gospel-propagation, into a promising country so comparatively near the original home of Aramaic.

It is not needful, of course, to assume that all the Christians among whom Pantænus found St Matthew's Aramaic Gospel were Aramaic-speaking persons. Probably their Christian predecessors had been such, probably their teachers at least had been such; but, if Jerome's representation be correct, it would seem, from the fact that Pantænus carried away with him what appears to have been their only copy to Alexandria, that it had become to them more an antique memorial of their past history than an instrument of present usefulness. In fact, one gathers from the story the impression that this community of Christians of St Bartholomew was at the end of the second century in a depressed, not to say moribund condition; that they were but the surviving remnant of a community which had seen better days; that they were fain to get help from any quarter; and that perhaps they found it easier, by reason of the regular marine trade with Alexandria, to communicate with the latter than with their own mother Church in Mesopotamia, from which they had long been separated. This, however, would not alter the fact of the accessibility of that region to Aramaic as a living, intelligible speech in the sub-apostolic age, and thus both the conditions involved in the narrative of Eusebius and Jerome seem to be satisfied. It will on all hands be admitted that in the population of the India of Alexander the Great there was a proportion of Brahmans; it will likewise, I trust, be admitted that a case has been made out in favour of the belief that in the same population, any time within the first two Christian centuries, Aramaic may well have been an intelligible language.

It is easy to see how Bartholomew's part in the matter found its way into history. The simple folk whom Pantænus visited held the belief, which probably all the ecclesiastical world then held, that in whatever country Christianity had found a footing, it must have been originally planted there by an apostle. The origin of Christianity in the famous land where they dwelt was to be ascribed, they said, to St Bartholomew. The mind of Pantænus received their tale as true, on what grounds of evidence we are not informed; and from Pantænus directly or through Clement the story was passed on to Origen, from whose writings it was duly copied by Eusebius and probably by Jerome and others.

The subsequent history of this apostle[16] is not irrelevant to our present inquiry. After having visited India, we are told, he returned to the north-west parts of Asia, and met St Philip at Hierapolis in Phrygia. Thence he travelled into Lycaonia, where he instructed the people in the Christian faith. His last removal was into great Armenia, where, preaching in a place obstinately addicted to idols, he was crowned with a glorious martyrdom. Some say that he was condemned by the Governor of Albanopolis to be crucified, while others tell us that he was flayed alive; and this last assertion has been perpetuated by art as well as by the devotion of the faithful. Who that has visited the cathedral of Milan, for example, does not remember its statue[17] of St Bartholomew in agony?

But, for perpetuating the name and influence of any defunct saint, nothing is perhaps more important than the destination of his bones. The relics of St Bartholomew seem to have had a tendency to travel westwards, away from the scene of his Indian labours. It is said that about the year

508 they were removed to the city of Dura in Mesopotamia; that, before the end of the sixth century, they were carried to the Isle of Lipari, near Sicily; that in 809 they were translated from Lipari to Benevento; and that finally they were conveyed from Benevento to Rome in 983, where they have ever since lain deposited in a porphyry monument under the high altar in the famous Church of St Bartholomew, in the isle of the Tiber.

Happily the early history of Christianity in India has not been encumbered with any question concerning the destination of the relics of St Bartholomew, no one having affirmed that they ever found a place on Indian soil. Whether he himself personally preached in any part of India is a sufficiently perplexing question. That he did so is not incredible. But no community of Christians calling themselves by his name, in India or elsewhere, after the date of Pantænus's visit, is known to history.

It would be doing injustice to this interesting story were we to withhold at the close of it a note of admiration for an excellent practice of the Oriental Church that it records. For the presence of an Aramaic Gospel among the Christians of St Bartholomew is but an illustration of her custom of habitually using from the first the Word of God as an instrument of persuasion and ingathering as well as of edification; and few facts in the history of the Greek, as compared with that of the Latin Church, are more gratifying than this, that the former put the Scriptures into the hands of so many of her children in their own mother tongue and granted them a free use of the same, limited only by the difficulty of multiplying copies. Had she been careful to follow up this wise and considerate step with an adequate provision for the instruction of her youth in schools and of all her people in their assemblies, her position in Asia might have been very different to-day.

CHAPTER VI.

PERSIA AND INDIA.

NOTHING is better fitted to give a clear and comprehensive idea of the extent to which Christianity had spread in the world by the end of the first quarter of the fourth century than to mark the dioceses of the three hundred and eighteen bishops who sat in the Council of Nicæa. The extreme West was represented by Hosius of Cordova, and the extreme East by James of Nisibis and John of Persia and Great India. The last is undistinguished in history. Nothing is known of him beyond the fact that he signed the acts of the first Ecumenical Council, the signature in full being—'Ιωάννης Πέρσης τῆς ἐν Περσίδι πάσῃ καὶ μεγάλῃ 'Ινδίᾳ.

The origin of the Church of Persia was due to the labour of Syrian missionaries, probably from

Edessa; and this historical circumstance was long commemorated by the fact that, though the speech of Persia during the Sassanian dynasty (226-561) was Pahlavi, the Christians used Syriac in their sacred services,—an illustration of "what an important part the Syriac language played in Asia, from the third to the ninth century of our era, after it had become the instrument of Christian preaching. Like the Greek for the Hellenic East, and Latin for the West, Syriac became the Christian and ecclesiastical language of Upper Asia."[1]

Of the details of the early history of the Persian Church we know but little; yet by the fourth century, when it effloresced in history, it was numerically strong, fully organised, and spiritually robust, not refusing to take its fair share of the public business of the Church at large, and to resist to the death the persecution that assailed it from without. It had its famous 'Persic School' at Edessa, where its clergy were taught the articles of the faith, and where they probably drank from the great stream of tradition that saturated the life of the Church there, learning the attractive story and becoming familiar with the precious relics of St Thomas.

The signature of Bishop John has received an amount of attention altogether out of proportion to its importance. It has frequently been referred to in proof or illustration of the idea that the presence of Christianity in India is due to apostolic intervention. This signature, it is affirmed, proves that there was a Church in Southern India at least as early as the fourth century, thus antedating that Church's origin by about two centuries, and bringing it so much nearer to apostolic times. It becomes necessary, therefore, to consider whether Bishop John can have intended any possible reference to Southern India.

It must be remembered that his bishopric fell within the period when the Sassanian dynasty swayed the destinies of Persia. The establishment of this dynasty meant the restoration of the purely Persian kings who were unseated in the person of Darius by Alexander the Great, and who, after the days of the Seleucidæ, were still kept for more than four centuries from their hereditary dignity by the brave and powerful dynasty of the Arsacids; and, although the Sassanians never acquired that extent of dominion and influence which Cyrus, for example, gained for the Achæmenidæ, yet they ruled one of the largest empires in the world. Roughly speaking, their territory extended from the Indus to the Euphrates, and from the Indian

Ocean to the Caspian Sea and the Hindu Kush. Now, it has been already shown that the provinces which lay between the Indus and the eastern frontier of Persia, and between the Indian Ocean and the northern boundary of Afghanistan, were anciently comprehended under the name of India, and were sometimes spoken of by authors as if they were the whole of India; and it seems to me that, in the designation of John's diocese, the name India is used in accordance with the *usus loquendi* of the period. The subjects of the Sassanian kings would without doubt use the name most naturally and most frequently, if not exclusively, to denote that India which formed such a large and important part of their own dominions. Bishop John was a Sassanian subject, and would most probably use the name in what may be called its Sassanian sense.

It does not appear that the epithet 'great,' introduced into the description of John's diocesan territory, is there used in any technical sense, like the epithets *major*, *minor*, and *tertia* or *middle* sometimes applied—though not uniformly or with a constant meaning applied—to India by writers in the middle ages. The first two of these epithets are used by Marco Polo and Friar Jordanus with

ST THOMAS'S MOUNT, NEAR MADRAS.

With Staircase leading to the Church at the top.

opposite applications, and none of them seem to have been in use so early as the days of Bishop John. The epithet 'great' would rather seem to be used by way of magnifying John's office. This India had the reputation of having, according to one tradition, a Church founded by St Thomas; according to another, a Church founded by St Bartholomew; and it was probably out of compliment to the memory of these two apostles, or out of respect to the tradition concerning them, that the name India was included in the designation of this bishopric; and it was probably for the same reason, and not merely on account of the physical extent of the diocese, that the epithet 'great' was originally applied.

To what extent the Church, which probably had some visibility in the end of the second century, survived till the days of John, we have not the means of determining. So far as appears, it was in a moribund condition at the date of the visit of Pantænus, and history has never granted a distinct view of that Church or a clear testimony as to its strength and activity. Certainly the use of the title, subscribed by John to the acts of the Council of Nicæa, does not carry with it, as has been commonly assumed, the inference that a Church existed even in this India in the year 325. It is easy to understand how the title should be retained in full long after that which originally gave it significance had become defunct; just as the Bishop of the Isle of Man is still known as the Bishop of Sodor *and* Man, although it is about five centuries since Sodor or the Sudreys (that is, the Southern Hebrides) formed any part of the area of his episcopal jurisdiction.

But in any case the diocese of John was 'great,' beyond the power of any single man to do justice to; and it is probable therefore that he held the rank of Metropolitan, with other bishops subject to his supervision. He himself was subject to the Archbishop and Catholicos of Seleucia-Ctesiphon, who was, in his turn, a man placed under authority; for this Catholicate "was, as it were, a vicarial jurisdiction of the see of Antioch, in the same manner that the Metran of Ethiopia was dependent on that of Alexandria."[2] The loose relationship here indicated between these two ecclesiastics, the one on the Orontes and the other on the Tigris, continued until the end of the fifth century, when Seleucia-Ctesiphon, which then ceased to be orthodox, itself became the chief seat of an independent patriarchate.

But, if we would estimate the strength of spiritual life in the Church of Bishop John, we must remember that he was contemporary with one of the most distinguished, if not the greatest, of the Sassanians. Shahpur II. was a posthumous child, and his birth was heralded by no common expectations. It is even said that the Magi went through the ceremony of crowning him before he was born. His political operations were undoubtedly carried to a high degree of perfection, and he is one of the men on whom history confers the name of Great. But with all this he was a religious zealot of an almost fanatical type. It must be remembered that the restoration of the purely Persian dynasty meant the revival of the Zoroastrian faith, which was endowed and propagated by the secular arm, such a union subsisting between Church and State as almost to amount to an identification. In the time of Shahpur II. also, the text of the Avesta—the Zoroastrian Scriptures—was restored, and every effort, including the persecution of Christianity, was made to render the supremacy of Zoroastrianism complete. Shahpur II. was as vehement a persecutor as Nero or Diocletian, and the record of his doings cannot fail to shock our Christian sensibilities as keenly as the Roman martyrologies do, or to awaken in our hearts as sympathetic an admiration of the constancy and faithfulness of the Church. Touching details are given by Sozomen,[3] who concludes a record of many individual cases of martyrdom with a reference to twenty-four bishops, whose names are enumerated, and to sixteen thousand noble Persians, besides many other persons of the middle and lower classes, who were called to surrender their lives.

In its conflict with the religions of the world Christianity offers to the student of history a very complex but most instructive problem. The external conditions of the problem change with the progress of the centuries, but the intellectual and spiritual elements are somewhat more constant and are of perennial interest. Of the conflict between Christianity and Zoroastrianism, we have been able to present only a few of the external conditions. In Zoroastrianism the religion of Christ had to contend with no common foe. Think what it might have been. "There were periods in the history of the world when the worship of Ormuzd threatened to rise on the ruins of the temples of all the other gods. If the battles of Marathon and Salamis had been lost, and Greece had succumbed to Persia, the State-religion of the empire of Cyrus, which was the worship of Ormuzd, might have become the religion of the whole civilised world. Persia had absorbed the Assyrian and Babylonian empires. The Jews were either in Persian captivity or under Persian sway at home; the sacred monuments of Egypt had been mutilated by the hands of Persian soldiers. The edicts of the great king, the king of kings, were sent to India, to Greece, to Scythia, and to Egypt; and if, 'by the grace of Aramazda,' Darius had crushed the liberty of Greece, the purer faith of Zoroaster might easily have superseded the Olympian fable."[4]

We have seen what it was in its revived form during the days of Shahpur II., and how it strove to exterminate its rival. Yet Christianity survived. Hereafter we shall see that the tide of public feeling and political action in Persia turned largely in favour of the Christians, though they enjoyed this favour on a somewhat precarious tenure. Nor did Christianity make such advances as to encourage the belief that within calculable time its upholders would succeed in possessing the land. Zoroastrianism indeed was crushed, but it was not "by the weapons of Roman emperors or by the arguments of Christian divines that the fatal blow was dealt to the throne of Cyrus and the altars of

Ormuzd. The power of Persia was broken at last by the Arabs; and it is due to them that the religion of Ormuzd, once the terror of the world, is now, and has been for the last thousand years, a mere curiosity in the eyes of the historian."[5]

Thus the interest of the story of Bishop John centres around his Persian rather than his Indian episcopate. But if the latter part of his official designation was then but an empty title, it was the symbol of a memory of what had been, and its retention perhaps embodied a hope and a prophecy of what was to be in the then not distant future, when the Church in which John presided should send forth spirited missions both to the Malabar and the Coromandel coasts of Southern India.

CHAPTER VII.

WHICH INDIA?

SOME historical errors die hard. There are writers who will cling to the notion of an apostolic origin for Christianity in Southern India, and who appropriate every passage in Church history which seems to them to carry the date of its origin back to a higher antiquity than the law of historical evidence is commonly understood to sanction. Thus the laborious, if not always concise, historian Hough[1] sets it down as "certain" that, through the efforts of a bishop of the name of Frumentius, the Indian "*peninsula* possessed a knowledge of Christ early in the fourth century;" and Hardwick[2] tells us that Theophilus, the Indian, "on visiting his native land and other parts of the *Hindu Peninsula*," in the third quarter of the fourth century, "was not surprised to meet with fellow-Christians, whose peculiarities attested their antiquity, as well as their comparative isolation from Christendom at large."

We shall see how far such representations accord with the sources from which they profess to be drawn; and whether the insertion of the words "peninsula" and "Hindu Peninsula" is not absolutely gratuitous.

I.

Rufinus, who is the authority for the story of Frumentius, was born in Italy about 345. He was at first an inmate of the monastery of Aquileia, and he afterwards resided many years at a monastery in Palestine, where he became intimate with Jerome. After remaining for about twenty-six years in the East, he returned to Italy in 397 and died in Sicily in 410. In his 'Ecclesiastical History'[3] he tells us that Meropius, a philosopher of Tyre, fired with the passion for travelling and encouraged by the example of Metrodorus, determined to pay a visit to India. He was accompanied on the voyage by his two young relatives, Frumentius and Edesius, whose education he was superintending. He probably thought that a voyage of discovery would help to perfect in his wards that liberal culture which it was his ambition to impart. After completing his researches in India and duly recording his observations, Meropius began his return voyage. He had occasion to touch at a certain port to take in water and other necessaries; but the savage inhabitants, who had just thrown off their alliance with the Romans, fell on Meropius and killed him and all his crew. Presently they found the two lads, his relatives, sitting under a tree, preparing their lessons; and, touched with compassion, they brought them to the king, by whom they were received with marked kindness. Frumentius, the elder of the two, seemed to be a lad of insight and wisdom, and gave promise of capability in administration; while Edesius, of less mental calibre, was distinguished for fidelity and goodness. The latter became the king's cup-bearer; the former his secretary, or chancellor; and both enjoyed high favour at court. But, when the death of the king was approaching, he bequeathed to them their liberty, and appointed the queen to act as regent during his son's minority. Pressure, however, was put on them both to remain after the king's death; and the queen had unbounded confidence in Frumentius and granted him unrestricted power; and the work of administration prospered in his hands, so that he became like another Joseph. As a Christian man, he felt that the moral and spiritual interests of the people had a strong claim on his regard, and so he instituted careful inquiries as to whether any of the Roman merchants that traded in the country were Christians; and, finding some such, he invested them with certain powers and advised them to build churches where the people might congregate for prayer; and much more did he himself try to promote the same objects and to act in every way so that "the seed of Christians might spring up in that place."

But when the royal youth, on whose behalf they took charge of the kingdom, attained manhood, they returned, says the historian, to 'our world,' although the queen and her son begged that they would stay. Edesius hastened to Tyre to see his parents and relatives, and was afterwards appointed a presbyter; but Frumentius, thinking it not right to "conceal the divine work," went to Alexandria, and explained to Athanasius, who had but recently been placed in the chair of St Mark, the whole matter as it occurred; and advised him to provide some worthy man whom he might send as bishop to the numerous Christians gathered together and to the churches erected in the land of the barbarians. Then Athanasius, considering with particular attention and favour the words and deeds of Frumentius, said in the assembly of his presbyters: "And what other such man shall we find in whom verily the Spirit of God is,[4] who can accomplish these things so well?" Having committed to Frumentius the sacred office, the young archbishop instructed him to return with the grace of God whence he had come. So Frumentius went, probably in the year 330, to India as bishop; and the historian, with a touch characteristically true to the notions largely prevalent in his time, adds that so great grace and powers are said to have been given him, that apostolic miracles were done by him and an infinite number of barbarians were converted to the faith. Wherefore, in various parts of India, multitudes of people became Christians, and churches were built and the priesthood began.

So far the story has been told as nearly as possible in the words of Rufinus, who took it down, as he tells us, from the lips of Edesius. The geography of Rufinus is hardly intelligible; but fortunately we possess contemporary sources of information which enable us to check his terms, and to determine the local limits of the bishopric of

Frumentius. Rufinus himself informs us that, while Parthia was assigned to St Thomas, Ethiopia to St Matthew, and India citerior to St Bartholomew, yet "no ploughshare of apostolic preaching had touched" India ulterior, until, in the time of Constantine the Great, it "received the first seeds of the faith" from Frumentius. Commentators like Pagi, while finding fault with the geographical nomenclature employed by Rufinus, tell us that by India ulterior he meant modern Ethiopia; and, though this might remain uncertain if we had nothing but the text of Rufinus to guide us, the writings of Athanasius and the records of the Abyssinian Church seem to put the question beyond dispute.

For nearly half a century, the brave, high-souled Athanasius held, as Archbishop of Alexandria, the highest ecclesiastical position in the Christian world of the fourth century; and, when persecution pressed him, as it persistently did—for he was banished five times by four successive emperors—he fled from the city, not uncommonly into the wilderness, where his active mind produced many of those writings by which he still speaks to the world. In the year 356, while he was in exile, he wrote his 'Apology to Constantius,' the time-serving son of the great Constantine. In that apology—the word being used of course in its primitive sense—he has occasion to complain of a rumour that had reached him about an alleged intention on the part of the Emperor to remove Bishop Frumentius from his see. The rumour was in due course confirmed by a letter addressed by Constantius himself to the 'tyrants' of Auxumis or Axum, the capital of Abyssinia. In that letter, of which Athanasius has preserved a copy,[5] the Emperor Constantius, whose prejudices were then all in favour of the Arians, and deeply embittered against Athanasius, ordered Æzanes and Sazanes to "send Bishop Frumentius as soon as possible into Egypt to appear before the most honoured Bishop George and the other bishops of Egypt," with a view to their determining how far he was influenced by the teaching of Athanasius. "For," adds the Emperor, "ye know and remember, unless ye alone pretend to be ignorant of those things which are confessed by all, namely, that it was by Athanasius that Frumentius was promoted to this grade of life." Thus, twenty-six years before the date of the Emperor's letter, Frumentius had been ordained Bishop of Axum by Athanasius; for upwards of a quarter of a century he administered the affairs of the Church of Abyssinia, whose records attest the gratitude with which his memory was long cherished as the founder of the Church, the translator of the Scriptures into the Ethiopic (*Geez*), and the doer of many other beneficent works. The letter of Constantius threatened the deposition of Frumentius, and there is some reason to think that the threat (as we shall see hereafter) was carried out. But however that may be, the province, whose ecclesiastical administration under the Pope of Alexandria was committed to the hands of Frumentius, was Abyssinia; and it was Abyssinia that Rufinus and his followers, Socrates, Sozomen, and other historians, called by the name of India.

Among the many Indias known to antiquity, therefore, there was an Ethiopian India. We shall presently see that there was also an Arabian India.

II.

The authority for the story of Theophilus, the Indian, is Philostorgius, a native of Cappadocia, who was born of humble parentage about the year 364. It would seem that he went to Constantinople in his youth to complete his studies, but it is uncertain whether he was educated for the Church or the Bar. In later life he composed a 'History of the Church,' comprised in twelve books, from the beginning of the Arian schism down to the year 425. The work itself is no longer extant; but we have an epitome of it compiled by Photius, who was appointed to the patriarchal see of Constantinople in 853, and under whom the schism between the Eastern and Western Churches was formally consummated. From this epitomised edition of Philostorgius we learn that in 356 Constantius resolved to send an embassy to 'Arabia Magna,' or 'Arabia Felix,' of which the metropolis was Saba, to a people known as Homeritæ. These Homeritæ were, according to Philostorgius, formerly called by the name of Sabæans, or Indians indifferently, and one of the names of their country was India, a name which he freely uses. In other words, Arabia Felix and India were used by Philostorgius as synonymous terms. The emperor wished to build churches for the benefit of the Romans who went thither by sea, and the inhabitants of the country who should embrace the Christian faith. He thought that, if he could conciliate the king of that people by magnificent presents and words of gentle persuasion, he could thence take an opportunity forthwith of sowing the seeds of religion. In despatching the embassy, therefore, he put on board the ship two hundred well-bred horses from Cappadocia, and sent many other gifts, with the double purpose of making an imposing show and of conciliating the feelings of the people. At the head of the embassy he placed Theophilus, the Indian,[6] who, being a native of the island Diu Socotra, had been sent in early youth by his fellow-citizens as a hostage to Constantinople, where he became a Christian, and embraced the true—that is, according to Philostorgius, the Arian—faith concerning God. He chose the monastic life, and was promoted to the diaconate at the hands of Eusebius, formerly of Nicomedia. Having undertaken this embassy, he was promoted by the men of his own party to the episcopal dignity.

Accordingly, Theophilus, on his arrival, finding that the Homeritæ, who were descended from Abraham by Keturah, not only practised circumcision, but also offered sacrifices to the sun and the moon and the gods of the country, endeavoured to persuade the ruler of the tribe to become a Christian. "Hereupon the customary fraud and malice of the Jews was compelled to sink into deep silence as soon as Theophilus had once or twice proved by his wonderful miracles the truth of the Christian faith." The embassy proved successful; for the prince of the nation, by sincere conviction, came over to the true religion, and built three churches in the district, not however with the money which the emperor's ambassadors had brought, but with sums which he voluntarily supplied out of his private resources, with a laudable strife to show that his own zeal was equal to the wonders performed by Theophilus. One of these churches he erected in a place called Tapharum (Zaphar), the metropolis of the nation; another at Aden, the mart of the Roman commerce "lying towards the outer sea," "where everybody is in the habit of landing on coming out of the Roman territories;" and the third in another part of the district, where the mart of Persian commerce stands "hard by the mouth of the Persian Sea."

Then Theophilus, having arranged everything among the Homeritæ according to his ability and circumstances, and having dedicated the churches and adorned them with such decorations as he could, went to pay a visit to his native island. Thence he made his way to "other districts of India" —*i.e.*, to other districts of Arabia Felix than that whose capital was Zaphar—and corrected many disorders among the inhabitants. They listened, it seems, to the Gospel in a sitting posture, and used other customs "repugnant to the divine law." But Theophilus, having corrected everything among them according to a religious rule, confirmed the doctrine of the Church. For, with regard to the doctrine of the Divine Being, he asserts, they needed no correction, inasmuch as "from the earliest antiquity they constantly professed to believe the Son to be of a different substance from the Father."

From this Arabia Felix, or India, where he found Arian Christians who practised irregular forms of worship, Theophilus proceeded to the Ethiopians, who were called Auxumitæ[7]; and, according to the Ethiopic Calendar,[8] he became Bishop of Axum in succession to Frumentius.

Arabian Christianity passed through a series of trying vicissitudes, until it was finally stamped out by the establishment and progress of Islam. For in 523 the throne of the Homeritæ was seized by a bigoted and dissolute usurper, named Dhu-Nowas (Dunaan). "A proselyte to Judaism, he perpetrated frightful cruelties on the Christians of the neighbouring province of Najrân, who refused to embrace his faith. Trenches filled with combustible materials were lighted, and the martyrs cast into the flames. Tradition gives the numbers thus miserably burnt, or slain by the sword, at twenty thousand. However exaggerated, there can be no doubt of the bloody character of the tyrant's reign. One of the intended victims escaped to the court of Justinian, and, holding up a half-burned gospel, invoked retribution. At the emperor's desire, the Negus, prince of Abyssinia, crossed from Adulis and defeated the usurper; and thus the Himyarites (Homeritæ) were supplanted by a Christian Government under an Abyssinian viceroy."[9] "If a Christian power had been maintained in Arabia," says Gibbon, by way of apology for introducing this story into the 'Decline and Fall of the Roman Empire,' "Mahomet must have been crushed in his cradle, and Abyssinia would have prevented a revolution which has changed the civil and religious state of the world." "But Abyssinian rule was distasteful to the people; an appeal was made to Persia; and, before the end of the sixth century, the Abyssinians were vanquished and expelled, and Yemen sank into a simple dependency of Persia."[10] In the following century Islam reigned alone in Arabia.

Thus on each side of the Red Sea, which was reckoned and named part of the Indian Ocean, there was an India; and these, not Southern India, are the lands to which Frumentius and Theophilus respectively went. The fact is that Southern India received Christianity, not from any of the ancient seats of the Church, not from Jerusalem or Antioch, not from Alexandria or Rome or Constantinople, but from the Nestorian patriarchate on the banks of the Tigris; not by way of the Red Sea, but by way of the Persian Gulf; not in the fourth century, nor until the beginning of the sixth.

THE NESTORIAN PERIOD

CHAPTER VIII.

THE PATRIARCHATE OF BABYLON.

The Syrian Church of Southern India was a direct offshoot from the Church of Persia; and, at the date of the planting of the South Indian Church, the Church of Persia was itself an integral part of the Patriarchate of Babylon.

To trace the development and extent of this great patriarchate, we must go back to the second quarter of the fifth century and glance at the great controversy of the day on the doctrine of the Person of Christ. It is well known how Nestorius, Bishop of Constantinople, was condemned by the Council of Ephesus in 431 for holding, as was alleged, not only that the epithet *θεότοκος* was objectionable as applied to the mother of our Lord, but also that in the Christ there were two persons as well as two natures, and that the incarnation was not the hypostatic union of the Logos with the human nature, but the simple indwelling of the Logos in the man as in a temple; how for many years thereafter he was persecuted by all the petty devices that imperial ingenuity could invent or imperial authority execute, and at length hunted to death like a beast of prey; how his works were ordered to be burned and his followers to recant; and how the Nestorian heresy was finally stamped out of the Roman Empire in consequence of stringent imperial edicts and the deposition of bishops hostile to compromise and union.[1]

But though the Nestorians were thus banished from the Roman Empire, they still lived and flourished. When they were persecuted under one government, they fled for protection to another; and although it might seem an imprudent step for them to betake themselves to a kingdom like Persia, which had been the home of persecution so long, yet in Persia they were welcomed, not because they were Christians, but mainly because they were, like the Persians themselves, the enemies of the Roman emperor. Preparation, moreover, was at an early stage made for them in the land of their adoption. Pains were taken gradually to educate the Persian mind. When, for example, the Church-teachers of Edessa were dispersed, owing to the tyranny of the orthodox, they diffused their tenets throughout the length and breadth of Persia; and King Pheroses was at length persuaded to issue a decree to the effect that Nestorianism was the only form of Christianity which would be tolerated within his dominions, a decision which was followed by a fearful massacre of all those who remained faithful to the orthodox Church.[2]

At last at a Synod, held at Seleucia in 498, the Persian Church wholly separated from the Church in the Roman Empire, and adopted the name of Chaldæan Christians[3]; while their chief assumed the splendid title of Patriarch of Babylon, his headquarters being in the first instance the double city of Seleucia-Ctesiphon, on the Tigris.

Periods of intolerance, however, on the part of the Sassanidæ were not unfrequent; as, for example, when they kept the patriarchal see vacant for twenty years till re-established by the elevation of Jesu-Jabus, who saw the last of that dynasty, and the subversion of their empire by the Arabs in the year 651.

On the first setting up of the Saracenic power, the Patriarch Jesu-Jabus succeeded in obtaining a guarantee of protection and religious liberty for the Christians on condition of their paying a certain tribute. From Omar he subsequently received a diploma of a more favourable character, by which the tribute was remitted; and these immunities were afterwards confirmed to his successor by the Caliph Ibn Abi Taleb, in a charter expressive of high esteem for the Christian religion, at least in its Nestorian form. When the city of Baghdad became the oriental metropolis about 762, the Nestorian Patriarch transferred thither his ecclesiastical see, where it continued during the existence of the caliphate. In fact, some of the earlier Mohammedan princes carried their goodwill towards the Nestorians beyond mere protection, so that they enjoyed in several ways the preference of the Caliphs, who favoured their commerce, employed them as secretaries and physicians, and raised some of them to municipal dignities.[4]

The Caliphs were doubtless well advised in securing the services of the Nestorians. The principle of selection was that of fitness. These Nestorians or Neo-Chaldæans would seem to have inherited the distinction for learning which characterised the ancient Chaldæans. Layard[5] tells us how we owe to them numerous fragments of Greek learning, as the Greeks were indebted to the ancient Chaldæans for the records of astronomy and the elements of Eastern science; how in their famous schools of Edessa, Nisibis, Seleucia, and Dorkena, both Chaldee and Syriac, as well as Greek, were taught, and that there were masters of grammar, rhetoric, poetry, dialectics, arithmetic, geometry, music, astronomy, and medicine, whose treatises were preserved in public libraries; how the attention of the Caliphs was attracted to the stores of learning translated into Chaldee from other languages and literatures, and how they were fired with a desire to have these and similar treasures translated into Arabic; how they employed for this purpose learned Nestorians who rendered, among other Greek works, those of Aristotle and Galen, besides original works from Chaldee, Persian, and Egyptian; and how Nestorian experts were sent into Syria, Armenia, and Egypt to collect manuscripts and to obtain the assistance of the most learned men.

But with all these instances of patronage, yet under the dominion of the Saracens, which endured for six hundred years, the Church had often to maintain its existence through oppression and injury, from the fickleness or cruelty of the reigning potentate, the avarice of local rulers, the jealousy of the Islamite doctors, and the hatred of the Mohammedan people at large to the Christian name.

Yet both before and after the dominion of the Caliphs began, the Church of the Chaldæan Christians did much for its own expansion; and its missionary labours, commencing so far back as the beginning of the sixth century, continued unabated till probably the eleventh or twelfth. These Chaldæans or Nestorians, says Neale, "pitched their tents in the camps of the wandering Tartar; the Lama of Thibet trembled at their words; they stood in the rice-fields of the Punjab, and taught the fishermen by the Sea of Aral; they struggled through the vast deserts of Mongolia; the memorable inscription of Singanfu attests their victories in China; in India the Zamorin himself respected their spiritual, and courted their temporal, authority." "The power of the Nestorian Patriarch," says the same authority, "culminated in the beginning of the eleventh century, when he had twenty-five metropolitans,[6] who ruled from China to the Tigris, from the Lake Baikal to Cape Comorin. Those who dwelt nearest to Baghdad met the Patriarch in yearly synod; those farthest sent their confession of faith to him every sixth year. It may be doubted whether Innocent III. possessed more spiritual power than the Patriarch of the city of the Caliphs."[7]

But the days of the destroyer were at hand. The Arab had found the Turk to be of service; and the Turk, being first a servant, gradually became a master. As in Europe the barbarians of the North crossed the mountain-backbone and swooped down on the plains of the sunny South, so Turk and Mongol came down from the heights of Central and Eastern Asia and carried all before them in the regions of wealth and ancient civilisation. When Hulaku Khan—the nephew of Chengis Khan—took Baghdad in 1258, the beginning of the end had come, and the Nestorians thereafter rapidly fell; and, when Timur about the year 1400 sent forth his conquering hordes, the Christians were either stamped out or driven for protection to the inaccessible mountain-fastnesses of Kurdistan, where a remnant of the Nestorian Church exists to this day.

Before passing from the general subject of the Nestorian Church, it is desirable to note one or two facts concerning it. In the first place, it was of vast extent. What may be called the home-Church covered thousands of square miles in Central Asia, while Southern India and Ceylon, Northern China, and Eastern Tartary may be regarded as its three great fields of foreign missions, and as daughter Churches. In the second place, its ecclesiastical position is worth observing. On this subject we may take guidance from Neale, who is by no means partial to the Nestorians, believing them, as he did, to be next to the Arians the worst enemies of sound doctrine. Neale says of them that, though heretical, they "can hardly be called schismatical, because they have constantly retained their (apostolic) succession, and for centuries had no branch of the true Church coexistent with them in their territories."[s] In all the wide territories occupied by Nestorians there was but the 'one altar.' Nestorianism and succession from St Thomas went together. Where the one was present, so also was the other. The Patriarchate of Babylon was, throughout its vast extent, Nestorian in doctrine, and in the line of succession from St Thomas. If St Peter claimed Antioch and the West, St Thomas claimed Edessa and the East. The Church of Southern India, therefore, which was a part of the

Patriarchate of Babylon, and of which we shall speak more particularly in the next chapter, was in the first instance Nestorian, and its members, deriving the succession of their ecclesiastical 'orders' from the carpenter-apostle, called themselves and were called by others Christians of St Thomas.

CHAPTER IX.

THREE PERSIAN CROSSES.

THE first unequivocal testimony to the existence of a Church in Southern India we owe to Cosmas, an Alexandrian merchant, who, having sailed the Indian Seas, was surnamed Indicopleustes, or the Indian voyager. He was a man with a hobby. His desire was to demonstrate that the world was formed after the pattern of the Jewish Tabernacle in the wilderness, and that the earth was a great rectangular plane, the length, as in the case of the table of shewbread, being double the breadth. When he had realised the hopes of a roving commercial career and had gathered all the observations he wanted in support of his impossible cosmical theory, he assumed the habit of a monk and retired to a monastery, where between the years 535 and 550 he wrote, in Greek, an account of his travels, exhibiting at the same time the details of his theorising vagaries. His 'Universal Christian Topography' is, as may be readily believed, a curious book, full of wild imaginings and strange distortions of Scripture. It has been characterised as a memorable example of that mischievous process of loading Christian truth with a dead weight of false science, which has had so many followers.

It has been compared to 'a continent of mud,' containing nevertheless a few fossils worth digging up for preservation in the museum of history. As specimens of such fossils, the following extracts may be taken. "Even in the Island of Ceylon," says Cosmas, "where the Indian Sea is, there is a Church of Christians with clergy and a congregation of believers, though I know not if there be any Christians further on in that direction. And such also is the case in the land called Malabar, where the pepper grows. And in the place called Caliana,[1] there is a bishop appointed from Persia." Speaking of Ceylon again he further says, "The island hath also a Church of Persian Christians who have settled there, and a presbyter who is appointed from Persia, and a deacon, and all the apparatus of public worship."

In this testimony we have the first scintillation

of historic light that penetrates the gloom wherewith the origin of the South Indian Church is shrouded. No more precious piece of evidence is to be met with in the whole of our researches. It is like a rock on which one may plant one's foot with firmness and survey the bearings of the situation.

In attempting to estimate the value of this testimony, one or two considerations are to be borne in mind. In the first place, it was in the year 522, or in the first quarter of the sixth century, that Cosmas visited the Malabar coast and found a fully organised Church there. The Church cannot have been of long standing, because the Persians, who from of old had a horror of the sea, had just begun to develop a capacity and a liking for navigation, and to work out schemes of commercial aggrandisement; and this enterprise on the South Indian coast was one of their earliest experiments. So that the maritime spirit of the Persian people, and the missionary spirit of the Persian Church, would seem to have grown together, and to have become active about the beginning of the sixth century. In the second place, Cosmas was himself a Nestorian, was personally on friendly terms with the Metropolitan of Persia, and was therefore as competent to report on the external relations as on the internal condition of the South Indian Church. He tells us that the constituency as well as the constitution of the Church both in Ceylon and on the west coast of Southern India was Persian; as neither, it would appear, had yet begun to associate the natives of the country in Church fellowship. In fact the Church of Ceylon would seem never to have done so, and probably for that reason had but a short-lived tenure in the island;[2] whereas, on the other hand, the Church of the Malabar coast largely cultivated the fellowship of the natives, and this was the main though not the sole cause of its permanence as a Church in the land; this and another cause to be described in a subsequent chapter[3] account, humanly speaking, for its being able to strike its roots so deep in the soil that it has weathered all the storms of adverse fortune which the vicissitudes of the ages have brought to bear against it.

But a point in Cosmas's testimony, which requires perhaps to be specially emphasised, is more of the nature of a suggestion than a statement of fact. Though he does not seem to have known of the planting of a Church on the Coromandel coast, yet in the first of the above extracts he suggests that possibly there may have been Christians 'further on in that direction,' as if he had heard something to that effect, but could not obtain sufficient evidence to warrant belief. At all events there was, as we know from other sources, a Church there which must have existed probably as early as the seventh century, or even from an earlier date. It would appear, in fact, that the Persian navigators, having established a connection at the beginning of the sixth century with the Malabar coast, proceeded thereafter, at no long interval, to establish a similar connection with the Coromandel coast. They touched at Mailapore, which was probably never a large place, but, being at the mouth of the Adyar river, it offered the most convenient access in that latitude to the busy centres of the interior. For it is worthy of note that none of India's great cities, except those built by the English, are built on the coast; so that, if you would see India aright, you must go inland and visit Delhi and Benares, Conjeveram and Madura, the temples of her gods and the palaces of her kings. It was Kanchipuram, the modern Conjeveram, that those Persian merchants were bound for. Kanchi was then one of the most famous cities of ancient India, magnificently built and strongly fortified, and it was the

PERSIAN CROSS IN CHAPEL ON ST THOMAS'S MOUNT.

Seventh or Eighth Century.

capital of a great and powerful empire. If the Persian merchants were attracted to the Malabar coast by the hope of sharing in the world-renowned pepper trade, so they must have been attracted to the Coromandel coast by the hope of a mutual exchange of products with the mighty empire of the Pallavas.[4]

Of the Christian settlement, which the colony established for itself at Mailapore, historical records are indeed peculiarly meagre, but they have been supplemented by a piece of monumental evidence of rare value, so far as it goes, which only quite recently became available. This monument helps to fix an approximate date for the settlement; it tends to show the identity of the Church at Mailapore with the stronger and more enduring Church on the coast of Malabar; and it casts some unexpected light on the doctrinal position of both Churches. The monument referred to is the cross which was discovered on St Thomas's Mount in 1547. The inscription, which is divided into two unequal parts by a mark like the plus sign in algebra, is in Pahlavi, the language of the Persian empire during the Sassanian dynasty, and, according to Dr Burnell, may belong to the seventh or eighth century. The same Pahlavi inscription appears on a similar cross of the same date in a church at Cottayam, in north Travancore. Of this inscription several renderings have been given, but probably the best is that of Dr Burnell,[5] which is as follows :—

> In punishment by the cross (was) the suffering of this One ;
> He who is the true Christ, and God above, and Guide ever pure.

Before remarking on this translation it should be noted that there is one more cross,[6] though of a much later date, in the same old church at Cottayam ; and this more modern cross, similar in form to the older cross in the same church, has in part the same inscription. In other words, it bears the second half of the Pahlavi inscription, "written in a sort of running hand" ; whereas the first part is replaced by a quotation from Galatians vi. 14, in Estrangelo Syriac, which is, "to judge from the MSS., of a period not older than *the tenth century.*" "Thus, if my reading be allowed," says Dr Burnell, "the whole would run :—

> (*Syriac*) Let me not glory except in the cross of our Lord Jesus Christ ;
> (*Pahlavi*) Who is the true Messiah, and God above, and Holy Ghost."

The meaning of this inscription it is difficult to make out with precision; but, in spite of the imperfect translations available, it would seem that a definite conclusion may be arrived at with regard to its general import. The inscription on a cross, set up as a symbol of Christianity within the limits of a church surrounded on all hands by heathenism, might be expected to exhibit the belief of that Church concerning the crucified One. To me, at least, it appears that the inscription does, in point of fact, set forth a view of the person of Christ characteristic of Indian Nestorianism; for in no other theological literature, so far as I am aware, will the notion be found which this inscription seems intended to convey. The first or shorter part speaks of the suffering Saviour, 'who,' continues the second part, 'is the true Messiah, and God above, and Holy Ghost.' Nothing can be inferred from the order in which the persons of the Trinity are here named, being the same as in the apostolic benediction;[7] but the second clause of the inscription seems intended to give expression to a doctrinal belief entertained in olden times among the Syrian Christians in Southern India, and often quoted from those books of theirs which were condemned as heretical by the Roman Catholic doctors at the Synod of Diamper (1599).[8]

The doctrine was to the effect that in the Christ each of the persons of the Trinity was incarnate. Thus in one book it is maintained that the union of the incarnation is common to all the Divine Persons, who were all incarnated; and in another the Lord Jesus is described as 'the Temple of the Most Holy Trinity'; and in several other works, quoted in the Diamper decrees, the same idea is set forth in similar terms.

The doctrine is peculiar—the Godhead, not the Logos only, being incarnate. It seems intelligible on Nestorian premises, but its genesis historically it is probably impossible to trace. On the one hand, it bears a certain resemblance to the Sabellian or Patripassian view; on the other hand, if we admit, what it seems impossible to deny, that Nestorians accepted the creed of Nicæa and were therefore trinitarians, we can hardly ascribe to them the monarchian view of the divine incarnation. But we must not look for perfect logical consistency on the part of these isolated Nestorians. However they may have come by this peculiar heresy, it seems never to have brought them into trouble. Though they blazoned it on their escutcheon, they did not fall out of communion or lose their succession.

But a point perhaps better worth insisting on than the historical or logical bearings of the doctrine exhibited on the cross, is the fact of the unity of testimony derived from the two oldest crosses. Both are Greek in form, both have the same ornamentation, both have the same Pahlavi inscription, and both exhibit the same peculiar doctrinal view of the person of Christ. In fact, it would almost seem as if these crosses had been originally set up, like the altar *Ed*,[9] to be a witness between the two Churches, separated by the breadth of a great peninsula; so that, in time to come, if circumstances should alienate them, or annihilate either, there might remain some visible token that they were both of the same stock, that they were not destitute of a zeal for doctrine, and that they desired to live in history.

So much for the older crosses; but the most modern of the three, which is supposed to belong to the tenth century, demands some notice separately, by reason of an interesting addition, not found in the older crosses. The slab on which the third of our crosses is cut, has a second or upper panel with a smaller cross, identical in form and ornamentation with the larger one below, and having on each side the figure of a peacock by way of heraldic support, the bill of each being in contact with one end of the transverse bar of the cross.

This arrangement is unique, and it becomes an interesting problem to determine what symbolic meaning is attached to the peacock in connection with St Thomas, or how it came to be adopted as a figure on his escutcheon. As the peacock is a native of Southern India, this piece of symbolism is less likely to have been imported, than to have been adopted after the connection of St Thomas's name with this province was established. At all events the local circumstances seem to supply the true explanation. For peacock-stories were often told to travellers by the Christians of Mailapore. Thus Marco Polo [10] informs us how he was told that one day, while St Thomas was praying in a grove, a fowler, who was engaged in shooting peacocks with bow and arrows, shot the apostle by mistake, so that he presently died, "sweetly addressing himself to his Creator." Again, John de Marignolli,[11] "who visited the place about the middle of the fourteenth century, tells a story he gathered on the spot, in which St Thomas is introduced on a supreme occasion riding on an ass and "wearing a shirt, a stole, and a mantle of peacocks' feathers;" and the tale concludes with an account of St Thomas's death essentially similar to that given by Marco Polo, though with many added details. And once more, Duarte Barbosa,[12] in the sixteenth century, was told a story showing how badly St Thomas was treated by the people, how he therefore often retired to the solitudes, and how one day "a Gentile hunter" who, having gone out with bow and arrows to shoot peacocks, and seeing many together on the slope of a hill, aimed at the bird in the midst of them, which seemed a peculiarly handsome creature, and sent an arrow through its body. Then the peacocks all "rose up flying," and in the air the wounded bird "turned into the body of a man." "And this hunter stood looking until he saw the body of the said apostle fall. And he went to the city, where he related that miracle to the governors, who came to see it, and they found that it was indeed the body of St Thomas; and then they went to see the place where he had been wounded, and they saw two impressions of human feet marked on the slab, which he left impressed when he rose wounded."

Now it is evident that these peacock-stories must have been invented for a purpose; and their creation marks the progress of decadence in the Church. The time of which we are speaking is not earlier than the tenth century. It may even be later. By that time the empire of the Perumals on the one side, and that of the Pallavas on the other, had passed away. Reinforcements from the mother Church had probably ceased; and the prosperity of the Indo-Syrian Church in temporal as well as spiritual things was probably on the wane. The thought of the Church began to turn upon itself. It sought to render to itself and to its neighbours an account of its own origin. Such questions could arise only long after all memory of its arrival in the country had perished. Generations must have passed away, and with them all tokens of their first coming to Southern India. The Syrians therefore wove this fictitious story of their pedigree. In doing this they had two considerations to guide them. In the first place, was it not the belief of the Church from the earliest times that St Thomas was the apostle of the Indians; and was this India in which they dwelt not to be adjudged to St Thomas? Was it not here that he fulfilled the commission which he received from the Saviour after the ascension? was it not here that he attained his consummation and won the crown of martyrdom? In the second place, were they not Christians of St Thomas? and was it not an ecclesiastical axiom, that, in whatever country Christianity might be found, it must have been planted there by an apostle? Who therefore could have planted the Church of St Thomas save the apostle whose name they had the honour to bear?

Such seems to have been the mental process through which they arrived at a conclusion still accepted by many in India. But it is full of fallacies. In the first place, these Nestorian Christians had forgotten, if they ever knew, that it was in India west of the Indus that St Thomas preached and performed miracles and planted churches, that from the date of his arrival in that country to the date of his death he never left it, and that no room is left by the writer of the 'Acts' for labours elsewhere, but that, on the contrary, all opportunity for such labours is excluded from the story. In the second place, they forgot what exactly is meant by the phrase Christians of St Thomas. It means merely that the Church to which they belonged, their mother Church on the Tigris, derived the grace of apostolic succession from St Thomas. If St Thomas planted the Church in Southern India, he did so, not by a personal visit, but by the agency of the Church which had adopted him as its patron saint, from whom, according to tradition (our only authority on this point), it received the chrism of ordination. The Church was planted in Southern India by Christians whose priesthood received their ecclesiastical 'orders' in the last resort from St Thomas. Their Church-standing was ultimately traceable to that apostle; and so, by a figure of speech, it might be said that St Thomas planted the Churches of the East; what was done by his followers in his name, whether in Southern India, or Northern China, or Eastern Tartary, was spoken of as if it had been done by himself; and thus it came to pass that, not St Thomas, but only the tradition migrated to these countries respectively.

For the development of these peacock-stories the spirit of rivalry and competition came into play; and the Christians of Mailapore probably felt that they were put on their mettle, and must not allow themselves in this matter to be outdone by their neighbours. The suggestion was derived from the mythology of the neighbouring Hindu temple; for it so happens that it has a peacock-story connected with it. The Purana of that temple tells how Siva's wife appeared there to her lord in the form of a *mayil* or peafowl; and that the place from this circumstance received its name, *mayil-a-pur* or peacock-town. Philologists may dispute concerning the etymology of this name if they please; but, whatever the historically correct origin of the name may be, it was the traditional view that became the popular belief, and it was the popular belief that operated so influentially on the minds of the Christians of St Thomas. They invented those peacock-stories, in which their apostolic patron figures somewhat ludicrously, for the purpose of adding prestige to their cause. They wished to carry back the beginning of their local history on the Coromandel coast to a time earlier than the foundation of the city, and to make-believe that it was not a Hindu but a Christian town, which owed its name to incidents in the history of St Thomas. It was he in fact that had made the place by having worked, and prayed, and died there; and his memory had been perpetuated in the name of the city. They wished to represent that the city was of Christian-apostolic and not of Hindu origin. Such was the intended effect of this clever appropriation of the peacocks;

and so it came to pass that the Indian peacock became the symbol of the Indian apostle.

It seems that the idea of appropriating the peacock as a symbol of St Thomas originated with the Syrian Christians on the Coromandel coast; but the fact that a representation of it in stone was set up as a piece of church decoration on the Malabar coast, shows that its acceptance by the Church was not confined to one side of the peninsula. It seems probable that, as in the seventh century two identical crosses were prepared and set up, one on each coast, so in the tenth century two identical crosses may have likewise been prepared and similarly arranged. But if so, the tenth-century cross on the Coromandel coast must have been lost, as the older cross on the same coast was for a time. It probably lies buried somewhere on St Thomas's Mount, to reward one day the labours of some industrious explorer.

CHAPTER X.

THE JEWS OF COCHIN.

OF Indian Jews there are in all about ten thousand. Perhaps the largest and most influential community of them is to be found in Bombay and Puna, where they have commodious and well-equipped synagogues. This body of Jews in our own time attracted the notice of royalty and received in the person of Sir Albert Sassoon the distinction of knighthood.

Perhaps the most interesting colony of Jews in India, however, is located on the western coast of the peninsula at a considerably lower latitude than Bombay. The Rajah of Cochin used to be called by the early Portuguese the king of the Jews, because of the conspicuous number of the stock of Abraham that dwelt within his dominions; just as the Zamorin of Calicut was styled, for a like reason, the king of the Moors or Mohammedans.

In the Cochin State there were, according to the census of 1881, some 1294 Jews[1]—including both the white Jews and the black—or about one-eighth part of all the Jews in India. In dress and outward bearing they hardly differ from their brethren in other places. The ladies are said to adopt the fashions of Baghdad; while the men, who all cultivate the long love-locks brought down in front of the ears in obedience to Leviticus xix. 27, wear a turban, a long tunic of rich colour, a waistcoat buttoned up to the neck, and full white trousers.

In speech, while they use Hebrew for purposes of religious worship, they employ for secular and common purposes the vernacular Malayalam of the place. They forsake not the assembling of themselves together on the seventh day of the week, and they put off their shoes before they cross the sacred threshold of the synagogue. Any one, however, who wears English boots or an English hat is not required or permitted to uncover. They separate the sexes in the house of prayer, and give to the woman a secondary place, every one of the circumcised meanwhile saying in a spirit, as it would seem, of self-gratulation, 'I thank Thee, O God, that Thou didst not make me a woman.' When public worship is being conducted, the rabbi stands on a platform in the middle of the synagogue, with his face towards Jerusalem, supported on either hand by a member of the congregation, and reads, chants, or snivels the service at such a rapid rate that it is difficult for an uninitiated spectator to understand how even the devout can profit or follow. In reading the law they do not venture to pronounce the name *Jehovah*, but substitute for it, according to a long-standing though by no means uniform practice,[2] the name *Adonai*—the Cochin theory being that 'Jehovah' was never pronounced in old times save by the high priest on the day of atonement. They observe the new moons and the annual feasts after a fashion, but modern Jews have no altars and no bloody sacrifices, and considerable modifications on strictly Mosaic ritual must in any case be made.

When I visited the colony in 1870, I asked what views prevailed among them concerning the Messiah—were they looking for Him? 'Yes,' said one who had visited Constantinople, Amsterdam, London, and New York; 'we are looking for

Him; daily, hourly, minutely looking for Him,'—language that may be compared with an article in the creed of Maimonides which runs, 'I believe with a perfect heart that the Messiah will come; and, though He delays, nevertheless I will always expect Him till He comes.' They have copies of the Pentateuch, both manuscript and printed. The prophecies, I believe, are rare; and the New Testament, I am told, they abhor, and will not allow a copy of it to come within their borders. Yet Claudius Buchanan relates that, when he visited the colony in 1807, he obtained 'in a private manner' an inspection of two translations of the New Testament into Hebrew—the one 'in the small rabbinical or Jerusalem character, the other in a large square letter.' The former, he adds, was rendered by a learned rabbi, who performed his task with stern fidelity because he had undertaken it, not to make the New Testament available to his kinsmen, but to confute it.

There is one touching feature in this little colony which can hardly escape the attention of even the most casual visitor. The cemetery, where their uncoffined dead sleep under the rustling leaves of the cocoanut-palms, in graves that run north and south, is called *Beth Haiim*, the house of the living.

In discussing the question of the coming of the Jews to Cochin, reference has been made by several writers with varying results to three different sources of information. The first authentic record of the contact of Jews with Dravidians is to be found in the Bible, 1 Kings x. 22, and 2 Chronicles ix. 21. Solomon's fleet, manned by Phœnician sailors, seems to have fetched from the Malabar coast of India "ivory, apes, and peacocks," as well as "gold and silver" to adorn his magnificent court. The subject has been much discussed,[2] but it is admitted that the names for *ivory*, *apes*, and *peacocks* are foreign words in Hebrew, as much as *gutta-percha* and *tobacco* are in English. Now, if we wished to know from what part of the world *tobacco* was first imported into England, we might safely conclude that it came from that country where the name, *tobacco*, formed part of the spoken language. If therefore we can find a language in which the name for (say) *peacocks*, which is foreign in Hebrew, is indigenous, we may be certain that the country in which that language was spoken must have been the country visited by Solomon's fleet. The discovery has been made. At all events, not a few competent scholars are agreed that the word used in the original text of the Bible for 'peacocks,' *tukki-im*, is simply the Tamil word spelt in Hebrew letters and supplied with a Hebrew plural inflection. Few can speak on this subject with more authority than Dr Caldwell. "The oldest Dravidian word," says the late learned Bishop, "found in any written record in the world, appears to be the word for 'peacock' in the Hebrew text of the books of Kings and Chronicles, in the list of the articles of merchandise brought . . . in Solomon's ships about 1000 B.C. . . . The ordinary name at present for the peacock on the Malabar coast and in Tamil is *mayil* (Sans. *mayûra*); it is sometimes called *śiki* (Sans. *śikhi*), a name given to it on account of its crest; but the ancient, poetical, purely Tamil-Malayâlam name of the peacock is *tôkei*, the bird with the (splendid) tail. *Śikhi=avis cristata; tôkei=avis caudata.*"[3] It seems reasonable, therefore, to infer that Solomon's historiographer became acquainted with the bird and its name in consequence of visits made by that great king's sailors to the west coast of Southern India. Nor is it improbable that similar visits may have followed in the course of the centuries subsequent to Solomon's time, there being no reason to disbelieve that Jews may have visited India, just as the Teutons visited Britain long before they actually settled there. A broad distinction, however, is to be made between the visits of traders and the coming of settlers; and there is no historical evidence of any actual settlement of Jews on the Malabar coast till more than a millennium and a half after Solomon.

The second source of information that falls to be considered is a document emanating from the Jews of Cochin themselves. It is a narrative, written in Hebrew, of the events relating to their first arrival in India which had been handed down to them from their fathers. Of this document they presented a copy to Claudius Buchanan in 1807. It is as follows: *After the second Temple was destroyed (which may God speedily rebuild!), our fathers, dreading the conqueror's wrath, departed from Jerusalem, a numerous body of men, women, priests, and Levites, and came to this land. There were among them men of repute for learning and wisdom; and God gave the people favour in the sight of the king who at that time reigned here, and he granted them a place to dwell in, called Cranganore. He allowed them a patriarchal jurisdiction within the district, with certain privileges of nobility; and the royal grant was engraved, according to the custom of those days, on a plate of copper. This was done in the year from the creation of the world* 4250 (A.D. 490); *and this plate of copper we still have in possession. Our forefathers continued at Cranganore for about a thousand years, and the number of heads who governed were seventy-two. Soon after our settlement, other Jews followed us from Judæa; and among these came that man of great wisdom, Rabbi Samuel, a Levite of Jerusalem, with his son Rabbi Jehuda Levita. They brought with them the* SILVER TRUMPETS *made use of at the time of the* JUBILEE, *which were saved when the second Temple was destroyed; and we have heard from our fathers, that there were engraven upon those trumpets the letters of the ineffable Name. There joined us also from Spain and other places, from time to time, certain tribes of Jews, who had heard of our prosperity. But at last, discord arising among ourselves, one of our chiefs called to his assistance an Indian king, who came upon us with a great army, destroyed our houses, palaces, and strongholds, dispossessed us of Cranganore, killed part of us, and carried part into captivity. By these massacres we were reduced to a small number. Some of the exiles came and dwelt at Cochin, where we have remained ever since, suffer-*

ing great changes from time to time. There are amongst us some of the children of Israel (Beni Israel) who came from the country of Ashkenaz, from Egypt, from Tsoba, and other places, besides those who formerly inhabited this country.[4]

In this narrative there are three notes of time: (1) that the Jews came to the west coast of Peninsular India just after the destruction of the second Temple by the Romans A.D. 70; (2) that their coming preceded by no long interval the date of their *sasanam*, or copper-plate charter, which they assign to the year of the world 4250 (A.D. 490); and (3) that their "forefathers continued at Cranganore for about a thousand years." Now these data seem to be mutually inconsistent, and cannot therefore be accepted without considerable modification.

Before, however, attempting to prove this, it is necessary to examine with some care our third source of information, namely, the *sasanam* or copper-plate charter referred to in the statement which Buchanan received at Cochin. It consists of two copper plates with three pages of text.[5] The character in which it is written is the Vatteluttu, which is believed to be an adaptation of some foreign (probably Semitic) character to a

Dravidian language; and is "the original Tamil alphabet once used in all that part of the peninsula south of Tanjore, and also in South Malabar and Travancore," though of course as different from the modern Tamil alphabet as the handwriting of Alfred the Great is different from the caligraphy of Queen Victoria.

The Jewish charter has often been translated, the oldest rendering of it being that given in Hebrew by the Jews themselves. "The Hebrew translator," however, says Dr Gundert, who was the first to unravel its true meaning, "seems neither to have understood much of the original Tamil, nor to have cared about rendering it faithfully." It confers, in the name of Bhaskara Ravi Varma, King of Malabar, the principality of Anjuvannam and all its revenues on Joseph Rabban, the head man of the Jewish community. It sanctions also the use of elephants to carry earth and water in marriage and other processions; the light by day, still highly prized by the ruling houses of Travancore and Cochin and other chieftains; the spreading cloth to walk upon; the litter or palanquin; the umbrella, a privilege so highly prized that the title 'lord of the umbrella' is hardly inferior to that of maharajah; the trumpet or conch-shell, which still figures in the emblazonments of the Travancore and Cochin rulers; the gateway with seats, probably the power of administering justice; ornamental arches, and similar awnings and garlands, still thrown across the paths taken by members of the royal houses.

But the grand distinction was the according to the head man of the Jews a rank co-ordinate with that of the local princes, which is implied in the fact that six of the latter appended their names as witnesses to the deed. Thus to Joseph Rabban, the owner of Anjuvannam, and to his posterity, sons and daughters, nephews and sons-in-law, these rights and privileges were given, "a hereditary appendage so long as the earth and moon endure."

"The actual date of this grant," says Dr Burnell, "cannot be later than the eighth century A.D., for of two other similar grants in possession of the Syrian Christians one presupposes its existence, and one of these I have ascertained to be of 774 A.D., while the other belongs to the beginning of the ninth century. Nor can the Jewish *sasanam* be older than the beginning of the eighth century, as the many Grantha letters in it are too developed to be of an earlier date." The date therefore has been set down approximately as 700 A.D.

Having thus ascertained the true date of the

Jewish *sasanam*, we may now recur to the consideration of those three notes of time found in the statement delivered to Claudius Buchanan.

In the first place, the Cochin Jews are known to have been expelled from Cranganore (of which more hereafter) in the year 1565; so that, if the 'thousand years' be taken as the nearest round number to fix the approximate date, then the coming of the first company of Jewish settlers may fall anywhere between the middle of the sixth and the middle of the seventh century. Again, the date of the *sasanam* as given in Buchanan's text is wrong. The true date is not 490, but 700. But the coming of the colony must have preceded the latter date by a considerable interval in order to give them time to show their own importance and the stuff of which they were made. They could not gain the goodwill of the king and the respect of the neighbouring chiefs in a day. If two or three generations should suffice for this process of habilitation, then the time of their coming would fall within the first half of the seventh century; if more were required, the date might still not go beyond the middle of the sixth century. On the whole it would seem that there is substantial agreement between the second and third notes of time above specified; but, for this very reason, they exclude the first. The date synchronising with the destruction of Jerusalem seems, not from any inherent improbability in the statement itself, but for the reasons just assigned, to be as apocryphal as the 'silver trumpets.' This amount of truth, however, may be supposed to reside in that first note: it may be held to record a lingering memory in the colony, of their having been originally urged to this migration by reason of persecution or war.

Having thus determined, within certain limits, the probable time of the coming of the Jews, the next question to consider is whence they came. On this point some light may be expected from a review of the political circumstances in which Jews were placed by the authorities in those countries of Asia that lie nearest to India and that border most closely on the great commercial highways by which intercourse with the West was maintained. It is well known, for instance, that Arabia had from early times become the chosen home of Jews. The sack of Jerusalem by Nebuchadnezzar, the attack of Pompey sixty-four years before the Christian era, with that of Titus seventy years after it, and the bloody retribution inflicted by Hadrian on Judea in the year 136, are some of the later causes which dispersed the Jews and drove large numbers into Arabia, where they long enjoyed the privilege of toleration. But on the rise of Mohammedanism all was changed. At first indeed Mahomet hoped to annex them to his cause; but, when it became evident to the prophet that his promises failed to win them, he had recourse to the stern proselytism of the sword. He sent them the peremptory alternative 'Islamism or war'; and there could be little doubt which of the two contending parties would ultimately win the day. Many of the Jews were slain, "but Mahomet reserved the right of exiling them according to his pleasure—a right which was afterwards exercised by the Caliph Omar, who alleged the dying injunction of the prophet, that but one faith should be permitted to exist in Arabia." "Some of the Jews of Khaibar," adds Dean Milman,[6] "were transplanted to Syria;" and it does not seem improbable that some may have found in India an asylum from Arabian persecution.

Similar persecutions were being carried on about the same time in Persia, where Jews had long dwelt and where they seem to have been sometimes oppressively treated. Especially severe was the persecution directed against them during the reign of Yesdegred III., the last of the kings of the Sassanian dynasty, and it was not to be wondered at, that many of them should have endeavoured to escape to countries where the hand of persecution would not be laid upon them, and where they would enjoy a measure of liberty in the pursuit of their chosen avocations. It seems therefore probable that the Jews, who obtained a charter from Bhaskara Ravi Varma, the King of Malabar, in the year 700, were refugees from the persecutions directed against them in Arabia or Persia.

In their adopted country the Jews enjoyed toleration; for the Brahman, the Musalman, and the Portuguese were all as yet equally unknown there; and, in so far as the people of Malabar had been influenced by Buddhism and Jainism, such influence was rather in favour of toleration than otherwise. With the blessing of toleration, denied them elsewhere, the Jews soon attained to a measure of material prosperity, social distinction, and political consequence, to which the circumstances that eventuated in the granting of their charter add a significance and a value that might otherwise escape notice. For we ought not to regard the recognition of the Jewish colony by the sovereign of the country and the promotion of its head man to a position of equality with the local princes, as being merely a transaction in which favour was granted on the one side and accepted on the other. It was rather of the nature of a bargain or contract. The Jews did not receive their privileges for nothing: it is probable that they gave a substantial *quid pro quo.* For the Jewish charter was granted "at or very near the time when the Western Chalukya raids into Southern India resulted in the dismemberment of the Pallava kingdom, and its three confederate and apparently subordinate dynasties, of which Kerala was one."[7] At such times the royal treasury might need replenishing and the ranks of the army require reinforcement; and the Jews, on condition of supplying, to an extent worthy of their proverbial resources, the sinews of war, and perhaps also a contingent of fighting men, would secure for themselves and the generations following both the status of a self-governing community and the right of freely carrying on domestic and foreign trade. The Perumal's extremity was the Jews' opportunity, and they made their bargain accordingly.

For nine hundred years the Jews of Cranganore

enjoyed the high standing set forth in the memorable deed; but no literary monuments of that prosperous period have survived the catastrophes which befell them in the sixteenth century, and by which they were finally expelled from Cranganore. It appears that in 1524, the year before Vasco da Gama's death, the Mohammedans, with the Zamorin's approval, made an onslaught on the Cranganore Jews and Christians, the reason alleged being that the followers of the prophet had resorted to various tricks for adulterating the pepper and other wares brought to market, and some Jews and Christians had been specially selected to discover such tricks and mete out justice to the offenders. Assembling from various quarters, the Mohammedans mustered a fleet of one hundred grabs and attacked Cranganore. They slew many Jews and drove out the rest to a village to the east; but, when they attacked the Christians, the Nayars of the place retaliated, and in turn drove all the Mohammedans out of Cranganore.

After this there seems to have been a respite for about forty years; but in 1565 the Zamorin and his allies again invaded the Cochin State. The enemy was victorious, the Cochin rajah and two princes were slain in battle, and the succeeding rajah shared the same fate only a fortnight later. In the same year the Portuguese enlarged and strengthened their Cranganore Fort; and the Jews finally deserted their ancient settlement of Anjuvannum and came to Cochin, near which they built Jews' Town, where they reside to this day. Even here, however, they did not escape chastisement at the hands of their enemies; for in 1661, on the siege of Cochin being raised, the Portuguese blamed the Jews for having helped the Dutch, and plundered their town of almost all it contained. What with the destruction of Cranganore, which they paint like the destruction of Jerusalem in miniature, and recite as if it were a chapter out of the book of Lamentations, and what with the wanton onslaught by the Portuguese at Cochin, the sacrifice of life and property to them must have been truly awful, and the destruction of all literary monuments is an irreparable loss to history. Soon afterwards the Dutch came into power on that coast, and after a hundred and thirty years gave way in their turn to the English. During the dominance of these two Protestant powers, the Jews have had all the advantages of a kindly toleration, and a frequent and friendly intercourse with their brethren in Europe.

Twelve or thirteen centuries have thus come and gone since this colony of Jews, who are fairer in complexion to-day than most Europeans, planted itself in the little Hindu State of Cochin. It has usually been believed that white races in India, after three or four generations, become sterile and die out; and some have inferred that the persistence of this colony at Cochin so long shows the common belief on this point to be destitute of adequate foundation. Yet the Jews of Cochin form no real exception to a rule so well established; for it is needful, in order to maintain the continuity of the colony, that fresh blood should be periodically imported from higher latitudes. It is the testimony of careful observers, who have lived on the west coast of Southern India, that no white Jews "of upwards of three generations," born in the country, of pure unmixed blood on father's and mother's side, can be detected.[8] The colony has been largely replenished from time to time by immigrants from Europe for at least two hundred years; and the law of periodic immigration as a condition of continuity doubtless goes much farther back in its history.

Nowhere have the Jews amalgamated with the people among whom they dwell. At Cochin this exclusiveness has operated peculiarly in connection with the formation of a synagogue of black Jews. These black Jews are converts to the faith from among the people of the land. It is said that, when the Jews settled at Cranganore, they purchased five hundred slaves, who became proselytes. In that case, the black Jews are the descendants of the five hundred together with those of accessions received afterwards. While the white Jews are traders and merchants, the black Jews gain their livelihood by practising various handicrafts, and are sawyers, blacksmiths, carpenters, bricklayers, bookbinders, tailors, fishermen, servants to the white Jews, or vendors of household necessaries. The black Jews have a separate synagogue of their own, but, if one of the white Jews were to enter, the chief seat would be at once vacated for him; and every relation in which they stand marks them out to be an inferior race, that have never yet risen above the servile origin from which they seem to have sprung. In these respects there is a marked contrast between the black Jews and the native Syrian Christians. The latter have some of the best blood of the land. But the synagogue never opened its door to the native. It told him to erect a synagogue for himself. The Church, on the other hand, freely opened its doors, admitted the natives to communion and to office, until the time came when the administration of Church ordinances, Church property, and Church offices from the highest to the lowest, fell entirely into their hands.

There seems to be no memory of any great men having arisen among the Jews of Cochin. A correspondent informs me that within the last half-century one of their number was made a judge by the rajah of Cochin, and was much esteemed also by the rajah of Travancore. "The brother of this judge," he adds, "became a Christian, and was very useful in service under the Church Missionary Society among the Beni-Israel of Bombay and Puna. . . . In commerce none have attained eminence, though there are two or three rich families still extant." For education they do not seem to care, either for its own sake or as a passport for admission to the public service. Efforts have been made from time to time by benevolent persons to encourage public instruction among them. The Church of Scotland maintained a mission to the Jews of Cochin from 1845 to 1857, but without success. Some ten or twelve years ago they petitioned the Dewan of Cochin for an English school, promising to send always fifty or a hundred boys. A district school in the neighbourhood of Cranganore, being no longer needed, was accordingly transferred to Mattancheri, within a stone's-throw of Jews' Town. On the other side of the backwater and ferry-free they have Government education available from the primary classes up to the standard of the First-in-Arts Examination of the Madras University. But they do not use their advantages. When the Mattancheri school was opened they sent about twenty scholars, varying in age from ten to twenty-eight. The elder ones fancied they could learn English in a year, but they proved too old to learn anything, and after a few months the numbers dropped to eight or ten; and now there are not over a dozen Jewish boys in the district school and the High School together. A school in which the Hebrew Scriptures and the Talmud are taught is maintained by the synagogue and aided by the native State, but it is a poor affair. The parents are contented if the boys learn to read a little Hebrew, and then turn their attention to trade or some other mode of money-making.

It deserves to be mentioned, however, that in 1884 a Jewish lad passed the Matriculation Examination of the Madras University, having been able to fulfil the requirements for matriculation in that particular year, because—not to speak of his educational equipment — the examination, which lasts for five days, began on a Monday morning, and did not therefore encroach on the Jewish Sabbath.

What the future of the Indian Jews shall be is a question bound up in the still larger question of the destiny of the Jewish people as a whole. They have been scattered over all the parts of the earth, but nowhere have they been absorbed. They remain as by miracle a distinct nation, six and a quarter million strong.[9] What is known in modern politics as the Eastern Question raises large issues with respect to the Jews. If, as many think, the Jews are destined in the latter days to return to their own land, then, when that grand reunion is effected, India will send its contingent of ten thousand to the great general assembly.

CHAPTER XI.

TWO COPPER-PLATE CHARTERS.

The history of the Church of Malabar is very different from that of the sister Church of Mailapore. The former has survived all the vicissitudes of its lot, and is at this day represented by a community of more than 400,000 people; while the latter had disappeared early in the sixteenth century, leaving a heritage of unhistorical traditions, to which the Goanese Roman Catholics promptly served themselves heirs.

The difference of fortune in the case of these two sister Churches may be accounted for mainly by the fact that the Malabar Christians acquired from the kings of that country a certain political status, including the right of self-government, in token of which they received two of those *sasanams* or copper-plate charters so familiar to the student of Indian history.[1]

Of these documents, the first that was granted to the Christians is a copper instrument—14¾ inches by 4—written on both sides in old Tamil characters mixed with a good many Grantha letters. The date of it, according to Dr Burnell's calculations, is 774. It is a grant made by King Vira Raghava Chakravarti to Iravi Corttan of Cranganore, making over to him, as representative head of the Christian community there, the little principality of Manigramam,[2] and elevating him to the position of sovereign merchant of Kerala.

The second *sasanam* that was granted to the Christians of St Thomas consists of five copper plates, bound together according to the usual custom by a ring passing through holes pierced in the ends of the several plates. These plates or leaves, as they are sometimes called, are of smaller size than the former, and contain seven pages of Tamil-Malayalam,[3] apparently written by different hands, and two pages of two other languages—Pahlavi and Arabic—in the Kufic character, with four Hebrew signatures. This deed was granted about the year 824 with the sanction of the palace-major or commissioner of King Sthanu

Ravi Gupta, who is probably identical with Cheraman Perumal, whose name is in the mouth of every child on the coast. It is a legal instrument by which one Muruvan Sapir Iso, who had obtained a grant of a piece of ground in the neighbourhood of Quilon, with several families of different heathen castes, transfers the same with due legal formality to the Tarasa Church and community.

From these two charters, compared with the Jewish charter, much may be learnt regarding the constitution of society in Malabar from the beginning of the eighth century to the end of the first quarter of the ninth. It will be sufficient to set forth here only so much of that constitution as may enable us to understand the position to which the Jews and the Syrian Christians were admitted by their respective charters.

The petty empire of the Perumals, or big-men, as the kings of Malabar were called, extended from Calicut in the north to Quilon in the south, and was known by the name of Chera, or—to use its better-known Canarese equivalent—Kerala. The great body of the people in this area, as well as the Perumals themselves, were then as now non-Aryans. But if the non-Aryans have always been the most numerous section of the population of Malabar, the Aryans have been the most influential. The introduction of Aryan civilisation into Malabar is due to the Jains, who were in that part of the country as early as the third century before Christ. Jain missionaries penetrated as far as Malabar in Asoka's time.[4] But though they established one of their peculiar styles of architecture and probably organised the community into corporate guilds, they seem to have made little impression on the religious beliefs of the people. This last result was reserved for the Brahmans, who seem to have first come to Malabar in the eighth century.[5] With that haughty indifference to objective truth in questions of divinity which led the Romans to admit into their pantheon the gods of the nations which they conquered, the Brahmans not only recognised the gods of the people over whom they obtained influence, but invented for them genealogies which connected them with their own proper divinities. Hence Malayali-Hinduism embraces, chiefly as divers manifestations of Siva and his consort Kali, all the demoniac gods originally worshipped by the Malayalis.[6]

The influence of the Brahmans, however, was by

no means limited to religion. It is interesting to mark how they contributed also to the development and perfecting of the organisation of the community for civil purposes. The old Aryan constitution consisted of the well-known four-fold division into Brahmans, Kshatriyas, Vaisyas, and Sudras; and it was on this model that the Brahmans sought to construct society in Southern India. It was not possible for them to carry out their scheme in all its symmetrical proportions; for, in dealing with the primitive population of Malabar, they were dealing with an alien race. They had no sufficient body of protectors of their own to fall back on, so they had perforce to acknowledge the native ruling race, whom they invested with the functions of Kshatriyas, but on whom they were apparently unable to confer a higher rank than that of Sudras. It was needful that there should be a protector or Kshatriya caste; so they promoted the ruling race to this distinction, and called them Nayars.[7]

As protectors their duties were to preserve all rights from being curtailed or falling into disuse. They were the militia, the police, and in some sense the *custodes morum* of the nation. Nor was this the only class of duties they had to perform. They were originally cultivators and belonged to the Vellala caste. In the development of the caste system they were made not only 'protectors,' but also land-agents and collectors of revenue, in which capacity the name applied to them was that of 'supervisors.'

Originally the Nayars seem to have been organised into 'six hundreds,' and each 'six hundred' seems to have had assigned to it the protection of all the people in a *nad* or county. The *nad* was in turn split up into *taras*—the *tara* being the Nayar territorial unit of organisation for civil purposes—and governed by representatives of the caste, who were termed *karanavar* or elders. The 'six hundred' was probably composed exclusively of these elders, and there seems to have been four families of them to each *tara*, so that the *nad* must originally have consisted of one hundred and fifty *taras*.

In compensation for the services rendered in the double capacity of 'protectors' and 'supervisors,' one share of the produce of the land, the amount of which cannot now be determined, was given to the 'six hundred' of the *nad*, and another to the king.

Now it will be comparatively easy to show in

what respect or to what extent the Christians of St Thomas were placed next or equal in precedence to the Nayars. In the charter of 774, it appears that the Christians were, like the Jews three-quarters of a century before, incorporated into the Malayali nation; while the charter of 824 shows that the position assigned to both Jews and Christians was that of practical equality with the 'six hundred' of the *nad* in respect to the two characteristic functions and the privileges that have been already indicated. For it was declared to be the duties of the Jewish and Syrian guilds, assembled in their respective headquarters at Anjuvannam and Manigramam, in association with the 'six hundred' of the *nad*, to protect the town of the Palliyar, or Church people. Further, it was the duty of the Church people to render to the powers above them, who were the king on the one hand and the Jewish and Christian protector guilds on the other, a trustworthy account of the shares of the produce of the land which respectively fell to them. "Let them, even Anjuvannam and Manigramam, act both with the Church and the land according to the manner detailed in this copper deed for the times that earth, moon, and sun exist."[8]

The circumstances which brought about this remarkable promotion of the Christian community in Malabar are historically interesting.

In the first place, there was a political necessity for this recognition. It was no feeling of favour towards the religion which they professed that induced the kings of Malabar to exalt the new-comers. The element of fear and of self-interest entered into the motive. For, as it was at the date of the Jewish charter, so at the respective dates of the two Christian charters, the Perumals had to fortify themselves against external enemies; they had to bethink themselves of every available resource whereby their seats on their throne might be preserved. The first Christian *sasanam* was granted "at or very near the time when the Rashtrakuta invasion of Southern India had resulted in the final subjugation of the Pallava dynasty of Kanchi (Conjeveram). Indeed the date of this charter (774) falls in the reign of Dhruva, the Rashtrakuta who hemmed in the Pallava host between his own army and the sea, and who, after despoiling them of their fighting elephants, seems to have let the opposing host go free in shame and contumely after making their sovereign 'bow down before him.'" "A few years later, about the time of the second Christian charter, it may be noted that fresh invasions of Kerala took place. It was, as the *Keralolpatti* tradition indicates, threatened from two sides at once. The Northern Kolattiri chief was appointed by the Perumal to stop the invaders — probably Kadambas or some other feudatory of the Rashtrakuta, — coming along the coast from the north, while the raid from the east, *viâ* the Palghat gap, probably by the Gangas or other feudatories of the Rashtrakutas, seems to have been defeated by the Enadi chiefs of the Zamorin's house." "At such times money may be required in large sums to buy off opposing hosts; and it is not therefore an improper inference to draw from the facts that, in offering assistance in this shape, the trading foreigners met the Perumal's wishes, and naturally enough secured for themselves a higher standing in the land in which they traded."[9]

Secondly, the numerical and material strength of the Christians of St Thomas had greatly increased; and therefore their help in the exigencies of the empire would be of considerable value. New colonies had arrived not long before the granting of each of the Christian charters. "The tradition of the existing Church is that a company of Christians from Baghdad, Nineveh, and Jerusalem, under orders from the Catholic arch-priest at Urahai (Edessa), arrived in company with the merchant Thomas in 745 A.D."[10] This Knaye Thomas or Thomas of Cana[11] and his following evidently made a deep impression on the popular imagination in Malabar. To him has even been ascribed the origin and not merely the reinforcement of the colony; and some authors have supposed that it was by confounding this Thomas with the apostle that the date of the origin of the Church has been thrown so far back as the first century—a supposition as inconsistent with history as the legend which it is intended to explain. Little light on the history of Knaye Thomas can be got from the stories that are still believed by the Malabar Christians. It is said that he had two wives—whether successively or simultaneously is not affirmed—and by each wife he had a numerous offspring, among whom his property was at last divided, those by his first wife receiving his northern estates, and those by the second receiving the southern. Hence there are two comprehensive divisions in the present day among the Christians of the coast, usually described as the Northists and the Southists respectively. Though they profess to believe the same doctrines and to obey the same bishops, they keep themselves perfectly distinct,[12] and avoid intermarriage with each other as carefully as if they were Hindus of different castes. The Southists are fairer of complexion than their brethren of the party of the North, and they boast of this as a proof of their more direct descent from the parent Church, and of their having genuine Syrian blood in their veins. This immigration preceded at no long interval the granting of the Christian charter of 774.

Besides this immigration of Christians under Thomas which settled at Cranganore, there was another which settled in the neighbourhood of Quilon. In 822 two Nestorian Persians, Mar Sapor and Mar Peroz, the former of whom is no other than the Muruvan Sapir Iso of the second Christian charter (*c.* 824), came with a large following and made a deep impression on the powers that were then in Malabar; and this circumstance helped to pave the way for the recognised and honourable place that they obtained in the society of that coast by the charter granted so soon afterwards.

These two immigrations, it would seem, form the historical grounds for the division of the community into Northists and Southists, although the legends which have mingled with the history have obscured the facts; and they are probably the last immigrations on any important scale from the mother Church in high Asia to Southern India.

But, at whatever time immigration from high Asia ceased, provision had been made otherwise for the continuity of the Church of Malabar. This Church was in some sense a missionary Church, and sought to share its spiritual possessions with the people of the land. It attempted, and it succeeded in the attempt, to build up a native Church. In the days of its prosperity, the expansion of the Church was probably rapid. Many converts came no doubt from among the employees and dependants of 'the sovereign merchant of Kerala'; but, in the subsequent decadence of foreign influences, the Persian element would die out or be absorbed; and, in the absence of fresh blood from higher latitudes, the native element would soon be left in sole possession.

The presence of a large native element from the first, nay the exclusively native composition of the membership, is attested in a characteristic manner by the author of the 'Brief History of the Syrians in Malabar.' This work, written by one of themselves about the year 1770, is of little worth in so far as it professes to set forth the facts of ancient history, but is valuable only as a record of the opinions of the people. Now the 'Brief History' asserts that St Thomas, during the thirty years of his sojourn in Malabar, preached the Gospel to the Brahmans, "and to the natives at large," that "many believing were baptised," that "two were ordained priests," and that, only when he had thus established the Church in Malabar, did the apostle feel free to carry the Gospel to regions beyond. The evidence of physiology as well as of history, testifies that the Christians of Malabar to-day are of Dravidian and not of Aryan or Semitic descent, unless the contention of the Southists, who are less than one-fortieth part of the whole Syrian Christian community, may be held in any degree to modify this general statement of fact.

In this connection, however, the term 'Syrian' requires careful definition. The members of the Church of Malabar are called Syrians, not because they have Syrian blood in their veins, but because they have a Syrian liturgy. They are not of the Syrian nation, but of the Syrian rite. The name in this case is not an ethnological or geographical designation, but is purely ecclesiastical. The Christians of St Thomas have from time immemorial used Malayalam for their vernacular speech;

and this Malayalam-speaking people, who had sat in darkness, received the light in a dark Syriac lantern. As Syriac was the sacred language of the mother Church in Persia, so it became the sacred language of her daughter in Malabar; just as the services in the Church of England were conducted for centuries in Latin through the failure of Augustine its founder to perceive that the same reason which required men to pray in Latin at Rome required men to pray in English at Canterbury. So the Christian Dravidians of Malabar have long, and not inconsistently with ecclesiastical usage, been called Syrians; but much confusion of thought has been created by the neglect, on the part of writers on this subject, to apply the word here only in its purely ecclesiastical sense. If it were the custom to call the Roman Catholic natives of Malabar by the name of Romans, no one would have any difficulty in perceiving the sense in which the name was applied, and no one would puzzle himself over the question of their race-connection with the men that peopled the 'city on the seven hills.'

The colonists who came from Persia and Mesopotamia to settle in Malabar made many mistakes, as those who make experiments in colonisation are sure to do; but, in so far as their aims were Christian, the developing of a native Church was the wisest thing they could have done for the perpetuation of their cause. Their worldly wisdom in discerning that the Perumals' extremity was their opportunity, and in striking a good bargain with the Perumals during the exigencies of the empire, gave a sort of stability to the Church they founded, which their neglect or incompetence on the spiritual side never availed to overthrow. To a long training in ecclesiastical customs and to an exalted social position, rather than to Christian learning and intelligent faith, is to be ascribed the permanence of the Syrian Church in Malabar.

CHAPTER XII.

THE LAST OF THE PERUMALS.

THE last Emperor of Kerala was Cheraman Perumal. The closing act in the drama of his life is remarkable, even after it has been stripped of sundry embellishments and reduced to a form in which it can be accepted both by the Hindus and the Mohammedans of that part of the country. It turned on a strange dream. Cheraman Perumal dreamt that the full moon appeared on the night of new moon at Mecca in Arabia, and that, when on the meridian, it split into two, one half remaining in the sky and the other half descending to the foot of a hill called Abikubais, where the two halves joined together and then set. Some time afterwards a party of Mohammedan pilgrims on their way to the footprint shrine at Adam's Peak in Ceylon [1] chanced to visit Cranganore, the

Perumal's capital, and were admitted to an audience and most hospitably treated. On being asked if there was any news in their country, Sheikh Seuj-ud-din related to the Perumal the apocryphal story of Mahomet having, by the miracle about which the Perumal had dreamt, converted a number of unbelievers. The Perumal was much interested and secretly made known to the Sheikh his intention "to unite himself to them."

When Seuj-ud-din and his retinue returned from Ceylon, the Perumal directed them to make ready a vessel and provide it with everything necessary for a voyage; and for the next eight days he busied himself in arranging affairs of State, and, in particular, in assigning to the different chieftains under him their respective portions of territory. This was all embodied in a written deed to be left behind him. He then embarked secretly in the vessel prepared for him, along with the Sheikh and his companions, and, touching first at Northern Kollam near Quilandy, and then at the island of Darmapattanam near Tellicherry, they made for the Arabian coast and landed at Shahr.

After remaining a considerable time at Shahr, during which the Perumal changed his name to Abdul Raman Samiri and married a wife named by some Rahabieth, by others Gomaria, he resolved to return to Malabar for the purpose of establishing his new religion, and of providing suitable places of worship. But before the ship which was to carry him back to his kingdom was built, he was seized with a dangerous disease, and, being convinced that there was no hope of recovery, he implored his companions not to desist from their design of going to Malabar to propagate the Fourth Vedam.[2] But they replied that being foreigners they knew little of his country, and were not likely to have influence therein, so he gave them writings in the Malayalam language to all the chieftains whom he had appointed in his stead, requiring them to give land for mosques and to endow them. "But," he solemnly charged them, "tell ye not my people of the violence of my sufferings, or that I am no more;" and, having finally enjoined them to land nowhere except at Darmapattanam, Quilandy, Cranganore, and Quilon, "he surrendered his soul to the unbounded mercy of God."

Some years afterwards, the pioneers of Islam in Malabar—Malik-ibn Dinar, his two sons Habib-ibn-Malik and Sherif-ibn-Malik, his grandson Malik-ibn-Habib, his grandson's wife Kumarieth, and their family of ten sons and five daughters—set out for that coast, bearing the Perumal's letters; and, concealing his death, they delivered them to whom they were addressed. They went first to Cranganore, where the officiating ruler received them hospitably, granting, in accordance with his royal master's orders, land whereon to build a mosque, together with a suitable endowment; and Malik-ibn-Dinar himself became first Kazi of the capital. At nine other places, including Darmapattanam, Mangalore, and Quilon, mosques were built and Kazis appointed; and thus, according to the dying wish of the last of the Perumals, Islam was established in Malabar.

Doubtful in detail as this narrative appears, considerations have been adduced which are supposed to confirm its general outline and substance. In the first place, Sheikh Zin-ud-din, writing on the subject, testifies that Cheraman Perumal's visit to Arabia took place about two hundred years after the flight of the Prophet. "It is a fact, moreover," he continues, "that the king was buried at Zaphar—and not on the Arabian coast of the Red Sea—at which place his tomb can be seen by any one, and is indeed now frequented on account of its virtues. And the king, of whom this tale is told, is styled by the people of that part of the world as Samiri, whilst the tradition of his disappearance is very common throughout the population generally of Malabar, whether Moslems or pagans; although the latter believe that he was taken up into heaven, and still continue to expect his descent, on which account they assemble at Cranganore and keep ready their wooden shoes and water, and on a certain night of the year burn lamps as a kind of festival in honour of his memory."[3]

Further, it has recently come to notice, from the information of an Arab resident near the spot, that the tomb of the Perumal still exists at Zaphar in Arabia, at some distance from Shahr, the place where he is reported to have landed; and that the inscription on it runs: "Arrived at Zaphar A.H. 212. Died there A.H. 216." As the former date corresponds to A.D. 827, this would imply that the Perumal remained two years at Shahr after his arrival there; and as the Malabar era, from which dates are still reckoned, is the 25th of August 825, it would seem not improbable that that era was fixed so as to coincide with the time when the last of the Perumals set sail for Arabia and the Persian Gulf.

It might be objected that such a change as is implied in the foregoing representation on the part of a people scattered over such a large area is altogether improbable; whether a community so large would have not only admitted so readily the representatives of a new faith amongst them, but actually adopted that faith in considerable numbers. This objection it would be difficult to rebut unless it could be shown that there was some previous preparation for the change. It is not improbable that such preparation existed; for it is well known that by the ninth century Arabs had penetrated, not to India only, but even as far as China, in the interests of trade; and that all the nine places, besides Cranganore, where mosques were erected, were either the headquarters of the petty potentates of the country, or places affording facilities for trade. It is probable that Arab traders had settled in these places long previously; and indeed a Mohammedan granite tombstone at Northern Kollam, near Quilandy, recites, after the usual prayer, how "Ali-ibn-Udthorman was obliged, in the year 166 of the Hej'ra, to leave this world for ever for the one which is everlasting, and which receives the spirits of all;" and the fact that Arabs had thus settled in the country suggests the belief that even in those early days alliances by Arabs with women of the country had been contracted, and that thus the beginnings of the mixed race, the Mapillas, who have played such an important part in the political history of the district, had already appeared.

This change in Malabar amounted almost to a political revolution; for no successor to Cheraman Perumal was nominated, the princes carrying on the government, for a time at least, in the belief that he was still alive. Soon of course that delusion passed away and every one looked to himself. So it came to pass in process of time that the Zamorin[4] of Calicut, the Rajah of Cochin who was the lineal descendant of Cheraman Perumal, and the Rajah of Travancore who still swears on attaining sovereignty that he holds the symbols of his high office only till the return of his uncle, survived as independent rulers on the west coast of Southern India.

As time went on, the Mohammedans multiplied, mostly in the northern parts of the district, having replaced Chinese traders in the Indian market and being patronised by the Zamorin, while the Jews and Christians were mainly concentrated in the territory of Cochin and North Travancore. The

Mohammedan ranks were replenished partly by immigration and partly by conversion. The latter process is still going on, not from among the Hindus moulded by the Aryan cult, but from the non-caste population. The low-caste man who adopts Islam is vastly raised thereby in the social scale. He obtains by conversion many substantial benefits, and is protected by the Mapillas from any oppression or interference at the hands of his former lords. Even within the ten years 1871-81, the accessions to the ranks of Mohammedans within the collectorate of Malabar alone, from the Cheramar and other low-caste people, amounted to about 50,000;[5] and there is reason to believe that the same process, if not to the same extent, is going on in other parts of the country. The adherents of Islam are increasing in number, but it is from the lowest ranks of the non-Aryan community that the increase is being drawn.

It is much to be deplored that the Mohammedans of Southern India, with some honourable exceptions, have as a rule been an ill-instructed race. Children in Malabar as elsewhere are taught to repeat without understanding scraps of the Kuran; and, in addition to this, elementary Malayalam handwriting is taught. At Ponnani there exists a Mohammedan college, founded, it is said, six hundred years ago, by an Arab named Zeyn-ud-din, who bore the title of Mukkhadam, signifying literally the foremost in an assembly. He married a Mapilla woman, and his descendants in the female line have retained the title, the present Mukkhadam at Ponnani being the twenty-fourth or twenty-fifth in the line of succession. The students at the college are supported by the Ponnani townspeople, the custom being to quarter two students in each house. The students study in the public Jammat or Friday Mosque, and in their undergraduate stage they are called mullas. There is apparently very little system in their course of study up to the taking of the degree of mutaliyar—*i.e.*, elder or priest. There is no examination for this degree, but the ablest and most diligent of the mullas are sought out by the Mukkhadam, and are invited to join in the public reading with him at the 'big lamp' in the Jammat Mosque. This invitation is considered as a sign of fitness for the degree, which is thereupon assumed without further preliminaries. The learning thus imparted is despised by genuine Arabs, of whom many families of pure blood are settled on the coast, and are themselves highly educated in the Arab sense. "Their knowledge of their own books of science and of history is very often profound, and to a sympathetic listener who knows Malayalam, they love to discourse on such subjects. They have a great regard for the truth, and in their finer feelings they approach nearer to the standard of English gentlemen than any other class of persons in Malabar."[6]

Still, uninstructed as they were, the Musalmans, under the ægis of the Zamorin, whose friendship they assiduously cultivated, were politically and commercially important in the society of Malabar. They fought the Zamorin's battles, they garnered his crops, they bought and sold for him at home and abroad. "The trade in Malabar products seems to have been exclusively in the hands of Mohammedan merchants, and it may be safely concluded that, after the retirement of the Chinese, the power and influence of the Mohammedans were on the increase, and the country would no doubt soon have been converted to Islam either by force or by conviction; but the nations of Europe were in the meantime busy endeavouring to find a direct road to the pepper country of the East. The first assured step in this direction was taken when Bartholomew Dias sailed round the 'Cape of Storms' in 1486. The Cape was promptly rechristened the 'Cape of Good Hope,' and the direct road to India by sea was won." [7]

But after the great upheaval in Malabar, consequent on the death of Cheraman Perumal, we are more interested to inquire how the Christians of St Thomas fared. The development of a Musalman power was not in their favour; yet so far as history reveals their mutual relationships, the Christians of St Thomas seem to have experienced less actual suffering from its hostility than the Jews did. The fact is that we hardly know anything of the history of Christianity on the Malabar coast during the next six hundred years. This was truly the period of the dark ages. When the Portuguese arrive on the scene, the recording of events historically interesting is resumed; but between the flight of the last of the Perumals and the coming of the Portuguese there is an almost total blank.

One interesting incident, however, has survived the reign of gloom. The Syrians seem to have cherished the tradition of having attained to the dignity of possessing a king of their own. This attainment may have been made in spite of, or because of, the confusion that succeeded the demise of Cheraman Perumal. Of Beliarte, the first Christian king of the Christians of St Thomas, whose capital was at Udiamperur near Cochin, they speak in terms of natural pride. How long the kinghood lasted it is impossible to say. The story, like so many parts of the story of this Church, ends with a sigh. Their royal crown fell to the hands of a neighbouring sovereign of superior strength. Their king dying, they plaintively relate, without heirs-male, the Rajah of Cochin came into possession by inheritance, and so they have been ever since a subject people, subject to the non-Christian rajahs of Cochin and Travancore.[8]

They might still as a Church, however, have held up their heads under this calamity, had they been inwardly fortified with a knowledge of the Gospel and faith in their own vocation as stewards of its mysteries. There is, alas! little reason to assume that they were so fortified. On the other hand, there is every reason to believe that they were particularly lacking in knowledge of the Scriptures and in desire to propagate such knowledge among their fellow-countrymen. Their training had not been favourable to the development of this side of their Christian character. For the provision of church officers and all the apparatus of public worship, they had mainly looked to a foreign source, and never cultivated the virtue of self-reliance in the matter, or the grace of conscious dependence on the Head of the Church. They had never worked out a single problem in Church life for themselves. The ceremonial, the traditional, the consuetudinary, bulked far more largely in their eyes than the doctrine and the ethics of the Gospel.

But more than this. Their eyes had been blinded and their hands tied in a manner which practically prevented them from being a self-propagating Church in the true sense of the term. They merely reproduced themselves, and their only ambition was to hold their own, if indeed they may be said to have done even that. The mill-stone which was hung about their neck and weighted them so heavily in the race of progress was, strange to say, no other than the copper-plate charters. Whether this was the intention of the givers and receivers of the charters is another matter. But there can be no doubt of the effect, and I am inclined to think that there may have been some such remote intention on the part of the advisers of the Perumals who granted the charters. Let it be remembered that these charters were granted under the pressure of a political necessity. Of this necessity the Brahmans, who appended their signatures as witnesses to the first Christian charter granted in 774, and who were the constant advisers of the royal mind in all matters political, social, and religious, would be prone to make a virtue. They were at least able to make provision for it in their scheme for the construction of Malabar society on Aryan lines. In Southern India to this day, Hindu society may be divided into two classes, Brahmans and Sudras. Both Kshatriyas and Vaisyas, where they exist at all, are numerically insignificant. But we have seen that, while the Brahmans regarded the Nayars in theory as Sudras, they gave them in fact the position and imposed upon them the duties of Kshatriyas. Towards the Christians of St Thomas they acted in a somewhat similar manner. Without these foreign settlers no section of the existing community could exactly be said to represent the interests of trade, and more especially of foreign trade, on anything like a national scale; and the kings, and probably their influential non-Aryan subjects, would be desirous of availing themselves of this source of gain and comfort. The Brahmans therefore made the best of the circumstances. If they had Vaisyas in the Aryan constitution, why should they not have a guild of traders in the constitution which they were trying to acclimatise in Malabar? Might not the formal recognition of these foreigners and their native dependants or associates as part of the body politic help to make the wheels of government run smooth, promote the interests of conciliation, and add prestige to the twice-born lords of creation?

We have seen what the privileges and functions of the Christians were under these instruments. The Christians were to all intents and purposes recognised as a caste; and they began—if not from the first, at least in course of time—to regard themselves in the same light. Had they not been in the days of the Perumals both 'protectors' and 'supervisors'? had they not acquired possession of certain heathen castes of the lower order, and were they not on the whole a superior class? Did they not learn thus to look down upon the lower castes? Did they not teach the lower castes to look up to them? And did they not in matters of diet and on questions of ceremonial pollution take up a position analogous to that of caste Hindus? Is it wonder, then, that this Church, holding such views of the relation of man to man, should have been indifferent to the spread of the Christian faith and the ingathering of the tribes? With little intellectual and less spiritual life amongst them, it is not surprising that their history for such a long period is a blank, and, with so little self-reliance or self-respect, that they were unable to hold their own among their neighbours.

Their fate is in some respects comparable to that of the mother Church in high Asia. As the Caliphs were favourable to the Nestorian Church in Persia and Mesopotamia, so the Perumals were favourable to the Nestorian Church in Malabar. The former Church was trodden down under the feet of Tartar and Mongol; but, as we shall see in a future study, it was reserved for a Christian power from the West to break the spirit of the Church of Malabar.

THE ROMAN PERIOD

CHAPTER XIII.

ROME'S FIRST WORK IN INDIA.

THE first Roman Catholic missionary to India, of whose work we have any account, was Friar Jordanus, of the Dominican Order. Jordanus was a Frenchman and a native of Severac. The dates of his birth, his first going to the East, and his death are undetermined. But it is ascertained that he was in the East in 1321-23, that he returned to Europe, and that he started again for India about 1330. He is best known as the author of the 'Mirabilia'; but whether this work was written on his first or on a subsequent return to Europe has not been satisfactorily ascertained, though there seems some reason to prefer the earlier date.

Two letters written by Jordanus are extant. The first is a sort of circular, dated October 1321, and addressed to fellow-missionaries of his own Order and the Order of St Francis, in Persia. It recommends India as a field for systematic missionary effort, and points out three stations adapted for the establishment of missions. Those stations were, to use modern geographical nomenclature, Surat, Baroch, and Quilon.

In his second letter, dated January 1324, Jordanus relates how he started from Tabriz to go to Cathay, but embarked first for Quilon, with four Franciscan missionaries; and how they were driven by a storm to Tana, in the island of Salsette, where they were received by Nestorian Christians. There he left his four brethren to go on a special mission to Baroch; but he was detained at Surat, where he received the distressing intelligence that his four brethren at Tana had been arrested. He therefore returned to aid them, but found them already put to death.

The story is interesting as a narrative of India's protomartyrs, and because of the curious sort of apologetic, coloured with fictitious miracle, which the author cunningly wrought into its texture. It appears that there was at Tana a Saracen of Alexandria, Yusuf by name, who summoned them into the presence of the governor of the land to give some account of themselves. "Being asked what manner of men they were, they replied that they were Franks, devoted to holy poverty, and anxious to visit St Thomas. Then, being questioned concerning their faith, they replied that they were true Christians, and uttered many things with fervour regarding the faith of Christ. But, when the governor let them go, Yusuf a second and a third time persuaded him to arrest and detain them. At length the Governor, and the Kazi, and the people of the place were assembled, pagans and idolaters as well as Saracens, and questioned the brethren: How can Christ, whom ye call the Virgin's Son, be the Son of God? Then set they forth many instances of divine generation, as from the sun's rays, from trees, from germs in the soil; so that the infidels could not resist the Spirit who spake in them. But the Saracens kindled a great fire, and said: Ye say that your law is better than the law of Mahomet; if it be so, go ye into the fire and by miracle prove your words. The brethren replied that, for the honour of Christ, they would freely do this; and brother Thomas coming forward would go first in, but the Saracens suffered him not, because he seemed older than the others. Then came forward the youngest of the brethren, James of Padua, a young wrestler for Christ, and went into the fire and abode in it until it was well-nigh spent, rejoicing and uttering praise, and without any burning of his hair even, or of the cloth of his gown. Now they who stood by shouted with a great cry: Verily these be good and holy men!

"But the Kazi, willing to deny so glorious a miracle, said: It is not as ye think, but his raiment came from the land of Aben, a great friend of God, who, when cast into the flames of Chaldæa, took no hurt; therefore hath this man abode scathless in the fire. Then stripped they the innocent youth, and cast him into the fire. But he bore the flames without hurt, and went forth from the fire unscathed and rejoicing. Then the Governor set them free to go whither they would. But the Kazi, and Yusuf, full of malice, knowing that they had been entertained in the house of a certain Christian, said to the Governor: What dost thou? Why slayest thou not these Christ-worshippers? He replied that he found no cause of death in them. But they say: If ye let them go, all will believe in Christ, and the law of Mahomet will be utterly destroyed. The Governor again says: What will ye that I should do, seeing that I find no cause of death? But they said: Their blood be upon us. For it is said that, if one cannot go pilgrim to Mecca, let him slay a Christian and he shall obtain a full remission of sins, as if he had visited Mecca. Wherefore the night following the Governor, the Kazi, and Yusuf, sent officers who despatched the three brethren Thomas, James, and Demetrius, to the joys of heaven, bearing the palm of martyrdom. And after a while, having made brother Peter, who was in another place, present himself before them, when he firmly held to the faith of Christ, for two days they vexed him with sore afflictions, and on the third day, cutting off his head, accomplished his martyrdom."[1]

By the help of a young Genoese, whom he found at Tana, Jordanus was enabled to remove the bodies of these martyrs, and, having transported them to Surat, he buried them in a church there as honourably as he could.

After being thus sorrowfully deprived of his companions, Jordanus again set his face towards Quilon; and, for his further history we must depend mainly on the 'Mirabilia.' In India the Less—which, according to Jordanus, comprehends "Sindh and probably Mekran and India along the coast as far as some point immediately north of Malabar"—he says, "There is a scattered people, one here and another there, who call themselves Christians, but are not so, nor have they baptism, nor do they know anything else about the faith. Nay, they believe St Thomas the Great to be Christ.[2] There, in the India I speak of, I baptised and brought into the faith about three hundred souls, of whom many were idolaters and Saracens. And let me tell you," he adds, "that among the idolaters a man may with safety expound the Word of the Lord; nor is any from among the idolaters hindered from being baptised throughout all the East, whether they be Tartars or Indians or what not."[3]

In another place he says, with reference to India, "that, if there were two hundred or three hundred good friars, who would faithfully and fervently preach the Catholic faith, there is not a year which would not see more than ten thousand persons converted to the Christian faith. For whilst I was among those schismatics (*i.e.*, the Syrian Christians, or Nestorians) and pagans, I believe that more than ten thousand, or thereabouts, were converted to our faith; and because we, being few in number, could not occupy or even visit many parts of the land, many souls (woe is me!) have perished, and exceeding many do yet perish for lack of preachers of the Word of the Lord. And 'tis grief and pain to hear how, through the preachers of accursed Saracens, those sects of the heathen be day by day perverted. For their preachers run about, just as we do, here, there, and everywhere over the whole Orient, in order to turn all to their own miscreance. These be they who accuse us, who smite us, who cause us to be cast into durance, and who stone us; as I indeed have experienced, having been four times cast into prison by them, I mean the Saracens. But how many times I have had my hair plucked out, and been scourged, and been stoned, God Himself knoweth; and I, who had to bear all this for my sins, yet have not attained to end my life as a martyr for the faith, as did four of my brethren. For what remaineth God's will be done. Nay, five preaching friars and four minors were there in my time cruelly slain for the Catholic faith. Woe is me that I was not with them there."[4]

The only remaining point of interest in the biography of Jordanus is found in a bull of Pope John XXII., dated 5th April 1330, addressed to the Christians of Quilon, and intended to be delivered to them by Jordanus, who was nominated bishop of that place. The bull begins: *Nobili viro domino Nascarinorum et universis sub eo Christianis Nascarinis de Columbo, venerabilem fratrem Jordanum Catalini, episcopum Columbensem, Predicatorum ordinis professorem quem nuper ad episcopalis dignitatis apicem auctoritate apostolicâ duximus promovendum,*[5] &c. The Pope goes on to recommend the missionaries to their goodwill, and ends characteristically by inviting the Syrian Christians in India, Nascarini, to abjure their schism, and enter the unity of the Catholic Church. This is probably the first claim definitely made by a Pope of Rome to ecclesiastical rights in India: we shall see in subsequent chapters it was not the last.

We may suppose that Jordanus proceeded to his see in Malabar by way of the Persian Gulf, the route which he had followed on his first visit to India; but how long he laboured there, or whether he had any successor, are questions which it seems impossible to answer, although it is tolerably certain that some at least of the churches which he planted survived his episcopate. John de Marignolli, who was sent out to China on an embassy by the Pope, reached Quilon, "where the whole world's pepper grows," on his return voyage about Easter 1347, and there he remained a year and four months.

"There is a church of St George there," he says, "of the Latin communion, at which I dwelt, and I adorned it with fine paintings and there taught the holy law."[6] But unfortunately this visitor did not leave any record of the number of Christians or churches, and still less of the state of Christian life on the west coast of Southern India in the fourteenth century.

For Rome's entering on her great work in India, the full time had not yet come. That was reserved to a later date, when a variety of historical circumstances combined to lead to large and decisive action. The doubling of the Cape of Good Hope for the first time by European navigators was an event not more important in geographical science and commercial enterprise than in the history of Church extension. While it vastly enlarged the dominion of Portugal, and furnished Camoens with a theme for his national epic, it lengthened the cords of the Roman Catholic fold, and introduced a new chapter into the annals of the Church. Her ranks had been greatly thinned by the off-break of Protestantism, and they must needs be replenished by foreign accessions. The counter-reformation of the Church from within was signalised not only by the formation of the Society of Jesus and the sittings of the Council of Trent, but also by the ingathering of many proselytes in foreign parts, to fill the gap made by the Protestant defection.

The way in which this aggressive work was carried out cannot in all respects be commended. Any means were thought lawful which had for their object the ingathering of outsiders, by whatsoever name known, under the protection of the Pope, the theory being that all persons beyond the pale of Rome were beyond the pale of salvation. Zealous for the conversion of the world on these terms, the decimated Church was ready to compass sea and land for the purpose of restoring the balance of power which had been disturbed by the loss of the most progressive race in Europe; and few regions offered a more promising field for this enterprise than India.

When Rome developed her plans for a really active propagandism on the Malabar coast, she sent forth the monastic orders, armed with the Inquisition. With all its intolerance and its terrors, the Inquisition was set up at Goa in the sixteenth century; and when it was resolved to subjugate the Syrian Church to Papal jurisdiction, this relentless institution was used to overawe it, and to prevent the arrival of bishops from Babylon. The subjugation was consummated by the Synod of Diamper in 1599, and for nearly two generations Rome's tyranny endured, until the splendid rebellion of the Syrians at the Coonen Cross near Cochin in 1653, achieved for them a new liberty and gave promise of better days.

CHAPTER XIV.

THE INQUISITION AT GOA.

The Holy Office of the Inquisition was established in India at the instigation of the first Jesuit missionary. In a letter dated 10th November 1545, St Francis Xavier begged John III. of Portugal to grant this favour on the plea that 'the Jewish wickedness' spread daily in his Indian dominions. The proposal commended itself to the royal mind, and the Inquisition was at length set up in 1560 at Goa, where for more than two hundred and fifty years it was maintained in terrible severity.

All the Inquisitors were nominated by the King of Portugal and confirmed by the Pope, from whom they received their bulls. Of the two that administered the duties of the Office at Goa, the one was always a secular priest, and the other a monk of the Order of St Dominic. The former was called the Grand Inquisitor and was the highest dignitary in the place, receiving more respect than the Archbishop or the Viceroy. The position must have been attractive to ambitious men who loved power and who were not over-burdened with feelings of humanity. But men were attracted into the office by motives more questionable. The property of the prisoners was almost invariably confiscated, and became, in whole or in part, the property of the Holy Office.[1] It would appear in fact that the officers of the Inquisition were much more anxious about annexing the property of their prisoners than about using suitable means to convict them of heresy, and that all steps towards the latter end were taken mainly with a view to accomplish the former.

The jurisdiction of the Inquisition at Goa extended over all the Portuguese dominions beyond the Cape of Good Hope; and the authority of the Grand Inquisitor extended over all descriptions of persons, both ecclesiastic and lay, except the Archbishop, his Grand Vicar (who was generally a bishop), and the Viceroy or Governor; but he could cause any of these to be arrested, after informing the Court of Portugal and receiving secret orders to that effect from the Grand Council[2] of the Inquisition at Lisbon. The Inquisition at Goa was more comprehensive in its sweep, more omnivorous so to speak, than similar institutions elsewhere. Besides hunting down heretics, Jews, new Christians,[3] and all who were accused of judaising (that is, conforming to the ceremonies of the Mosaic Law, such as not eating pork, attending the solemnisation of the Sabbath, partaking of the paschal lamb, and so forth), the Goanese Inquisitors also replenished their dungeons with persons accused of magic and sorcery (that is, of trying to divine, for example, "whether one is beloved by a certain person, the thief who has stolen what is lost, the issue of a certain undertaking or disease, and other things of a like nature"). This Inquisition also punished not only Christians who fell, or were accused of having fallen, within the cases under its cognisance; but Mohammedans, heathens, and other strangers of whatever persuasion, who committed any of the prohibited offences or who publicly exercised their religion in the countries subject to the King of Portugal; "for, though that prince tolerated liberty of conscience, the Holy Office interpreted the permission, that strangers might live in their own faith, but were liable to be punished as criminals, if they practised its ceremonies."

Now in the territories of the Portuguese in India, there were more Mohammedans and heathens than Christians; and the Inquisition, which punished apostate Christians with death, never sentenced to that penalty those who had not been baptised, though they should relapse a hundred times into the same errors, but generally commuted it for banishment, corporal correction, or the galleys. The dread of being liable to be sentenced to the flames hindered many from embracing Christianity; and the Holy Office, instead of being useful in those parts for the propagation of the faith, deterred people from the Church by rendering it an object of horror to them. But surveillance of 'Gentile' manners and customs on the part of the Inquisition and its attempt to control them with such a rigorous severity caused the Portuguese name to become nauseous to the people of the land. In consequence of the fears that the Inquisition inspired, sometimes almost the entire population fled and took refuge in British or French possessions, and there can hardly be a doubt that this was one of the main causes of the practical collapse of the Portuguese power on the coast. Nor was the jurisdiction of this Inquisition limited to the living. It professed to be the judge of the quick and the dead. A process might be instituted against a person who had been in his grave for years before his accusation; so that his body was exhumed and, on conviction, burned at the *auto da fé*, his estates seized, and those who had taken possession compelled to refund.

We possess a history of melancholy interest written by one who himself experienced the horrors of the Inquisition at Goa in the seventeenth century. M. Dellon was a young French physician who had already travelled much and was now preparing to make the tour of India. He was staying at Damaun, a seaport town and district in the collectorate of Surat, about eighty miles from Bombay, which was then and is still included among the Portuguese dominions. He proposed to rest there from the fatigues he had endured in various voyages, and to recruit himself for the more ample gratification of his passion for travelling. He lived with a friar of the Dominican order, and was incautiously free and affable in conversation. He had read with enthusiasm the Old and New Testaments, had some knowledge of scholastic theology, had freely disputed as a devoted Roman Catholic with heretics and schismatics, and indulged the same sort of free-lance policy at Damaun. He had an active mind and an eager temperament, and it hardly occurred to him that the freedom of speech in which he indulged was likely to bring him into trouble. He was only twenty-four then, and he believed himself to be perfectly secure against the calamity which ultimately befell him. On this point, however, he was undeceived in a manner as sudden and vexatious as it was cruel. He had given abundant occasion to the vultures of the Holy Office to pounce upon him for their prey; he had entered into a dispute with a priest of the Dominican order about the different kinds of baptism, denying, not so much on the ground of doubt or disbelief as for the sake of discussion, the efficacy of the baptism *flaminis*, and quoting John iii. 5 in support of his argument; he had refused to kiss, as was customary, an image of the Virgin on a box handed round for the reception of alms; he had said that we might honour images, but that, if we used the word 'worship,' it could only be with reference to those of our Saviour alone, whilst the adoration related only to the person represented by them, and he quoted the Council of Trent on the subject, Session 25; he had asked on one occasion, "Is this crucifix more than a piece of ivory?" And he had even dared to question the infallibility of the judges of the Holy Office: "Are the Inquisitors less human or less subject to their passions than other judges?" But while he rejoiced in the success of his argument and congratulated himself that, as "this severe tribunal had not been introduced" into France, he was therefore not subject to its jurisdiction, his conversations were exactly reported to the Father Commissary of Damaun, and a 'process' was soon out against him.

Yet he maintains that all these matters could have been easily adjusted, and that they were but the ostensible cause of his incarceration. The real cause lay in a foolish jealousy on the part of the Governor of Damaun, who had watched with much uneasy impatience "the frequent but innocent visits which I paid to a lady whom he admired, and by whom he was truly beloved, which I then knew not; and, as he judged from appearances only, he imagined that I was more favourably received than himself."

At all events, M. Dellon was arrested by order of the Inquisition on the 24th August 1673, and consigned in the first instance to the prison-house of Damaun, where he was detained in spite of all his offers of confession, conciliation, and compromise, until the first day of the following year, when he embarked in chains for Goa. This unexplained and unreasonable detention in a black-hole with a fœtid atmosphere was due to the treachery and wickedness of the Commissary. Dellon explains that this pretended friend of his own wished to do a kindness to the Governor at Dellon's expense. It appears that the *auto da fé*, or jail delivery, which usually takes place once in two or three years, was appointed in that year (1673) to be held in December, and that Dellon was intentionally kept in the local prison until this function at Goa should be over, so that he might not have the chance of obtaining his release for two or three years to come. However that may be, he was not admitted within the precincts of the Santa Casa till the 16th January 1674.

The first scene in the second act of this drama was in the audience-chamber of the Grand Inquisitor,[4] who, having made a note of Dellon's name and profession, and having asked him whether he knew the occasion of his arrest, exhorted him to confess it freely, but without receiving his confession then, dismissed him till a more convenient season; whereupon the Alcaide conducted him to a corridor where this official, assisted by a secretary, made a strict inventory of all his belongings, with the assurance, oft repeated, that everything should be restored to him on his release, which of course it never was. He was left with nothing but his rosary, his handkerchief, and a few gold-pieces providently sewn into his garters, which they neglected to examine; and the inventory being completed, he was conducted to his cell, where after a frugal supper, which two days of fasting enabled him to enjoy, he laid his weary body down and slept his first sleep in the Santa Casa.

His cell was ten feet square, vaulted, clean, and lighted by means of a small grated window, placed at a height above the reach of the tallest man. There were about two hundred such cells, and in each cell there were two platforms to lie on, as it sometimes happened that two persons were confined together. In addition to the mat which was given to each prisoner, Europeans had a checked counterpane, which served for a mattress, there being no need for a covering unless it were to protect one from the persecutions of mosquitoes, which were most intolerable; and, to add to his sense of degradation, M. Dellon was shorn of his flowing locks. On complaining of his poor accommodation, he was shown cells smaller than his own, dark and without any window, to make him feel that he might fare worse. The food, he admits, was fairly good and sufficient in quantity; in the event of sickness, competent medical aid was supplied; and, if death seemed imminent, confessors were admitted. Moreover, the Inquisitor, attended by a secretary and interpreter, visited every prisoner about once in two months, to inquire if anything was wanted, if the victuals were brought at the appointed times, and if there were any complaints against the officers; and as soon as answers were returned to those three questions, the door was instantly closed. "In effect," remarks M. Dellon bitterly, "these visits are made for no other purpose than to display that justice and goodness, of which there is so much parade in this tribunal; but they produce neither comfort nor advantage to the prisoners who may be disposed to complain, nor are they ever treated with more humanity in consequence. Such of the prisoners as are wealthy," he adds, "have no better allowance than those who are poor, the latter being provided for by the confiscations levied from the former; for the Holy Office seldom fails to seize all the property, real and personal, of those who are so unfortunate as to fall into its hands."

But the terrible stillness of the place, even more than its physical discomfort, was specially trying to an eager temperament like M. Dellon's. A perpetual and rigid silence was preserved in the Inquisition; and those who ventured to utter their complaints, to weep, or even to pray to God too loudly, were liable to be beaten by the guards who, on hearing the slightest noise, hastened to the spot from whence it proceeded to require silence; and, if a repetition of the order was not obeyed, they opened the doors, and struck without mercy. But what was probably most trying to M. Dellon was the lack of everything that could appeal to or feed his mind. "Was there ever any conduct," he indignantly asks, "so unjust as to shut up Christian people for many years in a narrow prison without books (since even the breviary is not allowed to priests), without any exhortation to encourage them to suffer patiently; without hearing Mass, either on holy days or Sundays; without administration of the Eucharist, even at Easter, which all Christians are compelled to receive under danger of committing mortal sin; and without being strengthened by the holy viaticum and extreme unction at the hour of death?" Nor did he enjoy the benefit of companionship, except for two short periods when another prisoner was placed in his cell to prevent him from committing suicide, which he had several times unsuccessfully attempted. On both occasions they were 'black' prisoners; the one stayed with him five months, the other, who was "much less civilised" than the former, for two; and this happened within the first year of his incarceration. The Inquisition was thus an experiment in solitary confinement on a large scale.

Those attempts at suicide on the part of M. Dellon were due, not only to the irritating nature of his confinement, but also to the exasperating character of his examination at the Inquisitor's tribunal. He was taken there on three several occasions within the first three months of his confinement; he was exhorted in each case to be his own accuser; he had confessed everything he could think of as a ground of accusation; and he had signed his name to the record made of his confessions before the tribunal. Having thus made a clean breast of all his offences, he expected that he would not have to wait much longer for his release. But for the next fifteen months he was not again called. At the fourth audience, the "Proctor, on reading the informations, stated that, besides what I had admitted, I was accused and fully convicted of having spoken contemptuously of the Inquisition and its officers, and even with disrespect of the sovereign Pontiff and against his authority; and concluded that the contumacy I had hitherto displayed, by neglecting so many delays and benignant warnings which had been given to me, was a convincing proof that I had entertained the most pernicious intentions, and that my design was to teach and inculcate heretical opinions." It is needless to say that M. Dellon was not furnished with the names of the persons who had evidenced this new charge against him, or granted the opportunity of confronting them for the purpose of cross-examination. Such practice was entirely foreign to the benevolent methods of the Inquisition. However, M. Dellon was not subjected to 'the question,' or compelled to taste of the torture which he was well aware from their cries that many of his fellow-unfortunates suffered, and which, as in the case of one of his temporary companions in the cell, crippled many of them for life. Moreover, the charge of his expressing disrespect towards his Holiness the Pope was not further insisted on, and was not recounted with the other charges, as we shall see, when he received his final sentence.

At length the *auto da fé* was at hand. It was fixed for Sunday the 12th January 1676, and intimation thereof was duly made in all the churches within the Portuguese dominions, so that if possible none might lose the benefit of enjoying this means of grace. But the prisoners had no intimation of the approaching event, and it came on them therefore as a surprise. A little before midnight on Saturday, M. Dellon's door was opened, and he received a particular dress, which he was instructed forthwith to put on. It consisted of "a jacket with sleeves down to his wrists, and trousers hanging over the heels, both being of black stuff with white stripes." At two o'clock in the morning the guards returned and summoned him to turn out into a long corridor, where about two hundred men, including only about a dozen 'whites,' were arranged in perfect silence against the wall. In another corridor the women, whose number is not specified, were assembled, apparelled in the same stuff. Presently other dresses of a more varied character were brought, intended to correspond to the nature of the offence or punishment of each; but none of the prisoners seem to have been sufficiently skilled in the mysteries of the Holy Office to interpret its symbols correctly, and they therefore received but the vaguest information from the character of these additional habiliments. The upper garment which M. Dellon received is thus described by himself. It was a sort of scapulary "made of yellow stuff, with crosses of St Andrew painted in red, both in front and behind." He adds, as the result of later information, that these particular vestments, which were named *sanbenitos*, were used to distinguish such as had committed, or were adjudged to have committed, offences against the Christian faith, whether Jews, Mohammedans, sorcerers, or heretic apostates. On this occasion these *sanbenitos* were distributed to twenty 'blacks' accused of magic, to one Portuguese who was charged with the same crime, and was moreover a new Christian, as well as to M. Dellon himself.

When all were duly accoutred according to the character of their respective offences, they were allowed to sit down on the floor in expectation of fresh orders. At four o'clock the prisoners were offered some nourishment in the form of bread and figs; but, though M. Dellon had taken no supper the previous evening, he did not feel disposed to eat and would have declined the proffered food, had not the guard whispered him, "Take your bread, and, if you cannot eat it now, put it in your pocket, for you will be hungry before you come back"—words which gave M. Dellon great satisfaction and dissipated all his terror by the hope which they inspired of his return. So he took the advice in the spirit in which it had been given, and was thankful.

At dawn, the prisoners were ushered one by one into the public hall, where the principal citizens of Goa were assembled to take part in the exciting function of the day. To each prisoner one of the citizens was attached as god-father. These god-fathers had the charge of the persons they were respectively attached to, and were obliged to attend them until the feast was concluded; and the Inquisitors affected that they conferred a high honour on any citizen whom they condescended thus to employ. M. Dellon's god-father was the 'General of the Portuguese ships in the Indies.' The procession set forth in double file, each prisoner and his god-father walking abreast through the streets of Goa. In front of all marched a company of Dominicans preceded by the banner of the Holy Office, on which the image of St Dominic, the founder, was represented with a sword in one hand and an olive branch in the other, over the inscription — which can hardly be regarded otherwise than as a mockery—*Justitia et Misericordia.* The prisoners walked with head and feet bare, and M. Dellon complains of his tender feet being badly cut by the sharp flints on the road, which caused the blood to stream forth. At length, "overwhelmed with shame and confusion, and fatigued by the walk," they reached the church of St Francis, where all the prisoners were arranged in due order and an immense concourse of spectators had assembled. On the right of the high altar, which was "hung with black and had six silver candlesticks with tapers of white wax burning upon it," a throne was erected for the Grand Inquisitor and his council; on the left, another for the Viceroy and his court. The ceremonies, which lasted the whole day, began with a sermon by the Provincial of the Augustins, who took occasion to compare the Holy Office to Noah's ark, pointing out however this difference, that the creatures which entered the ark left it on the cessation of the deluge with their original natures and properties; whereas the Inquisition had this singular characteristic, that those who came within its walls cruel as wolves and fierce as lions, went forth gentle as lambs.

When the sermon was concluded, the sentences of the prisoners were read out one by one from the pulpit, each prisoner standing forth in the middle of the aisle until his sentence was delivered, and then going forward to a side-altar to make, with his hand on the book, confession of his faith in a prescribed form. M. Dellon was summoned in his turn to stand forth to hear his sentence. "I found," he says, "that the charge against me involved three points, one of which was the having maintained the inefficacy of the baptism *flaminis*; another, having asserted that images ought not to be worshipped, and having blasphemed against a crucifix by saying that it was a piece of ivory; and the last, that I had spoken contemptuously of the Inquisition and its ministers; but, above all, the bad intention from which I had uttered these things. For these offences I was declared excommunicate, and, by way of atonement, my goods were forfeited to the king, and myself banished from the Indies, and condemned to serve in the galleys of Portugal for five years; and moreover to perform such other penances as might be expressly enjoined by the Inquisitors."

"Of all these punishments," he adds, "that which appeared to me the heaviest was the indispensable necessity of quitting India, in which I had intended to travel for some time; but this disappointment was in some measure compensated by the prospect of being soon delivered from the hands of the Holy Office."

When all the cases of the prisoners "to whom mercy was extended by the boon of their lives" were finally disposed of, the Inquisitor left his seat to put on alb and stole, and, with twenty priests bearing each a wand, went to the middle of the church, where, after the recitation of the appropriate prayers, he released these prisoners from excommunication by a stroke administered by a priest with his wand.

Yet even in those grim proceedings the comic element did not fail to intrude itself. "I cannot," says M. Dellon, "resist mentioning a circumstance which will show the excessive superstition of the Portuguese in matters relating to the Inquisition. During the procession, and whilst we remained in the church, the person who was my god-father (though I frequently addressed him) would not speak to me, and even refused me a pinch of snuff which I requested; so apprehensive was he that in so doing he should participate in the censure under which he conceived me to lie; but the moment I received absolution, he embraced me, presented his snuff-box, and told me that thenceforth he should regard me as a brother, since the Church had absolved me."

But perhaps the blackest acts of this unholy assembly have yet to be recorded. The cases of such as were doomed to be burnt had yet to be disposed of, and they were accordingly ordered to be brought forward separately. They were a man and a woman, and the images of four men deceased, with the chests in which their bones were deposited. The man and the woman were "black native Christians" accused of magic, and condemned as apostates. Two of the four statues also represented persons convicted of magic, who were said to have judaised. One of these had died in the prison of the Holy Office; the other expired in his own house, and his body had been long since interred in his own family burying-ground, but, having been accused of Judaism after his decease, as he had left considerable wealth, his tomb was opened, and his remains disinterred to be burnt at the *auto da fé*. The proceedings against these unfortunates were then read, which concluded in these terms: "That the mercy of the Holy Office being prevented by their relapse or contumacy, and being indispensably obliged to punish them according to the rigour of the law, it gave them up to the secular power and civil justice, which it nevertheless entreated to regard these miserable creatures with mercy and clemency, and, if they were liable to capital punishment, that it should be inflicted without effusion of blood!" "How benevolent is the Inquisition, thus to intercede for the guilty! What extreme condescension in the magistrates to be satisfied, from complaisance to the Inquisition, with burning the culprits to the very marrow of their bones rather than shed their blood!"

We may well throw a veil over the smoky spectacle on the banks of the river which seems to have attracted the Viceroy of Goa and his heartless retinue. Neither need we describe the punishments of those whose spared lives were robbed thereby of all peace and honour and usefulness. As for M. Dellon, he had only a few more days of detention. On the 25th of January he embarked for Lisbon, where he duly arrived; and he would probably have served his five years in the prisons there, had not a French physician, who possessed influence at the Court, interceded for him; so that, on the 30th of June 1677, he had the supreme satisfaction of hearing the welcome sentence: "Let him be discharged according to his request, and let him go to France."

In the list of penances to be observed by M. Dellon after his discharge from the Inquisition, the last item imposed on him the duty of being "inflexibly reserved" as to everything which he had "seen, said, or heard," or the treatment which had been "observed towards him, as well at the Board as in the other places of the Holy Office." But when, after nearly four years of prison life, M. Dellon again tasted the sweets of liberty in his own native France, he thought it his duty to communicate to the world a knowledge of the bitter experience he had passed through; and the story [5] which has just been related in outline is the result.

We get a curious peep into the Inquisition of Goa about the beginning of the present century, when the doom with which the Holy Office had visited so many was rapidly hastening on itself. It was in January 1808 that Dr Claudius Buchanan paid a visit to Goa, and his account of this visit is one of the most interesting chapters in his 'Christian Researches.' It appears that, at the date of Buchanan's visit, the forts in the harbour of New Goa were occupied by British troops—two king's regiments and two regiments of native infantry—to prevent its falling into the hands of the French. The British force was commanded by Colonel Adams of his Majesty's 78th Regiment, whose acquaintance Buchanan had made in Bengal. It happened also that Lieutenant Kempthorne, commander of his Majesty's brig 'Diana,' a distant connection of his own, was at that time in the harbour. By the former he was introduced to the Viceroy, and he soon made many influential acquaintances. Several of his friends accompanied him in the British Resident's barge up the river—a distance of eight miles—to Old Goa, where the Inquisition was, and which was a city of churches and inhabited by priests. There he was introduced, at the convent of the Augustinians, "to Joseph a Doloribus, a man well advanced in life, of pale visage and penetrating eye, rather of a reverend appearance, and possessing great fluency of speech and urbanity of manners." "After half an hour's conversation in the Latin language, during which he adverted rapidly to a variety of subjects, and inquired concerning some learned men of his own

Church whom I had visited in my tour, he politely invited me to take up my residence with him during my stay at Old Goa. I was highly gratified by this unexpected invitation; but Lieutenant Kempthorne did not approve of leaving me in the hands of an Inquisitor. For, judge of our surprise when we discovered that my learned host was one of the Inquisitors of the Holy Office, the second member of that august tribunal in rank, but the first and most active agent in the business of the department. Apartments were assigned to me in the college adjoining the convent, next to the rooms of the Inquisitor himself. I breakfast and dine with him almost every day, and he generally passes his evening in my apartment. As he considers my inquiries to be chiefly of a literary nature, he is perfectly candid and communicative on all subjects."

"I had thought for some days," adds Buchanan, "of putting Dellon's book into the Inquisitor's hands; for, if I could get him to advert to the facts stated in that book, I should be able to learn by comparison the exact state of the Inquisition of the present time. In the evening he came in as usual to pass an hour in my apartment. After some conversation, I took the pen in my hand to write a few notes in my journal; and, as if to amuse him while I was writing, I handed him Dellon's book, and asked whether he had ever seen it. It was in the French language, which he understood well. 'Relation de l'Inquisition de Goa,' pronounced he with a slow articulate voice. He had never seen it before, and began to read with eagerness. He turned over the pages with rapidity, and when he came to a certain place he exclaimed, in the broad Italian accent, '*Mendacium, mendacium!*' He continued reading till it was time to retire to rest, and then begged to take the book with him."

"Next morning after breakfast we resumed the subject of the Inquisition. The Inquisitor admitted that Dellon's descriptions of the dungeons, of the torture, of the mode of trial, and of the *auto da fé* were in general just; but he said the writer judged untruly of the motives of the Inquisitors, and very uncharitably of the character of the Holy Church; and I admitted that, under the pressure of his peculiar suffering, this might possibly be the case."[6]

But there were already indications that the beginning of the end had come; and accordingly, on the 16th June 1812, a decree was issued from the palace of Rio Janeiro, over the signature of the

Prince Regent Don José, ordering the final and total extinction of the Inquisition at Goa.[7] It is admitted in this decree that it was needful to do something towards the increase of the population and the improvement of industry within the Portuguese dominions in India, "by removing those obstacles which seem hitherto to have impeded the settling on the estates of persons belonging to various sects and nations, who are still intimidated by the deterrent remembrance of the ancient proceedings wherewith the Inquisition of Goa frightened the people of India." The decree, therefore, declares that in all the "estates of India" all the religions of its various populations will be tolerated, and it prohibits "the commission of any kind of violent acts towards the professors of any sects, conformably to the usage observed by the most civilised nations, which promote by such toleration the aggrandisement of their country." "Let it, however, be well understood," adds the Regent, "that the public profession of Gentile religions is allowed with the reserve exacted by the respect and veneration due to our holy Roman Catholic faith as the only dominant religion of Portugal, which I purpose to keep inviolable in all its purity and decorum."

Thus toleration was at last extended to the dwellers in the Portuguese dominions in India. But it was only the toleration of expediency, not of justice. It had yet to be acknowledged by Portugal that her Indian subjects are entitled to toleration as of *right.*

CHAPTER XV.

THE SYNOD OF DIAMPER, 1599.

THE Synod of Diamper is one of the most interesting and at the same time one of the most melancholy episodes in the history of the Syrian Church. The synod was held at a time when the office of metran, or bishop, of the Syrian Church was vacant. It was convened by the Archbishop of Goa under a brief from Pope Clement VIII. To this synod were summoned not only the archdeacon of the Syrian Church and "all the other priests of the same not hindered by age or some other just impediment," but also representative laymen. "Whereas," says the archiepiscopal citation, "by immemorial custom and right introduced into this diocese from its beginning, and consented to by all the infidel kings of Malabar, the whole government, as it were, and the cognisance of all matters wherein Christians are any way concerned, has belonged to the Church and the prelate thereof; and it likewise having been an ancient custom in the same to give an account to the people of whatsoever has been ordained in the Church, in order to its being better observed by all: we do therefore command all Christians in all towns and villages in this bishopric, and, where there are no villages, all that use to assemble at any church as belonging to it, immediately upon this our pleasure being intimated to them, to choose four of the most honourable, conscientious, and experienced persons among them to come in their name to the said synod, with sufficient powers to approve, sign, confirm, and consult in their name, so as to oblige themselves thereby to comply with whatsoever shall be determined in the synod."[1]

The objects of the synod were comprehensive and thorough. It was convened "for the increase and exaltation of the Catholic faith among the Syrians in Malabar; for the destruction of the errors and heresies which had been sown in the diocese by several heretics and schismatics; for the purging of books from the false doctrines contained in them; for the perfect union of this Church with the whole Church Catholic and universal; for the yielding of obedience to the supreme Bishop of Rome, the universal pastor of the Church and successor in the chair of St Peter, and vicar of Christ upon earth, from whom they had for some time departed; for the extirpation of simony, which had been much practised in the diocese; for the regulating of the administration of the holy sacraments of the Church, and the necessary use of them; and for the information of the affairs of the Church and the clergy, and the customs of all the Christian people of the diocese." It was in fact intended by means of this synod to revolutionise the whole doctrine and practice of the Syrian Church, to annex and assimilate it as far as possible to the Church of Rome, and to thrust on the acceptance of the Syrians the whole body of doctrine formulated by the Council of Trent.

It is much to be regretted that there is no history of this synod written by a representative of the Syrian community. The Syrian Christians, like their kinsmen the Hindus, have no annals. The Hindu mind, in bygone days at least, seems to have had no idea of time. India produced many poets, but no chroniclers. To the Greeks and Romans, to the Chinese and Arabs, to Christians and Moslems, to foreign litterateurs and foreign archæologists, the Hindu owes his knowledge of his own country. To foreign scholars the Syrians likewise owe their knowledge of the history of their own Church. Take away the history of the Syrian Church in high Asia, the 'Christian Topography' of Cosmas, and the great work of Assemanus,[2] take away the Persian crosses and the copper-plate charters, and the history of the Syrian Church in Malabar, at least till the coming of the Portuguese, would be an absolute blank.

But though we have no record of the synod from the Syrian standpoint, we have a very complete and authentic history of it from the Roman side. Its proceedings, and the events immediately preceding and following its sittings, were recorded by Antonio de Gouvea in his 'Jornada,'[3] published at Coimbra in 1606. Gouvea was an Austin friar, and reader of divinity at Goa. He enjoyed the confidence of the archbishop, who himself belonged to the same brotherhood, and under his direction and by command of the provincial of his order in Portugal, he prepared the history of the synod, to which he appended a copy of the original decrees as drawn up by the archbishop, with the assistance of the Jesuits. Whatever modifications may have, on account of his Roman proclivities, to be made on the representations given by Gouvea of the condition of the Syrian Church of Malabar at the end of the sixteenth century, it may be observed that Protestant writers have as a rule been fain to regard his representations as being rather creditable than otherwise to the Syrians. Nevertheless, it must be added that this favourable estimate on the Protestant side applies to the doctrine and not to the social life of the Syrians, and is based rather on a consideration of what the Syrians did not hold than on positive statements of their actual belief and practice.[4] As the interference on the part of Roman ecclesiastics with the Syrian Church proceeded on the erroneous assumption that the latter had more than a millennium previously gone from under the obedience of the Church of Rome, they probably felt no great temptation to exaggerate the departures from Roman usage which they discovered on the part of the Syrian Church. In only one case have we the means of definitely checking their accounts, and in that case they are, as I shall afterwards point out, found to be correct; and, though we have no account of the social condition of the Syrians from the Protestant side until more than two hundred years afterwards, yet on this score the accounts given by the missionaries of the Church Missionary Society, who were undoubtedly most friendly to the Syrians, are not essentially different from those given at Diamper. On the whole, therefore, I am disposed to accept the statement of facts made by Gouvea, so far as they came within the sweep of contemporary observation, as substantially correct, leaving my readers, each according to his own individual standard, to appraise the opinions and the policy he enunciates, at what they may respectively be worth.

The circumstances which led to the convening of this synod are most instructive. It will be remembered that, when the Portuguese arrived on the coast, the Syrians welcomed them with open arms, and the Portuguese on their part reciprocated the feeling. Cabral persuaded two of the Syrians, brothers,[5] to accompany him to Portugal; and in 1502 the Syrians presented a petition to Vasco da Gama praying him to take them under the protection of his Christian master, that so they might be defended against the injuries which they daily suffered from infidel princes; and, as a lasting testimony of their submission to the King of Portugal, they sent his Majesty a rod tipped at both ends with silver, with three little bells at the head of it, which had been the sceptre of their Christian kings. As a further proof of the confidence reposed in the Portuguese, which the Syrians thus intimated to the hero of the 'Lusiad,' their bishop handed over the six plates of copper, on which their ancient rights and privileges were recorded, to the Commissary of Cochin for safekeeping. These plates, consigned to the Portuguese soon after they settled on Indian shores, were kept until the memory of their existence had wellnigh perished, and were recovered only about the beginning of the present century after careful search in the Fort of Cochin by Colonel Macaulay.[6]

This mutual confidence led to considerable intercourse between the two races, and the Portuguese were freely admitted to the services of the Syrian Church, where they soon discovered a divergence of creed and ritual from those of Rome. A long period of more or less friendly intercourse enabled them to ascertain in detail the points on which the doctrine and practice of the Syrian Church were considered erroneous. First of all, their Scriptures varied from the Vulgate, and were therefore judged to be in need of correction or supplement. Apart from texts which were thought to have been intentionally corrupted to accord the better with Nestorian errors, such as 1 John iv. 3,[7] it was observed that in their copies of the Old Testament there were "wanting the books of Esther, Tobit, and Wisdom;" and that, in their copies of the New Testament, the second Epistle of Peter, the second and third of John, Jude, and Revelation,[8] were not to be found. The words of John's Gospel, viii. 1–11, and the trinitarian passage in 1 John v. 8, were likewise omitted, while the doxology was added to the Lord's Prayer in the sixth chapter of Matthew.

But if the Roman censors were dissatisfied with the text of Scripture as used by the Syrians, they were shocked by the contents of some of their theological and liturgical books. For the Syrians not only held the characteristic views of Nestorius with regard to the Virgin Mary and the person of Christ, but they asserted that the followers of Nestorius received their faith from the apostles, that this faith had been preserved in the Church of Babylon, and that the Nestorian patriarch of Babylon was the universal head of the Church immediately under Christ. They recognised the first two general councils; but the Athanasian creed, *Quicunque vult*, was altogether unknown among them; and they maintained that the Holy Ghost proceeds from the Father only, and not from the Father and the Son. Of the seven Roman sacraments the Syrians recognised only three—viz., baptism, the eucharist, and ordination. The doctrine of the sacraments and their uses those Malabar Christians were supposed entirely to misapprehend, and it was therefore judged impossible for them to obtain that spiritual benefit which these ordinances were fitted and intended to convey, and which their Portuguese friends seemed to think it their bounden duty to secure for them unasked.

With regard to baptism, the form of words used in the service by the Syrian priest was "N. is baptised and perfected in the name of the Father, amen; in the name of the Son, amen; and in the name of the Holy Ghost, amen;" and, being different from the Roman formula, this was judged altogether wrong. Moreover, proper fonts were not provided in the churches, the water was not blessed by the addition of holy chrism, the priest administered in his ordinary dress without surplice or stole, and the ancient custom of having godfathers and god-mothers "was not in use in the bishopric." Old Testament names were judaically given to the children, the ordinance was not administered on the eighth day after birth "according to the custom of the universal Church," but was often delayed for months and even years, and no baptism registers were kept. Great carelessness, it is alleged, was shown on every hand. Children in danger of death, the offspring of excommunicated persons, foundlings, infants exposed by their parents, adult slaves who desired baptism, and children of slaves, were not baptised, and no provision was made for the instruction and baptism of converts from heathenism. There were many persons in the diocese, and especially among them that lived "in the heaths" and far from any church, who, though they were not baptised, yet, being of a Christian race, professed themselves Christians, and when they came to a church received the holy sacraments with others, and, out of mere shame of letting it be known that they were not christened, died without baptism; and others, because they could not pay the fees that were simoniacally demanded of them. Nay, through this and similar acts of negligence on the part of the Syrian clergy, considerable sections of the community relapsed entirely into heathenism.

"Hitherto there has been no use," say the

Diamper decrees, "nor so much as knowledge of the holy sacrament of confirmation among the Christians of this bishopric, the heretical prelates that governed it having neglected to feed the people in a great many cases with wholesome Catholic food."

With respect to the eucharist, the Syrians communicated in both kinds, the bread being dipped in the wine and placed by the celebrant's hand in the mouth of each communicant. The bread happened often to be bread of rice and not of wheat; and, as for wine, they prepared an infusion of raisins and sometimes of dates instead of using the blood of the grape; and, even if they had real wine, it was "kept in glass bottles, where, being in small quantity and kept a long time, it necessarily decayed and turned to vinegar, thereby losing the essence of wine in the opinion of those who have good palates, with which they celebrated notwithstanding, not considering the danger there was of there being no consecration." They had wooden instead of stone altars, their cups were made of wood, or by the art of the potter, and not of metal, and the celebrant had not proper vestments; for hitherto there had been "no such thing as a surplice in the bishopric." The Syrian doctrine of the eucharist was most unsatisfactory to their new friends. They held that the true body of our Lord is not in the holy sacrament of the altar but only the figure thereof, that the holy eucharist is only the image of Christ, and is distinguished from Him as an image is distinguished from a true man; that the body of our Lord Jesus Christ is not there nor anywhere else but in heaven, at the right hand of the Father; that under the element of bread is only the body of Christ without blood, and under the element of wine the blood without the body; and that in this sacrament there is only the virtue of Christ but not His body and blood. Further, the priest seemed to call on the Holy Ghost to come down from heaven to consecrate the elements, "whereas in truth it is the priest that does it, though not in his own words, but in the words of Christ." It is evident, therefore, that transubstantiation, the sacerdotal function of the priesthood, and the sacrifice of the Mass for the living and the dead were altogether foreign to Syrian thought.

Of the seven orders of the Roman clergy, the Syrians knew only two, namely, the priest (*kasheesha*) and the deacon (*shumshana*); but the Syrian clergy, to the scandal of their Portuguese friends, were in most cases married men, some had married after they were in orders, "nay, had taken orders on purpose that they might marry the better, and had sometimes married widows." The Syrian position with regard to matrimony was that it "neither is nor can be a sacrament"; and it would have been well if it had been only in regard to the theory of matrimony that their Roman counsellors were able to lay a charge at the door of the Syrian Christians. For it would seem that inexcusable violations of the marriage law were but too notorious throughout the diocese.

The sacraments of penance, auricular confession, and extreme unction were, to the keen eyes of those Western ecclesiastics, conspicuous by their absence from Syrian usage.

So much for the sacraments. But errors or defects in other departments of doctrine, ritual, and practice could not be passed by without exposure. A few illustrations must suffice. "The holy water," say the Portuguese spies, "that has hitherto been made use of in this diocese has not been blessed by the priest, nor by any prayer of the Church, the sexton only throwing a little of the clay into it that is brought by pilgrims from the sepulchre of St Thomas, or from some other holy place relating to him; and, when such clay has been wanting, the said sextons have thrown some incense into it; whereupon, without any further consecration, it has been esteemed holy." Again, through the misgovernment of Nestorian heretics, it is affirmed, the Syrians lacked "the healthful use of pictures," they maintained that images are filthy and abominable idols, and ought not to be adored; the worship of the Virgin and the invocation of saints they abhorred. The Syrians were not accustomed to bow at the name of Jesus; "the greatest part of the people of this bishopric are not instructed in the doctrine, and they that are, know only the Pater Noster, and the Ave Maria in the Syriac tongue, which they do not understand, and most of the children know not how to bless themselves, nay, the clergy themselves are ignorant thereof, not being able to say the commandments;" and "in the remote parts of the diocese, as well towards the south as towards the north, the Christians that dwell in the heaths are guilty of working and merchandising on Sundays and holy days, especially in the evenings."

The Syrian theory of the intermediate state was somewhat peculiar. "The souls of the saints," they held, "are not to see God until after their bodies are raised at the day of judgment, and till then they are in a terrestrial paradise." "The soul of Christ, when He died, descended not into hell, but was carried to the paradise of Eden." "The wicked, when they die in mortal sin, are carried to a place called Eden, where they suffer only by the sense of the punishments they know they are to endure after the day of judgment," the fire of hell being, in Syrian thought, metaphorical or spiritual, not literal or material. Such a view of the intermediate state altogether precludes the idea of a purgatory. The insertion of the doctrine of purgatory in their creed must have been felt most seriously to dislocate some of the joints of the Syrian eschatology.

But reformation was needed in social as well as in ecclesiastical affairs. Faults great and small were patent to the eyes of fault-finding friends. A great many of the Christians had recourse to superstitious practices. When about to marry, for example, they consulted wizards and fortune-tellers to ascertain what success they should have, and governed themselves so much by what they were told as to break off matches already concluded and to make new ones at the pleasure of those wizards. During sickness they would send for such people to perform some ceremony whereby they hoped to have their health restored, and, in case of theft, to give a clue to the identity and whereabouts of the thief. Many Christians were in the habit of obtaining from wizards talismanic notes which they hung about their persons to cure their distempers, on the necks of their cattle to keep them well, and in their orchards to increase the fruit. In some parts of the diocese, when any of the baser sort touched the cisterns of the Christians, the cisterns were purified with ceremonies like those of the heathen. The Christians also forbore touching certain castes, and, if they did happen to do so, went and purified themselves by washing. Certain heathen festivals proved attractive to some of the Christians, who took part in some of the proceedings. Sometimes Christians also, when charged with a crime of which they were innocent, volunteered, in order to substantiate their innocence, to subject themselves to ordeals which were enjoined by heathen rulers on their own people, such as handling bars of hot iron, thrusting their hand into boiling oil, or swimming through rivers full of snakes, reckoning, if they were innocent, that none of those things could hurt them, but would certainly do so if they were guilty of the crimes laid to their charge.

CHURCH AND HERMITAGE AT THE LITTLE MOUNT, MADRAS.

In other matters the spirit of superstition, though more innocent perhaps, showed itself; for instance, in the making of circles with rice, into which they put persons about to be married, having given rice to children; in drawing out a thread when they cut a web of cloth; and in taking back two grains of rice after they had sold and measured it. Among other faults set down to the Syrians is that they were litigious, and often went to law before heathen judges; although it was "the ancient custom consented to by the infidel kings of Malabar that the whole government of the Christians of this bishopric, not only in spirituals, but temporals also, is devolved to the Church and the bishop thereof, who is to determine all differences that are among Christians." Another fault of which the Syrians were accused shows how agreeable to the oriental mind is the traffic in money. Charles Lamb would have had no hesitation in applying to the Syrians his comprehensive principle, that all mankind may be divided into two classes, borrowers and lenders. At all events, borrowing and lending seem to have been almost universal among them. But the Portuguese ecclesiastics could not away with their usurious practices. Syrian money-lenders were in the habit of charging one and sometimes two per cent per mensem for the use of money, whereas ten per cent per annum was the highest rate of interest that, according to the Portuguese, could come within the sweep of legitimate trade. Slavery as an institution was found among the Syrians, and this the Romans did not attempt to suppress; but two circumstances connected with it they deplored, and felt it a duty to try to restrain. The one was that "several poor wretched Christians, following the example of the heathen among whom they live, when they find themselves pinched with want, do, contrary to all right and reason, sell their children;" and the other was that baptised or Christian slaves were sometimes sold to 'infidel' masters.

The discriminating reader will judge how far the charges made against the Syrians were discreditable to them. I have not attempted to characterise in detail the evils laid at their door by the Portuguese. It may be enough to say that with much that was good, there were many corruptions, and, considering their circumstances, much excuse may reasonably be made for the Syrians. The explanation of so much divergence from Roman doctrine and practice was given by the Portuguese in a manner completely satisfactory to their own mind. "The Nestorians," they held, "by reason of the great communication they have had with the Greeks, have imbibed some of their errors." More particularly, the Syrian Christians of Malabar had long been subject to heretical and schismatical prelates, whose misgovernment might account for all doctrinal and ecclesiastical aberrations; while the fact that they had lived among the heathen and mingled with them for so many centuries was sufficient to explain the existence among them of so many superstitions and social disorders. But the cause of causes was that this Church had "been for 1200 years from under the obedience of the Holy Roman Church, the mistress of all the other Churches, and from whence all good government and true doctrines do come." In other words, it is pretended that up to the date of the General Council at Ephesus, which condemned Nestorius in 431, the Syrian Church had been subject to the Pope and loyal to Rome; and, by way of confirming this monstrous piece of history, the readers of the decrees of this notorious synod are obligingly informed that it was by order of the Pope of Rome that Cyril of Alexandria presided at Ephesus.

That there was much need of reform in the

Syrian Church every good Catholic was convinced: the only question was, how it could be brought about. To the monastic orders all naturally looked for such a service. The Franciscans were the first to move in this direction. They established a college at Cranganore, 1546, for the purpose of training up in the orthodox faith priests who should be set over the Syrian congregations. But the college was not a success, and its failure was set down by the Jesuits, who were far more aggressive than any of the other orders, chiefly to the fact that it did not pay sufficient attention to the Syriac language, "always regarded as most sacred by these people, being (as they maintained) the language spoken by their apostle St Thomas, and, further still, by our Lord Jesus Christ Himself when on earth." Passing by Cranganore, they selected a quiet spot on the isle Malankara. Here they erected in 1587 the famous College of Vaipicotta, in which special attention was given to the study of the Syriac language and literature. The place was well chosen, since, in addition to its having been the island where, according to tradition, St Thomas first landed, it was on one of the great water-ways leading directly to several of the churches of the interior, and not many miles from Angamalé, one of the most highly venerated strongholds of the native Christians. But, despite all their acquaintance with the Syriac language and the Roman doctrines, the young priests were rejected by the people for whose benefit they were intended; and this means of sapping the foundations of the Syrian Church was thus rendered abortive.

Such a state of things, however, could not be allowed to continue. If gentleness failed, force must be applied. A powerful ecclesiastic arose to lead the movement. Aleixo de Menezes, who had been appointed Archbishop of Goa and Primate of the Indies, had arrived with a brief from Pope Clement VIII., dated January 27, 1595, according to which he was directed to "make inquisition into the crimes and errors of Mar Abraham, and, in case he found him guilty of such things as he had been accused of, to have him apprehended and secured in Goa; as also to appoint a Governor or Vicar-apostolic of the Roman communion over his bishopric; and upon Mar Abraham's death to take care that no bishop coming from Babylon should be suffered to succeed."

Mar Abraham died in 1597, "contemning the sacrament of penance," and committing the care of his diocese to Archdeacon George. The time had, therefore, arrived for Menezes to carry out the papal brief, but it soon became evident that he had tough work to do. At an early stage of the negotiations Archdeacon George made bold to inform him that the Pope of Rome had no more to do with them than they had with the Pope of Rome; and, having made this declaration as for himself, he assembled a synod of the clergy and most substantial laity at Angamalé, the then metropolis of the diocese, where they all swore to stand by their archdeacon in defence of the faith of their fathers, to allow no alteration to be made in the doctrines of their Church, and to admit no bishops save such as should be sent by the Patriarch of Babylon; of all which they made a public instrument, and, having sworn to maintain it with their lives and fortunes, ordered it to be published. Would that they had proved as courageous in action as in speech! History searches in vain for their martyrs, their Hamiltons and Wisharts, their Ridleys and Latimers. The Syrians would murmur and protest and weep, but they would not burn. When Menezes came among them in person, with all his strength of will and wealth of resource, oriental-like they yielded. The archbishop, after a tour of visitation through the diocese the better to understand the state of feeling, convened a synod of the Syrians, over which he himself was to preside. It met at Diamper[9] on June 20, 1599, and sat for seven days. The meeting was opened with much solemnity, in presence of the dean and chapter of Cochin, and many other Roman ecclesiastics, the governor of Cochin, the commissioners of the Portuguese treasury, and the whole chamber of that city, besides several merchants of distinction; for the president evidently believed in having a strong platform. The proceedings were conducted partly in Portuguese and partly in Malayalam, and had eventually to be communicated to the congregations in the latter language. Jacob, a Syrian priest, was therefore appointed official interpreter to the president, who "had but little knowledge of the Malabar tongue," and to the holy synod, with Francisco Roz and Antonio Toscano, both of the Society of Jesus and of the College of Vaipicotta, as assistant interpreters; and every precaution was taken for giving to the synod as much of the appearance and as little of the reality of a free deliberative assembly as possible.

The synod having been constituted with a

solemn Mass and a sermon against schism, the first act which the members were required under heavy pressure to perform was to make, in their own name and in the name of all whom they represented, a profession of faith as it was henceforth to be taught among them. The Syriac Scriptures[10] were to be corrected and supplemented, while the Western form of the Constantinopolitan (Nicene) creed was accepted, together with all apostolical and ecclesiastical traditions, and the Church as the interpreter of Scripture. The Syrians acknowledged the seven sacraments with all their Roman interpretations and uses. The doctrines of the real corporeal presence, purgatory, the invocation of saints, indulgences, and the veneration of relics were all swallowed by the Syrians. They renounced Nestorius and all his works, holding the perpetual virginity of 'our Lady,' saluting her as the mother of God, and maintaining that in Christ there are two distinct natures and one person. The Nestorian saints' days were abolished and those of the Roman calendar put in their place. The Patriarch of Babylon was anathematised as being out of communion with the Church of Rome and beyond the pale of salvation; and the Syrians took an oath and protested to God by the Holy Gospel and the cross of Christ that they would never receive into their Church "any bishop, archbishop, prelate, pastor, or governor, unless appointed by the Bishop of Rome." The diocese was divided into parishes, each of which was to have a vicar and as many assistant clergy as were needful. Abuses and neglects in Church affairs were to be reformed, and heathen customs were to be abolished. A stricter moral discipline was to be introduced among the laity, and a higher standard of duty among the clergy. Lastly, the Syrians were placed under the protection of the Portuguese; the Jesuits were licensed to preach and administer the sacraments throughout the diocese, without the permission of the parochial clergy; and the people of this ancient Church were to submit themselves to the Holy Office of the Inquisition "in these parts established." Will it be believed that decrees to this effect were signed by a hundred and fifty-three cattanars, or priests, and six hundred and sixty lay procurators? Such was the influence of one strong-willed and resourceful European, supported as he was by all the local representatives of Portuguese civil and military power, over those unprotected orientals.

There were but few kindly touches in the proceedings of this synod, yet, such as they were, they perhaps ought in fairness to be mentioned. As there was no proper supply of wine for the performance of Masses in the diocese, the King of Portugal was petitioned to send "once a-year as an alms a pipe and a half or two pipes of muscatel wine of Portugal, to be distributed among the Christian churches;" and, pending a reply to this petition, the archbishop volunteered to supply wine at his own charges. He also undertook to supply the clergy in the same manner with proper official vestments; and, whereas simony had been largely practised in the diocese, and it was desirable to arrange "by the way of alms, collection, or assessment, or by the way of tithes, according to the people's ability," for the maintenance of the clergy without their having recourse to fee-collections for particular services, his Catholic Majesty, the King of Portugal, was entreated as "the protector of the Christians of these parts, and the only Christian king and lord in the Indies," to be graciously pleased, on account of their poverty, to provide for the vicars of the Church, allowing them at least fifteen thousand cruzados to be divided among them all besides what should be gathered for them in their respective parishes.

Some provision was also made for the poor in the congregations.

The most cruel of the synod's proceedings was the making of the decree about the celibacy of the clergy retrospective. After the manner of Hildebrand, Menezes compelled all married priests, on pain of excommunication, to put away their wives; and wives of priests — who were called cattaneiras, and held in honour as such, and partook of the revenues of the Church—refusing to leave their husbands, were to be deprived of all their church-living. But what history will least willingly forgive to this notorious synod is its wanton destruction of books. The liturgies were either destroyed or altered beyond recognition, and there is probably no entire copy now in existence which was used by the Syrians in Southern India before 1599.[11] Moreover, all other books that could be laid hold of and that contained heretical doctrine, were as a rule summarily committed to the flames, so that, apart from excerpts made from about twenty books given in the decrees of the synod, it is impossible to hear the Syrians of those days speak for themselves. Would that the archbishop had been content to send all the books, heretical or otherwise, to the Vatican!

With a view to carrying out, under his own personal supervision, some of the decrees, such especially as those just referred to, Menezes resolved to make a second tour of visitation through the diocese.

Only one fragment from the report of this tour seems of sufficient interest to deserve notice. While he was at Pallur, a farce—a diabolical farce, as Gouvea calls it—was enacted in the church there, which was afterwards enacted in other churches; and, though the construction of the play was of the simplest kind, the effect it produced on the spectators was very remarkable, and anything but agreeable to Menezes. There were three *dramatis personæ.* One of the speakers personated St Peter; another, St Thomas; and the third, who acted as umpire, St Cyriac, the patron of the church of Pallur. St Thomas began the dispute by bitterly inveighing against St Peter, and complaining of the wrong which that apostle had done him, in seducing the Indian Christians from their allegiance to himself, seeing that he had acquired a legitimate right over them by his preaching. "Your law," said he to St Peter, "was preached at Rome, and in Italy; your proceedings here, therefore, are most unreasonable. You have brought into this country an archbishop, a very enterprising man, who, by sheer violence, has maintained the cause of the Portuguese, and introduced your law among a people who owe you no allegiance. Your successors, the Bishops of Rome, can have no authority whatever in this country. We are both apostles of Jesus Christ; our power is therefore so equal that you have no more jurisdiction over my Christians than I have over yours." To such arguments, and others of equal force, St Peter was represented as returning a very feeble answer. He contented himself with asserting that his law was for all the earth; and that, although that of St Thomas was good, yet his own was much better. Upon this the dispute grew very warm, both the apostles becoming enraged. At last, however, bethinking themselves that, being the apostles of Jesus Christ, it was unbecoming their dignity to dispute in this angry manner, they moderated their wrath, and agreed that it would be better to refer the question to St Cyriac, to whom this church belonged, both promising to abide by his decision. St Cyriac, being called in, heard both cases, and decided immediately in favour of St Thomas, "because," said he, "the Christians of India do not depend on

St Peter, but on their true pastor, the Patriarch of Babylon. The Portuguese archbishop, who declares the contrary, is a heretic, against whom it is necessary that the Indian Christians should be on their guard. They ought not to surrender their faith to him; and the oaths he extorted at Diamper are manifestly null and void."

During Menezes' ten months' absence among the Christians of St Thomas, the Viceroy of Goa died; and on his return to the capital, the archbishop was called on by his sovereign to assume the reins of civil government. In 1601 he received a bull from Pope Clement VIII. confirming the provisional appointment of Francisco Roz, S.J., as Bishop of Angamalé; and four years afterwards Pope Paul V. translated the see of Angamalé to Cranganore and gave the title of archbishop to the prelate of that church, still retaining the primacy of India in the archbishopric of Goa. What more could the heart of Menezes wish to secure the permanency of his work? Presently, therefore, he "returned to Europe, where the respectability of his family, as well as his energetic character, and the elevated post he had filled in India, naturally led to his promotion to the highest offices both in Church and State. He was soon raised to the primacy of

Brague, nominated Viceroy of Portugal, under Philip III., which he held for two years, and was then made president of the council of the state of Portugal at Madrid, in which office and court he is said to have died in disgrace."[12] But the great work of his life was that which Gouvea recorded in his 'Jornada,' consisting of a couple of tours of visitation in the Syrian bishopric, with the Synod of Diamper between. These accomplished, he thought that he had made peace in the Syrian Church by reconciling it with the mother Church of Rome; but readers of this story will be reminded of the policy of the Romans so tersely described by Tacitus, *solitudinem faciunt pacem appellant.*

CHAPTER XVI.

AT THE COONEN CROSS.

The Portuguese never prospered after their subjugation of the Syrian Church at the Synod of Diamper in 1599. Of this let their own historians be the judges. Portuguese chroniclers divide the history of their nation's prosperity in India into three periods. The period of its infancy extends from the end of the fifteenth century, when Portuguese intercourse with India began, down to the year 1561. From that time to the year 1600, they regard as the period of its manhood or full vigour. At the last date they reckon its old age to have commenced; and it has since become so decrepit as to be only the shadow of a great name. It is the old story: prosperity begat luxury, self-indulgence, and all kinds of moral weakness; and, where the carcass is, there the vultures assemble. Towards the close of the sixteenth century the Dutch threw off the Spanish yoke in the Netherlands; and, the ports of the Iberian Peninsula being thenceforward closed against them, they turned their attention to the commerce of the East, where they soon became formidable rivals to the Portuguese. In 1595 they captured Java, where they founded the city of Batavia, the capital of their possessions in the Eastern Archipelago. This success was followed in a few years by the capture of Formosa, Amboyna, Sumatra, and several smaller islands. In the year 1603, they began trading with Ceylon and soon had a large commerce in its productions. For some years they seem to have limited themselves to these peaceful occupations, but in 1632 their ambition stretched beyond the bounds which had hitherto confined them; and, when in 1636 their designs of conquest became known to the King of Kandy, he invited them to help him to effect his deliverance from the arrogance and tyranny of the Portuguese. Accepting this invitation, the Dutch lost no time in sending a strong armament to the king's assistance; and, after a long struggle, Colombo, the capital, yielded; the power of the Portuguese in Ceylon was destroyed; and they were expelled from the island.

In 1660, four years after the capture of Colombo, they took Negapatam from the Portuguese and made it the capital of their possessions on the Coromandel coast. They next turned their attention to the Portuguese maritime towns in Malabar, the possession of which they considered essential to the safety of their commerce. They succeeded in taking Quilon about the end of the year 1661; and, in January of the following year, they captured by assault the town of Cranganore, which was the residence of the Jesuit archbishops, who then ruled over the Syrian Christians, in place of their own metrans. The taking of Cranganore was followed by the siege of Cochin, which submitted to the Dutch in January 1663. This was the deathblow to the Portuguese power in India. After this it never rallied. Its possessions shrank within a very small area, being reduced to the city of Goa and a few places of minor importance to the north. The glory had departed. Another sun had arisen in all its splendour on the coast. Fresh hopes inspired the breasts of the Syrian Christians; for practically the whole area within which the ancient Church was planted fell under the dominion of a European Protestant power. The Dutch had known themselves what it was to be persecuted in their own land. In a spirit of obedience to the royal law, they refused to persecute their subjects in foreign parts. To the Syrians at least they extended an easy toleration.

But, before this political change occurred, one of those hopeful outbursts of indignation, which serve to show what might have been, was manifested on the part of the Syrians. They had not been accustomed to strict ecclesiastical discipline; and they could not endure the rigid rule of the Jesuit archbishops of Cranganore. Nothing, they thought, could be worse than that; and they resolved that, whatever should be the consequence, they would make an end of what they were accustomed to call their Babylonish captivity. They accordingly prepared for action, and they certainly made a demonstration which their foreign ecclesiastical rulers could not fail to understand. They assembled one day in thousands round the Coonen Cross, in a village near Cochin, and took an oath that they were done with Portuguese bishops and would never again acknowledge them. This was in 1653.

The immediate occasion of this demonstration was that one Atalla or Ahatalla (*i.e.*, Theodore), a bishop, having been sent by the Patriarch of Babylon to India, and having landed at Mailapore, had been seized by the Portuguese and put on board ship to be conveyed to Goa and consigned to the Inquisition. When the Syrians became aware that the bishop intended for them was thus doomed to destruction, their indignation knew no bounds; and the numbers being so great that all could not touch the cross in taking the oath, they connected themselves with the venerable symbol by means of ropes along which the current of 'virtue' might flow to sustain them in the brave stand which they resolved to make for liberty. Then and there, too, they appointed a provisional government for the diocese, choosing Archdeacon Thomas as their bishop, and taking such further action as seemed necessary for carrying on the work of the Church.

Not all the Syrians, however, renounced Roman jurisdiction on that day. They were then divided into two parties, some in favour of the Syrian *régime*, others contented with the Roman. The former accordingly reverted to the Syrian rite; the latter continued to be Romo-Syrians. The names by which they were thenceforward distinguished in Malabar are respectively the Puthencoor or new community, and the Palayakoor or old community, —the relative proportions being probably then as now about three to one.[1]

It was ten years after this memorable incident that the Dutch became masters of Cochin; and though they did nothing directly for the benefit of the Syrians, they undesignedly did them a great kindness, when, to serve their own ends, they ordered all foreign ecclesiastics of the Roman rite to leave their newly won territory.

Released from the tyranny of the Portuguese priests, the Syrians might have been expected to look forward to an independent future and to solve once for all the problem of self-government. But they did not avail themselves of the splendid opportunity which Providence gave them, and from that day to this they have shown a degree of indifference on the point only too characteristic of the Oriental. Leading-strings they loved, and in leading-strings they were content to walk. If the supply of bishops from the Patriarch of Babylon was hopelessly cut off, they would not refuse a bishop from any other oriental sect, and so they were fain to take the first that came their way. He happened to be a Jacobite, but such as he was they vastly preferred him to any bishop from the West.

THE JACOBITE PERIOD

CHAPTER XVII.

THE SYRIAN JACOBITES.

I.

To trace the origin and progress of the Syrian Jacobites we must go back to the days of the controversy concerning the constitution of the Person of Christ in the fifth century, and especially to that phase of it which connected itself with the name of Eutyches, an Egyptian monk. The question of the period was: Are there in the one person of Christ two distinct natures, or only one? Eutyches adopted the latter alternative; and thus became, however unfitly, the representative of a theory which engaged the attention of three synods, and was finally condemned and disposed of as a heresy by the famous Ecumenical Council of Chalcedon in 451.

But among those who were adjudged heretical

on the question at issue, two views prevailed. The Armenians embraced the Eutychian view that the divinity is the sole nature in Christ, the humanity being absorbed; while the Egyptians and Abyssinians held to the doctrine, which is specially called Monophysite, that the divinity and humanity make up one compound nature in Christ. The West Syrians, or the Syrians of Syria Proper, were ultimately drawn into the adoption of the Monophysite view chiefly by the influence of Severus, Patriarch of Antioch.

Now it came to pass in the days of the Emperor Justinian that the Monophysite party in Syria was threatened with becoming gradually extinct; when a man arose among them whose indefatigable zeal did much to revive and extend the Monophysite communion. This was Jacobus Zanzalus, commonly surnamed Baradæus, or the man in rags, from the circumstance that he went about in the guise of a beggar. Ordained by certain imprisoned bishops to be the metropolitan of their Church, he visited the Syrian and neighbouring provinces, ordained clergy for his party, and gave them a Patriarch of Antioch for their superior. For more than thirty years he continued his labours with great success till his death in 578. It was from him that the Syrian Monophysites were called Jacobites, and it was by his ordination of Sergius as successor to his master that the heretical succession was kept up.

Though the head of the Monophysite sect claims the rank and prerogatives of the Patriarch of Antioch, it is to be remembered not only that he is both a heretical and schismatical patriarch, but also that there are other three Church dignitaries who all claim the same title. These three are: first, the orthodox Patriarch of Antioch, who sits on the throne of St Peter and St Ignatius, and lives to-day at Damascus; second, the head of the Maronites, who dwells in the monastery of Kanobeen, in the district of Khesrowan, in Mount Lebanon; and third, the Roman anti-patriarch, who dwells in Aleppo. The Jacobite Patriarchs of Antioch, being unable to reside at that city while it remained in the power of the Emperors, settled themselves at Amida (Diarbekr) on the Tigris, where they still have their headquarters. They also pass much of their time in the monastery of St Ananias, near Mardin. Since the end of the sixteenth century they have invariably taken the name of Ignatius.

It is wellnigh impossible to estimate the number

of Christians subject to the Jacobite patriarch. As many as a hundred and three episcopal and twenty metropolitan sees are reckoned as having belonged to him. But at the end of the sixteenth century there were not more than twenty of both kinds; and at a later period only five metropolitans, viz., those of Diarbekr, Mosul, Maadan, Aleppo, and Jerusalem.

The Jacobite Church has not been distinguished for great theologians or great works in theology; but the Syro-Jacobite liturgies are very numerous, no fewer than forty-one being described by Neale. Gibbon finds only one name of eminence among them, and on Abulpharagius, otherwise known as Gregorius Bar Hebræus, he has pronounced a well-deserved panegyric. He adds, however, that "the sect which was honoured by the virtues of Abulpharagius appears to sink below the level of their Nestorian brethren." "The superstition of the Jacobites," he continues, "is more abject, their fasts more rigid, their intestine divisions are more numerous, and their doctors (as far as I can measure the degrees of nonsense) are more remote from the precincts of reason."

II.

Such then are the Jacobites; and it was one of their number, Gregorius, styled Metropolitan of Jerusalem, that the Syrians of Malabar had the pleasure of welcoming among them when their Church was thought to be in a state of widowhood. It was in 1665 that Gregorius arrived, and he was cordially received by metran and people as giving encouragement to their feeble hope of regaining connection with an Oriental Church. Gregorius seemed to them to be sent by Providence in answer to their prayers. As the officiating bishop, whom we may now call Mar Thomas I., had never received the formal rite of episcopal consecration, it was deemed advisable that he should undergo this solemnity at the hands of Gregorius. For twelve years Mar Thomas I. had administered the see without imposition of hands, having received only such call and consecration as his fellow-believers could give. But now, having among them, as they believed, a duly consecrated dignitary of the Jacobite Church in high Asia, there was no longer any reason for the omission of this formality. The consecration was accordingly performed, and Gregorius seems to have exercised a sort of joint rule along with the native metran till death, in which they are said to have been divided by the space of only two days. It is by no means certain whether they or either of them had previously consecrated a successor; but it may be admitted as probable, although there is certainly no historical evidence on the point, that Mar Thomas II. was likewise consecrated by Gregorius. Meanwhile several other foreign prelates came to Malabar, but the information available concerning them is peculiarly meagre. One Mar Andrews is said to have come in 1678, but no ecclesiastical act is ascribed to him and no good service of any kind. His whole known history is summed up in the suggestive words of Paoli, *ebrius in flumen prolapsus mortuus est.* In 1685, the year to which the death of Gregorius is commonly assigned, Mar Basilius Catholica, Mar Ivanius Episcopa, two Armenian priests, and others arrived in Malabar from foreign parts; but from what parts or with what credentials history leaves us uninformed. Mar Basilius died very shortly after his arrival in the country, but Ivanius had a career before him; for Mar Thomas II., having been struck by lightning, suddenly died; and the administration of the see seems to have fallen for a time to Ivanius. Presently he consecrated and appointed Mar Thomas III. as metran of Malankarai; but, as the latter enjoyed this dignity for only two years, he next consecrated the Anandaravan[1] of the deceased as Thomas IV.; and having done much to free the Syrian Jacobite churches from practices which had crept into them by long contact with Nestorians and Jesuits, he died in 1694, and was buried at Mulanthuruthu.

During the time of Mar Thomas IV., Mar Gabriel, a Nestorian bishop, came to Malabar. He is described by Paoli as an *implacabilis hostis Jacobitarum.* On account of his creed neither the metran nor his people acknowledged him, nor would they allow him to preach in their churches. Nevertheless some of the Syrians clave to him and thereby made factions; and for twenty-three years, or till his death in 1731, this man managed to retain a position and to take some part in the administration of the Church. Mar Thomas IV., without consulting Mar Gabriel, consecrated his own Anandaravan with the designation of Mar Thomas V., by whom he was succeeded in 1728. In 1747 Ezekiel, a Cochin merchant, brought from Bassorah Mar Ivanius, of whom little seems to be known, except that Paoli calls him a Jew. But in consequence of his interference with images in the church, the metran and the people united in opposition to him, and "resolved that, since it was the practice for prelates, who had up to that time come from foreign parts, to be subject to the metran and archdeacon of Malayalam, a proper prelate should be got down." A letter was accordingly despatched to the Jacobite Patriarch of Antioch, who sent Basilius Catholica, Gregorius, and Ivanius, who with some others arrived in Cochin in 1751, bringing with them many copies of the Jacobite liturgy. A letter from the patriarch to Thomas V. seems to show that the latter had questioned the necessity for imposition of hands under authority from Mardin. "You wilfully contend," writes the patriarch, "that the perfection of your dignity is not needed," and he goes on to allege that Mar Thomas V.'s consecration had consisted in the placing of the episcopal mitre on his head by a priest. Further on, the metran is exhorted to become obedient, and "get his episcopal title confirmed." Whether the patriarch's letter had the desired effect, and whether Mar Thomas V. submitted and was reconsecrated, are questions which we have not the means of satisfactorily answering; but, if he was reconsecrated, the act must have been more of the nature of extreme unction than a qualification for admission to office, for he died soon after the date of the alleged reconsecration.

In 1761 Mar Thomas V. raised his Anandaravan to the dignity of episcopa as Mar Thomas VI. and died in 1765. Though the reconsecration of the former by foreign prelates is probably apocryphal, yet their reconsecration of the latter seems to be an admitted fact. It took place in 1770, and, strange as it may appear, this is the first and last occasion when any ordination of a metran of Malankarai took place by admitted authorisation of the Jacobite Patriarch of Antioch. In the case of those that follow, no one pretends that any of them were consecrated by authority derived from the patriarch; and, as for those that precede him, we shall presently sum up our finding.

From the date of his reconsecration, Mar Thomas VI. governed the diocese for upwards of thirty-seven years; and, being a man of considerable influence and administrative capacity, is not unfrequently referred to as Dionysius the Great. In 1796 he consecrated Matthan Ramban as Mar Thomas VII., and the latter succeeded to the administration of the see in 1808; which, however, he held only for one year, when he died. Soon afterwards, that is in 1813 or 1815, the Palamattam family appears to have become extinct, and at all events it supplied no more bishops for the see of Malankarai.[2]

III.

It is unnecessary to pursue the detailed history of these native metrans. Enough has been said to show how loosely the whole of the ecclesiastical business was conducted; how dependent the Syrians were on the services of foreign bishops; and how dear to their heart it was to see a prelate from high Asia among them. The services of these foreign prelates were so given and received as to exhibit on both sides a ludicrous attempt to keep up a show of apostolic succession, and the way in which it was done was enough to reduce apostolic succession, at least in Malankarai, to a farce.

It is important to notice that most of the foreign prelates that came to Malabar were mere adventurers and not a few of them unscrupulous men, altogether unworthy of the position to which they aspired. Those who performed episcopal acts, as well as those who did not, have left behind them no evidence to show that they were duly accredited representatives of the Jacobite Patriarch of Antioch. And so it came to pass that when the whole case of the succession was recently sifted in the courts of Travancore, no evidence of authorisation in favour of any of the bishops was forthcoming until we come down to those who reconsecrated Mar Thomas VI. Even the documents produced in *their* favour are not unanimously accepted by the judges of the Royal Court. Of Gregorius, who consecrated Mar Thomas I. and perhaps also Mar Thomas II.; of Ivanius, who consecrated Mar Thomas III. and Mar Thomas IV., not a shred of evidence is producible to free them from the suspicion that they came on their own account and to serve ends of their own. In fact the coming of the latter prelate, with a companion who died soon after their arrival, is described by the two Hindu judges in the Royal Court as being "from foreign parts, but from what parts the histories do not clearly say, but, from the circumstances attending their reception by the people of Malabar, it is only fair to presume that they must have come" from the Jacobite Patriarch of Antioch, or under directions from that dignitary. And even if we admit the validity of the claims of the reconsecrators of Mar Thomas VI. as genuine representatives of the Jacobite Patriarch, it appears that—from 1653, the year in which the Syrian Church asserted its independence of Rome, down to 1852, the year in which the first native of Malabar that ever received consecration direct from the hand of the Patriarch, was installed as metran—there was found, in the mass of documents recently laid before the Courts of Travancore, only one which could be construed as a sort of proof of ordination by delegation from the Patriarch. Thus the net result of two hundred years' connection with the Jacobite see of Antioch is that one metran was reconsecrated by delegation of the Patriarch, and another consecrated directly by the Patriarch's own hands. All the rest were, so far as documentary or other legal evidence is concerned, without authority; and there is no proof that they were bishops at all.

But not to press this point, let us assume for the sake of argument—what cannot be conceded on any other ground—that all who came to Malankarai from foreign parts and performed episcopal acts in the Syrian Church, or took part in the ordination of metrans, were bishops duly authorised in that behalf by the Jacobite Patriarch of Antioch, what ecclesiastical position was acquired thereby? The answer to this question cannot be very satisfactory to those among the Syrians who try to uphold the formal continuity of apostolic succession in their Church. By their acceptance of the services of those foreign prelates, they became Jacobites; they became connected, that is to say, with a heretical and schismatical Church. I am not here using my own words in describing the Church of the Jacobites. Dr Neale, an expert in ecclesiastical archæology, has shown that the Jacobites, having derived their existence as a sect from Severus, the heretical and schismatical Patriarch of Antioch, were themselves both heretics and schismatics. It is a moot point in ecclesiastical law whether schism does or does not nullify ordination and cause the Church, which is the subject of it, to lose the notes of a true Church. But, according to Newman, there can be no doubt about what 'the traditional view' on this subject was. In the preface to the third (1877) edition of the 'Via Media,' § 32, the late Cardinal wrote: "As regards schismatical ordination, as of the Donatists: on this occasion, Rome stood firm to her traditional view, and Augustine apparently concurred in it; but the African bishops on the whole were actuated by their sense of the necessity of taking the opposite line, and were afraid of committing themselves to the principle that heresy or schism nullifies ordination." So that according to this *dictum*, the Syrians of Malankarai by becoming Jacobites did, wittingly or otherwise, link themselves on to a Church which, on the ordinary traditional mechanical theory of apostolic succession, for which they have always been sticklers, was no part of the Church Catholic and did not possess the grace of orders. That is the position from which there seems no logical escape.

But let us waive the point. Let us assume for the sake of argument—what cannot be conceded on any other ground—that the Syrians of Malankarai were linked on, not to the heretical schismatical Church, but to the orthodox Catholic Church of Antioch, and that the contention which they sometimes erroneously make about their ancestors having come from the place where the disciples of our Lord were first called Christians, were admitted, what follows from their voluntary acceptance of this position? It follows that they have departed from the line of apostolic succession in which the Church of their fathers subsisted; they have chosen to be of the Church of Antioch, and to desert the Church of Babylon; they have preferred succession from St Peter to succession from St Thomas. The Syrians of

Malankarai would therefore do well to remember that the acceptance of Antioch means the rejection of St Thomas. Whatever right their fathers may have had to call themselves Christians of St Thomas — and I for one believe that, according to ecclesiastical usage, they had the right — the modern Syrians have now no right, nor have they had for more than two hundred years the right to assume that designation. They have been disloyal to St Thomas, and have set him aside; so that, if their own contentions and those of the Jacobite Patriarch of Antioch were admitted, they would now be Christians of St Peter, for Antioch is St Peter's Eastern chair.

Such are the results which seem to me to follow logically from the application of that merely mechanical theory of apostolic succession which has hitherto been of so much account in the treatment of ecclesiastical questions on the part of the Syrians and those who have had the regulation of their affairs. It will be shown in a future study that the Syrians of Malankarai, by adjusting themselves to new bearings, might still take up a true and effective position as a spiritual society and hold an honoured place among the Churches.

It is enough here to remark that they passed from

the one extreme of Nestorianism to the opposite extreme of Monophysitism at a single bound, without a moment's thought on the question of doctrine involved. A Church that sits so loose to doctrine, which is the nutriment of spiritual life and the guide of Christian practice, cannot be spiritually strong. The Syrians were exasperated by the rigid rule of the Jesuit archbishops of Cranganore and were prepared to purchase freedom from it at any price. Had they fought their battle on the basis of theological principles, or attempted to work on the lines of a rational Biblical theology, the revolution we have chronicled might have been a forward movement. As it was, they only exchanged one *-ism* for another and lost their apostolic succession into the bargain.

CHAPTER XVIII.

THE ENGLISH MISSION TO THE SYRIANS.

When the Portuguese Roman Catholics began to reform the Syrian Church, the first step they took was the establishment of a college for the training of the Syrian clergy. When the English Protestants began their reform, the first step they took was the planting of a similar college. The plan of establishing such a college originated with Colonel Munro, the British Resident at the Court of Travancore and Cochin (1810-19). It so happened that the ways and means for carrying out such an undertaking were not far to seek. The Resident found that a certain amount of money was available through the foresight of his predecessor in office. During the episcopate of Mar Thomas VI., a sum of three thousand star pagados (Rs. 10,500) was recovered by Colonel Macaulay, through the

Travancore Government, on account of injuries inflicted on the Syrian Christians by their non-Christian neighbours; and this sum was invested by him with the Government of Madras at eight per cent a-year, for the benefit of the injured community. The accumulations of interest were sufficient to erect the structure, and the Ranee of Travancore not only provided land for a site, but gave also land and money for an endowment. The college building is a quadrangle in which the apartments open into a verandah, or covered gallery, which runs round the whole of the interior. It was finished in 1813, and students presently began to frequent its halls.

With this nucleus, Colonel Munro made an earnest appeal to the Church Missionary Society to send missionaries to begin the work that was so needful for the renovation of the ancient but down-trodden Church. The way for this appeal had been paved by the writings and the personal influence of Claudius Buchanan,[1] and we shall see that it was not made in vain. But before we introduce the missionaries on the new scene of their labours, let us glance at the field into which they were called to work, and describe the plan of the operations which it was intended they should carry out. The field had undergone considerable transformation since we surveyed it in connection with the proceedings of the Synod of Diamper. That notorious assembly had borne fruit. So much so that, while the Portuguese Roman Catholics had in those days traced all the evils of the Syrian Church to her isolation from Rome, the mother of all the Churches, the English Protestants, on the other hand, considered that if only the Roman elements, which had been introduced by the Synod of Diamper, could be eliminated, and the Syrian Church could return to her ancient canons, there would be a glorious exhibition of primitive purity in doctrine and worship. Never was there a greater mistake, although the mistake was to a large extent excusable. Certainly the ecclesiastical aberrations of the Syrian Church under Roman influence were very conspicuous, but they were accompanied with much religious apathy, much theological error, and many social vagaries of a grave and serious character. Prayers were offered to the saints, to the Virgin, and for the dead, the communion was administered only in one kind, the clergy were celibates; the Scriptures, though theoretically not withheld from the people, were, like the liturgy, in Syriac, a tongue wholly unknown to the people, and no further understood by the clergy as a rule than that they could spell the words and parrot-like repeat the services. Simony was still prevalent in the diocese. The clergy yielded to the temptation of eking out their incomes by means of the *chattum*, a funeral service for the departed, and even the metran did not disdain to aim at providing a revenue consistent with his rank and dignity by granting ordination indiscriminately to the sons of the wealthy for the sake of the fees. The church fabrics were in a bad state. Some fifty-five churches needed repairs; others, having gone to ruin, required to be rebuilt; and a few had fallen into the hands of the Roman Catholics, for which reason an arbitration had to be appointed, and two out of four churches then lost to the Syrians, viz., the great church at Cottayam and the church at Puruwum, were restored. Above all, priests and people were ignorant to an inordinate degree. Their lack of enterprise, "the loss of the martial spirit of their ancestors," and their indolence, which prevented them from making the best of what was given to them in the good land,—these things were grievous to the hearts of their English friends, and their grief was still further aggravated by the evils of Sabbath profanation, adultery, the abuse of intoxicating drinks, and occasional participation on the part of Christians in heathen ceremonies.

The plan of reform was simple and definite, subject to such modifications as time and experience indicated. The object was to reform without disintegrating the Syrian Church, to help it in fact to reform itself from within. "The business of the Society's missionaries," said one of themselves, "is not to pull down the ancient Syrian Church and to build another on some plan of their own out of the materials; our object is to remove the rubbish, and to repair the decayed places of the existing Church. We are but advisers and helpers and instructors of such as are willing to hear." Their policy, said another, was to "alter as little as possible, so that the character and individuality" of the Church might be preserved. The Syrian Church had fallen into hard hands, and the Church Missionary Society played the part of the good Samaritan towards it.

The first triumvirate of English missionaries to the Syrian Church of Southern India were Benjamin Bailey, Henry Baker, and Joseph Fenn. They came to Malabar 1816-18, and gave themselves devotedly to work out the policy we have just sketched. They received liberty from the metran to preach in the Syrian churches, a liberty of which they freely availed themselves, using the vernacular Malayalam in the services. In their preaching they were silent on those points of the Syrian ritual and practice which all Protestants would condemn, leaving it to the gradual spread of evangelical knowledge to undermine, and at length by regular authority to remove such things. On the question of the celibacy of the clergy, however, a more positive course of action seemed practicable. The metran and his malpan were secretly of opinion that the single life was the highest and holiest; nevertheless they admitted that matrimony was lawful to the clergy according to the ancient rules and practice of the Church, and, moreover, that it seemed to them the only cure for the dissolute habits of many of their order. To encourage the movement of restoring to the Syrian clergy the right to marry, the metran published that he himself would gladly perform the nuptial ceremonial in the case of any cattanars who were willing to enter 'the holy state'; and Colonel Munro offered a reward of four hundred rupees to the first cattanar who should come forward to be married. So that by the year 1820 forty cattanars out of a hundred and fifty had become married men.

Possessing diversity of gifts, the missionaries soon saw the propriety of making a division of labour. In addition to the services in the Syrian Church already referred to, the work of the missionaries was mainly educational and literary. Bailey gave himself at once to literary work and the instruction of the cattanars. He translated the Scriptures and the Book of Common Prayer into Malayalam; he made two dictionaries of the vernacular language; with the aid of a native blacksmith he got types and punches made and a wooden press; and so the work of printing was begun. His version of the Scriptures still survives, though sorely in need of revision; and the work of revision has in fact been going on during a longer period than Bailey, with such coadjutors as he could obtain, required for the original version.

Baker gave himself to the establishment of village schools in connection with about seventy-two congregations which were not under the heel of Rome, and which were willing to be helped. These were carried on in Malayalam, and Scriptural instruction was given throughout. At Cottayam a superior grammar-school was erected, where English was also taught; and similar grammar-schools were established at Mavelikara and Alleppy. These were all under Mr Baker's supervision, and were intended as feeders to the seminary.

The work of the seminary or Old College, as it is now called, for the training of the Syrian clergy, was placed under the principalship of Mr Fenn. The instruction given included the elements of a general education as well as special instruction for the work of the ministry. The students studied the Latin, Greek, and Syriac languages, construing by means of English and Malayalam. They also made considerable progress in mathematics. And, whatever may be thought of the propriety of weighting the curriculum with European classics, it was evidently the design of its framers that the college should turn out men well equipped for their sacred profession. An arrangement had been made moreover, with the consent and approval of all parties concerned, that the metran would accept no applicant for ordination unless he produced a certificate from the principal of the college, showing that he had gone through the regular course of study, and had acquitted himself satisfactorily.

The Church Missionary Society was thus making an experiment, and its work attracted visitors. The first of these visitors came in 1820 in the person of the Rev. James Hough, for some years a chaplain in the service of the East India Company, and the author of a valuable 'History of Christianity in India.' His testimony was most explicit to the effect that the missionaries had not interfered with the observances of the Syrian Church, and were highly esteemed by the metran and his clergy generally.

The next visitor was Dr Middleton, the first Bishop of British India, who, from his point of view, was not disposed at first to regard this particular mission with favour. He did not see that it was right, unless under very special limitations, for one Church to enter the diocese of another, and to attempt to effect changes in the latter. In the course of his pastoral visitation in 1821, Bishop Middleton "had heard it stated that there was great reason to hope for a rapid approximation of this ancient and venerable community to the doctrine and discipline of the Church of England, that it was actually in contemplation to introduce the English Liturgy into the Syrian service." So, in returning from Bombay, he halted at Cochin, where he invited the metran to meet him. It was in reference to this interview that Middleton wrote: "I was with the Syrian bishop yesterday from seven till nine A.M., having no other person present but an interpreter, whom I could trust. The result is that the Syrians are much in the same state in which I left them four years and a half ago; that there is no visible approximation to the Church of England; and that, if ever there should be, it will be communicated to the bishop of that Church in India. The Church missionaries do indeed expound in their own church to all who will hear them; and this is well received by the people, to whom it is something new; but the bishop assures me that nothing is done which he has any reason to complain of."[2]

In 1822, Dr Mill, Principal of Bishop's College, Calcutta, visited the Mission largely with the view of searching for copies of the ancient liturgies used by the Syrians previous to 1599. In this quest he was wholly disappointed, but he gave cordial testimony to the satisfactory character of the work of the missionaries and to the soundness of their policy.

When Major Mackworth visited the Mission in 1823, an attempt was made to impress him with a show of that military character and status which, it was assumed, their ancestors possessed. He was met at Puruwum by the malpan with all the state his limited means could admit. He was escorted by a small troop of boys, armed with swords and shields, who preceded him with measured step. On their arrival at the church, half-a-dozen iron pots filled with gunpowder were discharged, giving a report like a small cannon, and two or three ancient matchlocks were fired off on the occasion. "The metran, who then usually lived in the college at Cottayam, gave a state reception to the gallant Major. He wore on the occasion a mitre; whilst a pastoral staff of polished blackwood, mounted with gold, and ornamented with a strip of silver descending spirally from the top to the bottom, was carried before him by an attendant. After a short time he took off his outer robes, and kept on only the usual one of crimson silk. His suite of apartments, and the furniture which adorned them, were of the most primitive order; he had a little bedroom containing a cot, three chairs, a small table, a wooden chest, and a brass lamp; from the canopy of his cot some dresses of ceremony were hanging, and a few books lay on the chest opposite the small window. He had one other room, not much larger and nearly empty." The metran allowed unreservedly the state of wretched ignorance in which the Syrians were plunged prior to the coming of the English missionaries; and since then, by converse with them, he had made the discovery that he himself had everything to learn, everything was new to him.

So far all had gone well. All this apparatus of reformation was benevolently provided for the Syrians and cost them nothing. Many of the contemplated reforms were easily carried out at first, partly through the friendly attitude of the metran, but largely because the British Resident, who wielded immense power, was strongly and avowedly on the side of the cause of progress. The missionaries were happy, and the work they had undertaken seemed full of promise. To those early days, to the greater part of the first decade, they looked back in after years with feelings of gratitude and joy. But this happy period was not destined to last very long, and a second decade saw the end of this friendly alliance. Altogether it lasted for a period of about twenty years, and what remains of the story will have for the most part to trace the development of those untoward circumstances which led to the final rupture between the Syrian Church and their evangelical friends from the West.

In the history of Indian Missions, one has always to reckon with the climate and its deteriorating influence on the health and vigour of European missionaries. And by the end of the first decade the triumvirate that saw the beginning of the work was broken up by the enforced retirement of Mr Fenn on the failure of his health; and, though vacant places thus caused may be speedily filled up, there is a distinct loss, for a time at least, when men have to retire with all their dear-bought experience, and their places have to be filled by novices. But, apart from the question of the continuity and efficiency of the missionary staff,[3] other conditions developed that acted unfavourably on the plans and prospects of the Church Mission. Some of the Syrians on their part were apt to be critical and suspicious. Too much, perhaps, was being done for them without any cost of labour, self-denial, or money; and there are always evil-disposed persons ready to resist a forward movement and to incite the halting to do the same; and the opportunity for an outburst of ingratitude, discontent, and wilfulness in due time came.

The native metrans were at first distinctly favourable to the co-operation of the missionaries. Of such metrans there were three during the period of the confederacy, each of whom assumed the title of Dionysius, the name of their respective villages being prefixed for the sake of distinction. They were Pulikote Dionysius, Punnatharai Dionysius, and Cheppat Dionysius. The first of these is said to have been at the outset somewhat suspicious of the intervention of English ecclesiastics, but a little intercourse with the missionaries soon dispelled his fears and he offered them every encouragement. But he did not long enjoy his episcopal dignity, having survived his consecration only about eighteen months. His successor, Punnatharai Dionysius, who was consecrated by the same prelate, is described as having "a pleasing and dignified appearance, a good address, and a fine countenance, expressive of mildness and good sense, yet with a meek, subdued look, which secured sympathy." Like his predecessor, he went heart and soul into the plans and purposes of the missionaries; so that the work of church reform and church extension was going on apace, when it was mysteriously arrested in 1825 by the sudden death of the metran, caused by an attack of cholera.

The ceremonies connected with the death and funeral of this prelate are interesting as illustrative of the manners and customs of the Syrians of Malankarai. Immediately after he expired, the bells of Cottayam church tolled, and shouts of lamentation and wailing were heard throughout the place. Having wiped the body with a moist cloth, the priests dressed it in full pontificals, and placed it in a chair. Thus seated it was removed into the church (which belonged to the Northern party of the Syrians), and placed at the foot of the chancel steps with the face looking westward. During the whole day dirges were chanted by the priests, and at four o'clock in the afternoon they carried the deceased metran round the church, followed by his state and private palanquins. The body, on being brought back into the church, was carried to the central altar, and then raised nine times towards the north, and three times towards the south; and, when it was returned to its place, men, women, and children were allowed to come forward and kiss the hand of the departed bishop. When Mar Philoxenos[4] at length arrived from Anjur, he could not suppress exclamations of grief while he took away from his deceased brother his wig, pastoral staff, and cross. He then seated himself in the chancel. The body being placed in a large wooden chair, a wooden cross was hung round the neck, another placed in the right hand, and the pastoral staff in the left; in this position the body was interred in a grave within the church, on the north side of the chancel, opposite that of Mar Gabriel the Nestorian; and, after the body had been lowered, Mar Philoxenos, supported by two or three friends, came forward and poured a small bottle of olive-oil on the head. For forty days after the funeral, Masses were performed by some of the priests. On the twentieth day after death, a *chattum* or funeral feast was given, at which deputies, lay and clerical, attended from all the churches. Food was provided for ten thousand persons, and it was calculated that more than six thousand actually partook of the good things provided. No meat or fish was allowed to be eaten; but there was rice in abundance, ghee, curds, oils, pulse, pickled mangoes, sweetmeats and preserves, milk, cakes, and pancakes fried in ghee and sugar.

After all the funeral ceremonies were over, steps were taken to fill up the vacant office of metran. That was not now so simple a matter as it had been till recently. Within the generation which witnessed the death of Punnatharai Dionysius, there had been some important innovations. In the first place, the office had ceased to be hereditary. The Pálamattam family, which had from time immemorial furnished all the Metrans of Malankarai, had become extinct. Since this happened, appointments had been made in a manner altogether new. The person generally supposed to be the fittest was selected by some of the senior cattanars and tacitly accepted. That is to say, there was no formal popular election, no plebiscite. But as there were in connection with such appointments certain malcontents, who endeavoured to agitate and carry an appeal to the Patriarch of Antioch for the exercise of his supposed prerogative, the Resident fell on the expedient of causing the person, selected for the office, to be proclaimed as metran by a royal proclamation. The substance of such proclamation was to the effect that So-and-so was appointed Metran of Malankarai, and that his people were to obey him according to custom. Thus an end was put to all disputation, but whether this device was in the long-run for the good of the church may admit of some question. At all events, when a successor to Punnatharai Dionysius was wanted, an unprecedented circumstance emerged. There were three candidates for the office, and it was curiously decided to make the selection by lot. The lot fell on Philippus Malpan, who was presently consecrated by Philoxenos of Tholiyur as Cheppat Dionysius. It was hoped by the missionaries that the new metran would walk in the steps of his predecessor. But in this they were destined to be disappointed.

The development of his hostile policy, however, was slow and cautious, and meanwhile he had himself to pass through an experience of sharp trial. He soon became aware that his own mitre was not over secure on his head. Complaints were being quietly sent by some of the people to the Jacobite Patriarch of Antioch regarding ecclesiastical irregularities in Malabar, and more especially about the insufficient ordination, as they thought, of their metran. In response to these communications the patriarch took a most unwarrantable step. Without any attempt to verify the representations that had been made to him, he resolved to supersede the native metran, and to replace him by a foreign ecclesiastic. Athanasius Metran and Abraham Episcopa were accordingly sent to take charge of the government of the Syrian Church of Malankarai. At Bombay they met with Bishop Heber, who happened to be there on a tour of visitation. The English Bishop was ill advised enough to honour this man Athanasius as if he had been an angel of light. At the communion in St Thomas's Church, he placed

Athanasius in his own chair within the altar rails, and afterwards sent him on his way to Malabar with a present of £30 to pay his travelling expenses. When he reached what he regarded as his diocese, he showed himself to be a veritable firebrand, and was deported along with his attendant colleague by order of the Government of Travancore; and the native metran was established on his throne by royal proclamation. So far there was peace. But the new metran began to show the cloven hoof. He was an exceedingly avaricious man, ordaining mere children for the sake of the fees. No friend to the reform which the missionaries sought to effect, he even forbade them the use of his churches. The missionaries themselves had begun to fear that the relation which they had tried to establish between the English and Syrian Churches could not much longer be maintained.

So matters continued in this unsatisfactory state till the coming of Bishop Wilson, the first Metropolitan of British India, on a tour of visitation in 1835. He was enthusiastic and hopeful, and perhaps slightly domineering. At all events he held a conference with the metran and cattanars in which he mildly laid down the law, hoping and perhaps believing all the while that his counsel was being accepted in the spirit in which it was offered. He recommended (1) that those who should be ordained by the metran should be so only after they had been instructed in the college, and had obtained certificates of learning and good conduct from the principal, the agreement between Colonel Munro and the then metran having apparently fallen into disuse; (2) that all the lands, funds, and other property belonging to the Syrian Church should be examined, and an account of them sent to the Resident that he might see that all was in order; (3) that some arrangement should be made to provide adequate salaries for the Syrian clergy, so that they might be able to abjure the custom of collecting fees for prayers for the dead; (4) that schools should be multiplied so that there should be at least one school for every church; (5) that the Gospel should be explained to the people on Sundays in Malayalam; (6) that the prayers should likewise be said in the vernacular language; and, at the instance of Mr Bailey, (7) that the plan decreed by Colonel Munro should be revived, viz., that all official letters on church affairs and to the churches should be signed conjointly by the metran and the senior missionary.[5] Looking back on this day's work, or rather on this visit, the Bishop recorded in his journal, "Never in my life, I think, was I permitted to render a greater service than to these dear Syrian churches." But the worthy Bishop was unable to penetrate below the surface of the inscrutable Syrian countenance. He did not read the thoughts of the people. Hardly had his back been turned when all his counsels were set at naught, and the thousand rupees he had left as a mark of his love to the Church were returned. So things went from bad to worse, till at length, in 1837, the metran summoned a synod of his Church at which he managed to drown the voice of the reforming party, and carried a resolution to cut off all connection with the Church Missionary Society, and to have nothing more to do with its aims and objects.

A formal dissolution of partnership was thus effected between the Syrian community and the C. M. S. missionaries, whose verdict on the occasion was expressed in the words of St Paul, 'from henceforth we will go unto the Gentiles.' "These ancient Christians must now seek us, not we them. We sought them for twenty years, and the separation was at their instance, not ours. Our schools and churches cannot but be open to all, and our clergy will use their discretion as to admitting such as may desire it to our communion on proper evidences. But no attempt at anything like proselytism must be thought of either as to clergy or laity."[6]

One step more, and the severance of the ties that had bound them together for twenty years was complete. The metran, the missionaries, and the Travancore Government appointed a committee of arbitration to allocate the several properties hitherto held in common. The arbitration was completed in 1840; and it assigned certain properties "to the Reverend the Missionaries at Cottayam and their successors, the Secretary *pro tempore* to the Corresponding Committee of the Church Missionary Society (Madras), and the British Resident for the time being or such person as the latter may authorise to act on his behalf, to be held by them in trust for the exclusive benefit of the Syrians;" while it assigned certain other properties "to the metran to be held in joint trust by him and two others, an ecclesiastic and a respectable layman of the Syrian persuasion, to be selected by that community itself, for the exclusive benefit of the Syrians."

The Syrian Church was thus much richer after the separation than before the alliance; but unhappily this property, which was intended to be a means of helping the ancient Church forward on evangelical lines, has now become an apple of discord between different parties of Syrians; and, so far as one can judge from present appearances, it will likely be used in the future to maintain the influence of the reactionary party, and thus to retard the very cause it was intended to promote. Such is the Nemesis of kindness unregulated by self-restraining discretion.

CHAPTER XIX.

MAR ATHANASIUS MATTHEW.

THE first native of Malabar that ever received consecration as Metran of Malankarai directly at the hands of the Jacobite Patriarch of Antioch was Mar Athanasius Matthew. This Matthew was a student in the old Syrian college at Cottayam, when it was under the charge of the Church Missionary Society, and was one of the deacons selected in 1837, as its most prominent students, to be further trained in the Church Missionary Society's institution at Madras. After some years' study there he was dismissed as unfit for the ministry. Then he proceeded to Mardin in Armenia to visit the patriarch, as well as the churches and convents in that region. He was graciously received by his Holiness, who entertained him under his own roof for seven months.[1] It so happened that, at the time of

Matthew's arrival, the mind of the patriarch was perplexed in regard to the state of things in Malankarai by some doleful and perhaps not altogether unprejudiced accounts that he had just received from that diocese. It appears that between 1825 and 1842 the Syrian community, or rather the Adullamite section thereof, had addressed the patriarch eleven times, soliciting that a metropolitan should be sent there, and stating that they were as sheep having no shepherd; that the Syrian Church in Malabar was in a state of widowhood; that, being without a duly constituted metropolitan and priests, they were deprived of the benefit of baptism, absolution, mass, and other sacred rites; that they had no morone (holy oils); that a priest ordained a priest and a priest consecrated a metran; that the patriarch should prohibit the priest, Mar Cheppat Dionysius, who wore the sacerdotal habit of metropolitan, from wantonly transgressing the canons of the Church; and that a metropolitan should be sent, reputed for piety, wisdom, and discretion, provided with the necessary holy oil and religious books. Accordingly, in the staticon or commission given to Matthew, the patriarch says: "While we were labouring with all these thoughts, as to who should be sent to Malayalam, there came our dear son Matthai from you in peace. On seeing him we were much pleased with him, and said that, as one had come from among them, it is best above all that he should be the father and ruler of them. So first we ordained him as deacon, thereafter as cattanar, subsequently as ramban or archdeacon, and afterwards as metropolitan."

This was in 1842. In the following year Mar Athanasius arrived in Malabar to take possession of his see. But then his difficulties began. There was already a metran in possession. Mar Cheppat Dionysius, holding as he did a royal proclamation which recognised him as the regular accredited bishop of the Syrians, declined to vacate his see in favour of the new claimant. In these circumstances Mar Athanasius made appeal in a series of letters, year after year, to the British Political Resident at the court of Travancore. His plea was that he had been properly ordained by the patriarch, and that the Syrian community were longing to see him invested with the tokens of his rightful authority over them, whereas Mar Cheppat Dionysius had never been properly ordained, having received consecration neither from the hands of the patriarch direct nor by delegation from that dignitary, and that he had not a majority of the

Syrians in his favour. The Resident, however, seems to have turned a deaf ear to all his pleadings.

Meanwhile Mar Cheppat Dionysius and his cattanars were by no means idle. They were busily engaged in sending to Mardin representations of the life and doctrine of Mar Athanasius Matthew very damaging to him; so that the mind of the remote patriarch was as much perplexed as ever. He therefore sent Mar Koorilos (Cyril) to make inquiries on the spot. It appears that Koorilos was intrusted by the patriarch with blank papers, signed and sealed by him, for such use as he (Koorilos) might have occasion, such for instance as to issue an interdict if he found Mar Athanasius guilty of heretical practices and to grant a staticon to one who should take his place. Armed with these instruments Mar Koorilos arrived in Malabar, and, after an interview with Mar Cheppat Dionysius, declared himself metropolitan of Malankarai duly consecrated and appointed by the patriarch, to supersede Mar Athanasius, showing as his credentials a staticon in his own favour which he had forged on the blank papers intrusted to him. There is no doubt that Mar Cheppat Dionysius lent himself to this most daring and sacrilegious act, to defeat the aspirations of his opponent. At all events he made over the charge of his office to Mar Koorilos and gave intimation of that fact to the British Resident.

It became necessary therefore for the Sirkar to take some action, and accordingly a committee was appointed to inquire and report. The circumstances under which the committee was appointed are interesting. "A proclamation having been issued by the Acting Dewan of Travancore in January 1848 to the effect that, whereas both Mar Athanasius and Mar Koorilos, who arrived in this country in the years 1843 and 1846 respectively, have produced to the British Resident credentials from the Patriarch of Antioch, appointing them severally metropolitans of the Syrian Church in Malabar, and that, whereas one party of the Syrian community desire to receive Mar Koorilos as their metropolitan, alleging that the documents produced by Mar Athanasius are not genuine, and the other party desire to receive Mar Athanasius as their metropolitan, alleging that the documents produced by Mar Koorilos are not genuine: the Sirkar, before recognising either of the two persons above mentioned as the Syrian metropolitan, deem it necessary that inquiry should be made into the dispute between the two parties;

and with that view have appointed, with the concurrence of the British Resident, four Sirkar officers to form a committee for the purpose of instituting such inquiry, and that Mar Athanasius and Mar Koorilos together with two cattanars and four principal parishioners of each of the Syrian Churches are required to attend at Quilon (on a given date) to answer such questions as may be put to them by the said committee."

The finding of this committee was that the documents submitted by Mar Koorilos were forgeries; that he had lent himself to acts which no man of principle would be guilty of, thereby compromising his character and the dignity assumed by him; that the charges which were made the grounds for the alleged supersession of Mar Athanasius were entirely unfounded; that, independently of the staticon possessed by Mar Athanasius being unquestionable, his selection as a native of the country being in strict accordance with former precedents, it was but just and reasonable that he should be recognised and proclaimed by the Sirkar as metropolitan of the Syrian Church.

Thus the pretensions of Mar Koorilos were finally disposed of; Mar Dionysius resigned his dignity on account of old age; Mar Athanasius was by royal proclamation declared metropolitan, he having brought a letter from the Patriarch of Antioch for that dignity; and all comprising the Puthencoor Syrians in the diocese were enjoined to acknowledge him as such, and to "conduct themselves in conformity with past customs." This happened in 1852, so that, after ten years of painful waiting and struggling, Mar Athanasius attained the summit of his ambition.

During the sittings of the Quilon committee, however, and before the royal proclamation of 1852, fresh trouble arose. A letter from the Jacobite Patriarch of Antioch, addressed to Mar Cheppat Dionysius and based on representations made by Mar Koorilos and others, intimated that he had sent Mar Athanasius Stephanos Episcopa, and with him Ramban Simon. "Therefore let them rule with you and with Mar Koorilos, our spiritual son," wrote his Holiness, adding that he had sent with these officers service books to be copied and placed in the churches, and holy morone, and that he had further instructed them to collect the *Rasisa*, an ecclesiastical tax "due to the chief Preceptor of the Apostolic See."

Stephanos, having duly reported his arrival in

Malabar to the British Resident, was informed by that officer that it appeared to him that the patriarch in sending Stephanos must have been acting on most incorrect information; that neither the money intended for the Syrian College at Cottayam nor any funds derived from the Syrian community were at the disposal of the patriarch; that the College funds were controlled exclusively by the local authorities in Travancore and no foreign prelate could have any right to meddle with them. Besides, to carry out the patriarch's wishes would be in direct violation of the order of the Madras Government, to which he would refer. What action, if any, the Madras Government took is not known. However, Stephanos was not to be put down. He entered the Syrian churches and preached, whereupon a quarrel arose, and the Dewan interfered to quiet the disturbance. A further appeal to the Resident being of no avail, Stephanos addressed the Honourable Court of Directors in London, who sent a despatch in which they repeat that their policy of "absolute non-interference with religious matters must be adhered to." Such matters, they add, are to be determined by the Syrian Church alone, "and it is for them to recognise or not the pretensions of any ecclesiastic who may be hereafter sent into the country by the Patriarch of Antioch." This despatch was dated 13th May 1857, after which Mar Athanasius Matthew seems to have been allowed to reign in peace for the next eight or nine years.

But in 1865 another native of Malabar, said to be "connected with the Palamattam family by relationship," and henceforth known as Mar Dionysius Joseph, went to the Jacobite Patriarch of Antioch at Mardin and got himself consecrated and appointed as Metran of Malankarai. The patriarch appointed him metropolitan because complaint of heresy and objectionable practices had been received, though as usual not verified, against Mar Athanasius Matthew. In the following year Mar Dionysius Joseph returned to his native land, where he hoped to be in due course established on the episcopal throne. With a view to attain this desirable end he addressed the Dewan of Travancore on the subject of his appointment to the metranship and of Mar Athanasius's deposition, and prayed for recognition by the Sirkar and the granting of facilities for his installation. But he received no redress. The Sirkar's principles were those of perfect neutrality in religious matters. To this official declaration the Dewan (4th July 1866)

MAILAPORE CATHEDRAL.

Chapel under Dome at east end said to contain Grave and Relics of St Thomas.

added his advice that "the only satisfactory course for the dissentient parties to pursue would be to effect a compromise, and, failing that, to go to law. If the case of one Church were taken to court and there decided, the principle involved would be settled and would apply to all similar cases."

Such a man as Mar Athanasius Matthew could not be supposed, however, to watch the tactics of his rival, and to sit still with folded hands. He determined to checkmate Mar Dionysius Joseph, if he could, and so in 1868 he consecrated his cousin Thomas as his successor. On that occasion he invited his neighbour, Mar Koorilos of Tholiyur, to unite with him in the act of ordination; and thousands of his own people were present from all parts of the diocese to witness the interesting spectacle and to show by their presence how thoroughly they approved of their metran's act for securing the succession in accordance with the 'use and wont' obtaining in Malankarai. Mar Athanasius Matthew also took the precaution to make a will, so that in the event of his death his cousin Thomas might quietly enter on the duties of the offices of metran and joint manager of the property held in trust for the benefit of the Syrian community.

In 1869 Mar Dionysius Joseph addressed a memorial to the Government of Madras complaining of his anomalous position and begging redress. But his Excellency in Council did not see his way to interfere with the possession of the Syrian churches then avowedly in the hands of Athanasius, and referred the petitioner to the advice given by the Dewan of Travancore, already quoted. At the same time the Government of Madras ordered that the moneys lying in the Resident's treasury to the credit of the Syrian Church, including thirty years' accumulations of interest since the date of the arbitration, should be paid over to Mar Athanasius.

But the mind of the resourceful rival was still restless. In 1874, as a last resort, he made his appeal to the Patriarch at Mardin; and that dignitary warmly espoused the cause which was identified with that of his own supremacy in Malabar. He determined to leave no stone unturned till he should see his authority fully established (we cannot say *re*-established) in Malankarai. With this view he undertook, what must have been to him a novel task, a journey to London by way of Constantinople, his object being to associate with himself at the latter place the Jacobite Metropolitan of

Jerusalem. In London he had interviews with all from whom he expected help. In certain circles he was fêted, and some may remember him during the season of '74 as he moved about, the guest of appreciative hostesses at garden-parties and evening gatherings, always noticeable by his dignified demeanour and picturesque dress. But on the whole his visit was disappointing. The Archbishop of Canterbury met him at his residence in Addington Park, near Croydon, and, after a short service in the private chapel, read to him a letter, being a reply to the patriarch's, which he afterwards handed over to his Holiness. The Archbishop's attitude on the question was perfectly distinct. He had been in communication with the Bishops of Calcutta and Madras on the subject, and he had come to the conclusion that Mar Athanasius, and not Mar Dionysius, ought to be supported as Metran of Malabar; and that the cause of true religion would be safer in the hands of Athanasius, who, he was assured, had the confidence of the great majority of the native Church, and who represented the principle of that Church's independence and its desire for reform. His Grace suggested, for the consideration of his Holiness the Patriarch, the question whether it was desirable to endeavour to maintain over the Syrian Christians of Malabar a control which could only be nominal over so distant a Church, with which communication must be difficult, and the members of which seemed entitled to independence in the selection of their own bishops. The Archbishop further showed the relation in which colonial Churches stood to the mother Church of England, and concluded by seriously recommending "some similar readjustment of the relations at present existing between your Holiness' see and the Christians of Malabar."[2]

The English visit having resulted in practical failure, his Holiness of Mardin next turned his steps towards Southern India, where he hoped in some degree to overawe Mar Athanasius Matthew by his presence; and, at all events, to obtain an interview with the authorities in Travancore and with representatives of the Government of Madras. He arrived in Travancore at the beginning of 1875 and exerted himself in the interests of his Church as much as possible. His success was considerable. He accomplished three things, all of which tended powerfully towards the establishment of his ecclesiastical supremacy in Travancore. The *first* of these achievements was a change in the attitude of the Sirkar towards the appointment of metrans of Malankarai. This was brought into practical effect by the withdrawal of the royal proclamation made in 1852 in favour of Mar Athanasius Matthew. That proclamation had been interpreted as securing the metran's position against litigation; but now, on the 4th of March 1876, a new royal decree was issued proclaiming that, "whereas representations have been made that the Patriarch of Antioch or his predecessor claims to have deposed the said Mar Athanasius and to have appointed another metran, this is to inform all whom it may concern that the former proclamation is not to be considered as in any way precluding the courts of law from deciding on the rights to churches or church property or the power of appointing or removing officers connected with the Church." "The action of his Highness the Maharajah's Government," it went on to say, "will be confined to the maintenance of peace and good order, and any apparent connection with appointments relating to the Syrian Church, which proclamations issued under times and circumstances now altered may seem to indicate, will henceforth be avoided." This action on the part of the Sirkar did not immediately affect the state of affairs in the Church, but the patriarch promptly followed up his first success.

Accordingly, the *second* great achievement of his Holiness during his sojourn in Travancore was to convene a meeting which was dignified with the name of a synod, but which was really of the nature of a caucus. It was held at Mulanthuruthu in June 1876, when, to the discomfort of all concerned, the south-west monsoon was at its height. It was moved that his Holiness, Maran Mar Ignatius, Peter III., Patriarch, the chief authority on the Apostolic Throne of Antioch and the Holy Father of the Jacobite Syrians of Malankarai, should be requested to preside over the deliberations of the assembly, which he was pleased to do. In his opening speech he intended possibly to give a veracious account of the situation, but in this respect at least he was not successful, and it is difficult to acquit him of the charge of deliberate prevarication. He not only thought it consistent with his dignity to brand Mar Athanasius Matthew with the title of Beliar (Belial), but also to represent the Sirkar as saying in its recent proclamation, "since the patriarch has dismissed him (Athanasius), we also dismiss him from the Church." By this wickedly false rendering of the royal proclamation, coming from the lips of such a high dignitary, the simple folks who heard him must have been grossly misled.

Without attempting to give anything like an exhaustive account of the proceedings at Mulanthuruthu, I shall content myself with the following *précis* of the resolutions, which may be accepted as fairly indicative of the nature of the caucus. It was resolved (1) that the people of each respective parish should execute and register a deed of covenant binding themselves to be subject to, and never to transgress the mandates of, the see of Antioch; (2) that lists should be made of the families in each congregation and that of their Karanavar (elders), that a book of canons should be printed and a copy placed in each church, and that a register of baptisms, marriages, and burials should be kept in all parishes; (3) that an association of the whole race should be formed and called the Syrian Christian Association, of which the present Holy Father and his successors should be patrons, and the ruling metran, the president; (4) that whereas it would be difficult for all of them (*i.e.*, the whole race of the Syrians) jointly to carry on the affairs, a chief committee composed of eight priests and sixteen laymen, with the ruling metran for president, should be formed, with a paid secretary and a cash-keeper; that they should be "made responsible as managers and responsibility-bearers to manage and control all the religious and social concerns of the whole of the people in general;" and that, in particular, they should be responsible for the collecting and remitting *Rasisa* to his Holiness the Patriarch, and for collecting the moneys due to the ruling metran by the churches; and (5) that, as it would be difficult for all of them (*i.e.*, the chief committee of twenty-four) jointly to conduct and carry on all the litigations arising generally as to religious or social matters, the president, Mar Dionysius Joseph, metropolitan, should be the person who should have power to carry on all such and to collect the moneys necessary for the purpose, and that the members of the committee should be auxiliaries to him therein.

Such is the gist of the proceedings of the meeting at Mulanthuruthu as reported by those who took part in it. Some further questions may fall to be discussed in the next chapter concerning this caucus. But it would appear that the practical outcome of these proceedings was to invest Mar Dionysius Joseph with a sort of power of attorney to act on behalf of the Syrians who agreed with him, in the matter of the approaching litigation, which now seemed imminent.

The *third* strategic move made by the patriarch during his Holiness' sojourn in Travancore, was to divide the province of Malankarai into seven dioceses,[3] that number having been fixed on probably from the consideration that St Thomas was believed to have planted seven churches in Malabar; and, having assigned to Mar Dionysius Joseph, who had been consecrated in 1865, the charge of the church of St Thomas at Quilon and the surrounding churches, he proceeded to consecrate six more metropolitans, as they are called in their staticons, and to assign to each of them a see. From the documents it would seem that the seven metropolitans were intended to be of co-ordinate rank and all directly responsible to the patriarch; yet the seniority of Mar Dionysius Joseph would naturally secure for him a precedence over the other six and make him at least *primus inter pares.* And it is probable that the patriarch intended this. At all events, the other six metropolitans recognise Dionysius as such, and testify that to him belongs not only the charge of the diocese of Quilon, but also "what is comprised in the Cottayam seminary and all general matters in the whole of Malayalam."

There is one curious circumstance connected with the consecration and appointment of these six metropolitans. In the staticon given to one of them (and it is the same for all), there occurs this remarkable sentence: "Should he show defiance, and infringe the canons of the fathers and the true faith, he would not only render himself, in terms of the written deed of consent passed by him at his consecration, excommunicated and accursed; but he would also be tried in terms of the temporal registered deed he has passed, and would be declared to have forfeited his dignity." And correspondingly in the said 'temporal registered deed' the following occurs: "It is competent for your Holiness to dismiss me from all churches, and to publish that I am a liar so that I may not be believed anywhere, if I should violate in any way this agreement executed by me of my own free will and consent. . . . When such is done by your Holiness or your Holiness' successors, I bind myself to pay two thousand eight hundred and fifty (2850) British rupees to your Holiness or successors."

This appointment of additional metropolitans was intended to be a "counterforce against the (hitherto) absolute authority of the prelates of

Malayalam," and it would largely tend to give roots to the patriarch's authority in the province. What view Mar Dionysius Joseph may have privately taken of this arrangement is not recorded. It must have greatly altered his prospect of being the sole Jacobite metran in Malankarai, but it is possible he may not have objected to this. His patriarch's will in the matter may have been his pleasure. But, if Mar Dionysius Joseph did not suffer from the pangs of wounded ambition, he must have groaned under the heavy bills of costs he had to pay. Being mainly responsible for having sent the patriarch to England to interview the authorities there on the subject of his grievances, and for having brought that dignitary to India, he was held responsible both for the heavy travelling expenses of his Holiness with a retinue suitable to his position, and for the legal expenses incurred during his temporary stay in Travancore. On this phase of the subject a curious side-light may be allowed to fall. We are told by one of the missionaries of the Church Missionary Society,[4] who was in Malankarai at the time, that the patriarch's "conduct was so violent and his greed of gain so insatiable, that even Mar Dionysius, who had invited him into the country, was at length unable to work with him, and there was a rupture between them;" and the same authority adds, by way of illustrating the above characterisation, that at the Church of Parur the patriarch opened the grave of an eminent Church dignitary in the hope of finding treasure.

At length, however, towards the end of 1876, after a sojourn of about two years in Travancore, his Holiness returned to Mardin.

In July 1877, Mar Athanasius Matthew passed away. His death, heralded by violence, and disorder[5] in his diocese, was due to blood-poisoning, caused by the bite of a rat. For a quarter of a century he had occupied the episcopal throne of Malankarai; and, more than any of his predecessors, had attempted to reform his Church. The sympathies of his manhood were those he imbibed in the course of his early training. During his *régime*, "every encouragement was given to the reading of the Scriptures, translated by the missionaries; prayers in the church were conducted in many instances in the vernacular; invocation of saints and worship of relics with other superstitious practices, introduced into the Syrian worship by the Roman Catholics, were excluded; Sunday schools, Bible-readings, preaching, and other active efforts to spread the truth were fostered and encouraged,"[6] and all the ordinary apparatus of evangelical work was used for promoting the good of the Syrian Church. Among his last instructions he gave orders that, though it was customary for the Syrians to bury their metrans in a sitting posture, robed as on state occasions, within the chancel of the church, this ceremony should be dispensed with in his case as tending to superstition. He ordered a coffin to be prepared some days before his death, and expressed his desire to be interred in the open graveyard of the Maramena Church, beside the grave of his uncle, a once famous malpan of that Church, and the father of reformation amongst the Syrians.

It is not easy, however, to make an analysis of the character of Athanasius altogether creditable to him. He was undoubtedly a man of ability, who managed to attain to the highest position in his Church and to hold his own to the last against considerable opposition. The phase of his character which may be most easily assailed is the palpable inconsistency of his maintaining — previous to 1852, when a royal proclamation was issued in his favour — that he held his office in virtue of his consecration by the Patriarch of

Antioch, and that the Patriarch of Antioch was supreme in matters spiritual in Malabar; while at a later stage, when the patriarch, for reasons satisfactory to himself, wished to depose Athanasius, the latter denied his authority and held his ground in spite of his Holiness of Mardin. His action in this matter has been severely criticised by the judges in the courts of Travancore, and there is no doubt that he laid himself open to the charge of double-dealing. On the other hand, it is at least possible that the Bishop's change of opinion may have been an honest change. The missionaries of the Church Missionary Society, who had ample means of watching him, seem to have believed in him to the last. Moreover, he received the approbation of the English Bishops of Madras and Calcutta, and, finally, of the Archbishop of Canterbury.

The death of Mar Athanasius Matthew opened the way for fresh action on the part of his rival. In 1878 another caucus, on the same lines as the meeting at Mulanthuruthu, was summoned to meet, under the presidency of Mar Dionysius Joseph, at Parumalai, at which the preparations for litigation were completed.

CHAPTER XX.

TEN YEARS OF LITIGATION.

A CASE of disputed succession in the bishopric of a Christian Church running the gauntlet of a series of law courts[1] in which most of the judges were non-Christians, is a phenomenon of considerable historical as well as legal interest. The leading parties in the case were Mar Dionysius Joseph, plaintiff, and Mar Athanasius Thomas, defendant. On the death of Mar Athanasius Matthew, the latter had quietly entered on the office of metran, discharging all the duties thereof, and managing, along with two others, the trust-property for the benefit of the Syrian community. To oust Mar Athanasius Thomas from the position which he had thus acquired, and to secure the recognition of his own episcopal dignity and the management of the trust-property were the objects which Mar

Dionysius Joseph had in view. His plea was that he had been duly consecrated Metran of Malankarai by the Jacobite Patriarch of Antioch in 1865; that he had been appointed president of the Syrian Association Committee; that he had been accepted by the Syrian community; and that, although during the lifetime of Mar Athanasius Matthew he had been unable so assert his rights and enter on his office, he was entitled at least on the death of that prelate to have his position recognised and to receive facilities for accession to office. The contention on behalf of Mar Athanasius Thomas was that he had been, in accordance with use and wont, consecrated by his cousin in 1868 with the approbation of the Syrian community; that, when his cousin died in 1877, he had, in accordance with the terms of his will, entered on the management of the trust-property; and that he had discharged the duties of the office of metran for nearly two years before the institution of this suit. Judgment in each court was given in favour of the plaintiff, with this modification, however, that, in the Court of Final Appeal, the English judge dissented from the finding of the two Hindu judges, and decided in favour of the defendant.[2]

In the course of these ten years, many strange things came about. One of the most interesting, though most irrelevant items in the proceedings, was a series of issues involving questions of heresy. Though there was no reference to heresy in the plaint, though no supplementary plaint was put in, and though no motion was made to amend the plaint, still some crude issues on the subject were irregularly imported into the record. The only judge that thought them worthy of discussion on the merits was Mr Justice Arianayagom Pillay. He discussed them with that amount of learning which Pope dubbed a dangerous thing, and with that sort of zeal which St Paul attributed to many of his kindred. He found it proved that invocation of saints, adoration of the Virgin, and prayers for the dead, had been deliberately omitted by the late Mar Athanasius Matthew from certain service-books of the Syrian Church, and that those omissions were approved of by the defendant. But he did not inquire how the said doctrines had got into the Syrian service-books, or whether there existed any standard of Syrian doctrine similar to the Thirty-nine Articles, or the Westminster Confession of Faith, by which to test whether the said omissions were or were not a return to ancient Syrian orthodoxy. He was probably not aware that the doctrines in question were all foisted on the Syrians by their Roman Catholic oppressors at the Synod of Diamper in 1599; he would probably have refused to admit that the Syrians acquired the right to eliminate all Roman elements from their creed when they threw off the Roman yoke at the Coonen Cross in 1653; and he would probably have denied that the Syrian Church, which was no more beholden to the Patriarch of Antioch for a system of doctrine than to the Archbishop of Canterbury, had the right to make from time to time in a regular manner such changes in its creed as its own wisdom might dictate, irrespective of foreign intervention. He therefore concluded that a person with the defendant's views could not only not be a bishop, but he could not even be a member of the Syrian Church. It followed of course that the defendant and his adherents were not Syrians at all, and so were disqualified for making any claim to the plaint property. This decision, or rather fragment of a decision, was, however, unanimously set at naught by the Royal Court, and the issues on Articles of Faith rejected as irrelevant. But Mr Justice Arianayagom Pillay's eloquence probably prejudiced the defendant in the same way as a dog's interests are damaged when one gives him a bad name.

But the great issue in the case was whether the plaintiff was the lawfully appointed metropolitan of Malankarai, and whether he was as such entitled to recover possession of the properties specified in the plaint.[3] Both parties agreed in their respective pleadings that to constitute a duly appointed metropolitan of the Syrian Church two conditions must be fulfilled, namely, (1) proper consecration, and (2) acceptance or acknowledgment by the people.

I.

With reference to the requisite consecration, both parties agreed that it must be performed by a bishop belonging to a Church holding the apostolic succession, by imposition of hands. But plaintiff-respondent affirmed and defendant-appellant denied that such consecration must be either by the Jacobite Patriarch of Antioch or by some bishop duly authorised by that patriarch to make the consecration. No issue could be more distinct, but the disposal of it involves a somewhat elaborate investigation; for no authoritative canons of the Church or books of procedure were produced by either side to show what was the state of the law within the Syrian Church, the fact being that the Syrians of Malankarai never possessed any code of laws, or, if they did, the code must have been lost.[4] The only course remaining therefore was to find out the Syrian 'use and wont' in affairs ecclesiastical by referring to such works on the history of the Syrian Church as were available, and by calling such witnesses as could speak to the past practice of the Church. In both these lines of research the courts were particularly unfortunate. The quasi-historical works that were filed are most unsatisfactory productions, three-fourths of them, moreover, having been written after the controversy that led to this litigation was begun[5]; and most of the witnesses[6] were either so ignorant or so prejudiced that their testimony was worthless.

Both parties strongly, though of course erroneously, maintained that the Church of Malabar was founded by St Thomas, the apostle, in the first Christian century, so that it was at the first an independent local Church. But how long it remained independent of foreign control, neither party could make out exactly to its own satisfaction. The Chief Justice and Mr Justice Sitarama

Iyer, the two Hindu judges in the Royal Court, seem to think there is reason to believe that, from a very early date indeed, the Indian Syrian Church became subject to the Church of Antioch, and that this relation to Antioch was quite firmly established by the date of the first General Council at Nicæa (325). These two judges describe the Council in a manner which must be pronounced at least uncommon. With the help of Ittoop, they find that "the Council of Nicæa, among other matters relating to the revival and establishment of Christianity, revision of the Scriptures, and framing a code of faith and rituals, settled the jurisdiction of the several ecclesiastical heads who were charged with the due carrying out of the acts of the Council." In other words, the Patriarchs of Rome, Constantinople, Alexandria, Antioch, and Jerusalem (such is the order in the text of the judgment) were appointed, the fifth or last of these being subordinate to Antioch. After this, one would be prepared for a good deal. But it is really too much to be asked to believe that the following is one of the decrees or acts of the Council: "*It was also laid down, that the Catholica appointed at Tigris (Baghdad) to manage the affairs of the Eastern Churches subject to Antioch was common and could exercise all the functions of patriarchs.*" Whether this is a correct quotation from *any* collection of the acts of the fathers of Nicæa, is extremely doubtful[7]; but, waiving that point and assuming the substantial correctness of the alleged quotation, two or three remarks are demanded.

In the first place, the two Hindu judges, who accept this fragment from Ittoop, do not seem to be aware that the sentence, which after their example I have printed in italics, belongs to a set of forged decrees of Nicæa. In collections containing both the genuine and the spurious decrees of the first Christian Council, this particular decree appears sometimes as thirty-third and sometimes as thirty-eighth; but it is well known that there are only twenty genuine decrees,[8] and that the remainder, seventy or eighty in number, were collected from the Synods of the Greek Church; though, judging from the equal reverence with which the whole code is received by all the Eastern communions, it was probably finished before the schism of the Nestorians and Monophysites. Further, the title of 'patriarch' was not admitted into regular ecclesiastical usage at the date of the Council of Nicæa, or for more than a hundred years afterwards; and, as for the insertion of 'Baghdad,' which we probably owe to the ingenuity of Ittoop, the city did not exist till about four centuries after the Council.

In the second place, though it is true that John, who appended his signature to the acts of the Council of Nicæa, and described himself as bishop (or metropolitan) of Persia and Great India, was at that time subject to the Archbishop or Catholicos of Seleucia (*not* Baghdad), the latter being himself subject to the Patriarch of Antioch; and, though it is clear that the Indian Christians under John were *a fortiori* under the Patriarch of Antioch, yet it is not perceived by the two learned Hindu judges that the Indian Christians subject to the jurisdiction of Antioch in 325 A.D. were living under Sassanian government, and that their India was, not Malabar, but India, west of the Indus. The Church of Malabar did not then exist.

In the third place, although the Catholicos of Seleucia was, at the date of the spurious Nicene decrees, subject to the Patriarch of Antioch, he did not always remain so. Before the end of the fifth century (498), the churches under the Catholicos, having by that time become Nestorian, met in Synod at Seleucia, and proclaimed themselves independent of Antioch, and gave to their chief the splendid title of the Patriarch of Babylon. This happened before the Church of Malabar came into existence; and the Church of Malabar was founded by the Patriarch of Babylon, who was Nestorian in doctrine and independent of the see of Antioch.

It has pleased the two Hindu judges in the Royal Court of Travancore to ignore altogether the relations subsisting between the patriarchate of Antioch and that of Babylon; and they never realised that the latter is, or rather was, the true mother Church of Malankarai. It is almost needless, therefore, to follow the reasonings of these two judicial authorities any further about the external or foreign relations of the see of Malankarai during the middle ages. Yet one or two remarks may not be altogether superfluous. In the first place, they represent that Thomas of Cana "made the power of the Patriarch of Antioch supreme in Malankarai about twenty years after the Council of Nicæa," although as matter of fact there was at the date in question no Church in Malabar at all. Thomas of Cana came at a much later date, and was probably a Nestorian and had nothing whatever to do with the Patriarch of Antioch. But however this may be, the whole story of Thomas of Cana "is far too shadowy and unsubstantial to be made the foundation of a legal judgment." In the second place, these two judges ignore the invaluable evidence of Cosmas, whose testimony is the first piece of historical illumination that helps to break up the darkness in which the origin of the Syrian Church of Malabar is otherwise involved; and who, himself a Nestorian, was on friendly terms with the metropolitan of Persia, and was able to define to the world the exact relationship of the see of Malankarai to the patriarchate of Babylon. Nothing can be more unsatisfactory than the flagrant misreading of the history by these Hindu judges, who refuse to see the historical bond that connected the Church of Malankarai with the Babylonian patriarchate. True, we have not many references to the Syrian Church of Malabar in the literature or among the monuments of the middle ages, but every authentic reference goes to connect it with the Church of Persia, which was Nestorian and subject to the Patriarch of Babylon—every authentic reference from Cosmas of the sixth century to Vasco da Gama, the Indicopleustes of the sixteenth.

Mr Justice Ormsby by consulting, in accordance with the Evidence Act, works of general interest on the subject, not produced in the atmosphere that engendered the particular controversy on which he was called to adjudicate, protected himself from the delusions which darkened the minds of his two Hindu colleagues. He declined to have his hands tied by the cords woven by Ittoop and his congeners; and so with a free hand he cut his way clean through the meshes in which the facts had been entangled. He saw, what every one who keeps his eyes open to all the facts of the case must see, that there have been three distinct periods in the history of the Syrian Church, namely, the Nestorian period, from *c.* 500 to 1599; the Roman period, from 1599 to 1653; and, after twelve years' interregnum of exemption from foreign interference, the Jacobite period, from 1665 to the present day.

Now we have already seen that it was only from the second half of the seventeenth century that the Church of Malankarai began to have any, even a nominal, connection with the Jacobites. We have seen moreover that, during the first two hundred years of this connection, only one metran was consecrated by the patriarch's own hands, and that this did not take place until the last decade of the said period of two centuries;

while, in the course of the other nineteen decades only one metran, who had first been consecrated by his predecessor, received reconsecration at the hands of a foreign bishop believed to have been delegated by the Jacobite Patriarch of Antioch. It cannot be maintained surely in the face of these facts that anything more than the barest and most nominal connection had been established between Malankarai and Mardin until the present generation. During those two hundred years the bishops of Malabar were as a rule consecrated each by his predecessor, those consecrated by foreign bishops, professing to be delegates from the patriarch, being few in number and entirely exceptional.

It seems clear that the precedents of two centuries of bishop-making should be sufficient to attest the use and wont of the diocese, and therefore to show that Mar Athanasius Thomas was consecrated in an orderly and valid manner;[9] and it is not for an interloper, like the Patriarch of Antioch, to come in at the request of a few malcontents, and, by a combination of high-handedness and bigotry, to upset the precedents of two centuries, and to subject the people to a foreign yoke fitted to repress all spiritual progress in Malankarai.

II.

The second condition to be fulfilled by a metran of Malankarai was his acceptance by the people. This was admitted by both parties at the bar and adopted as a test by the bench in trying the case. But it is not pretended by any one that this is a law of the Church, and it is absolutely destitute of precedent in the Church's history. From time immemorial down to an early date in the present century, the office of Metran of Malankarai was hereditary in the Palamattam family; so that, while this particular family furnished metrans for the see, there was no occasion for the people to express their acceptance; and as a matter of fact such acceptance was never asked or given. On the other hand, when the Palamattam family became extinct and the office of metran ceased to be hereditary, a new device was introduced by the Resident. He arranged that the person nominated and consecrated by the preceding bishop should be proclaimed by a royal proclamation, which enjoined on all the people the duty of obedience to the new metran according to the custom of the see. This practice continued down to Mar Athanasius Matthew, who was the last of the royally proclaimed metrans. So long as the practice of issuing royal proclamations lasted, the idea of a formal expression of acceptance by the people is nothing short of ludicrous. In fact it was the abolition (1876) of the practice of making proclamations in favour of particular bishops that seems to have suggested the application of this idea of popular acceptance. The Chief Justice and Mr Justice Sitarama Iyer say that "this contention of the parties (*i.e.*, about acceptance) seems to us to be a new idea, and is due, probably, to a precaution on their part to prevent foreigners sent by the patriarch from assuming the management of the temporalities of the Church, without the consent and against the wishes of the community. . . . It was only after the proclamation, under which the Sirkar disclaimed all connection with the appointment and removal of Syrian metropolitans and explained the effect of its proclamation in favour of any particular metropolitan, that acknowledgment by the people was thought of as the best and safest substitute to adopt. . . . The first case under that system," they add, "happens to be the present." What could more clearly prove that, for this condition of acceptance by the people, there is absolutely no precedent? It forms no part of the law or the past practice of the Church.

Whether it was invented by "the parties" or not, it is a mere phrase and does not amount to a formulated proposition; and, when it came to be expanded and applied to details, neither the judges on the one hand were agreed among themselves, nor the parties on the other. In fact the two Hindu judges who formed the majority in the Royal Court, so expanded the phrase and so defined 'acceptance,' as to its nature and effects, that their ruling will probably be quoted hereafter as a precedent and will acquire all the force of law. Several points, as will appear in further discussion, were practically enacted, but the main point is that it is acceptance by the people which admits a duly consecrated metran to the enjoyment or control of the temporalities of the see. Due consecration qualifies for the exercise of spiritual functions, popular acceptance admits to the management of church property; that is the present ruling.

It does seem strange that the courts should have adopted, as an essential condition of the validity of an appointment to the bishopric of Malankarai, what had never, until the institution of this particular suit, been heard of as a condition for such appointment. The function of the courts of law is to interpret and apply the law to particular cases, not to make it. The courts of Travancore are not, however, the only law courts in the world which have, especially in ecclesiastical cases, framed decisions on the basis of judge-made law.

But we have next to consider the use made of this piece of judge-made law in its application to the circumstances of the present case. It appears that the courts below regarded the question of acceptance by the people as having been settled at the meeting at Mulanthuruthu (June 1876). This announcement, it must be admitted, is surprising; for, in the record of the proceedings of that assembly, there is not a syllable from beginning to end about the acceptance of Mar Dionysius Joseph as metropolitan; and, as a matter of fact, the name of that person occurs only once in the record, and that in an altogether different connection. It appears, however, that the mere fact of his having been *called* metropolitan in the record is what is relied on as binding the individuals who signed it. And this might pass. But before it could be held to bind the whole Church or community to such acceptance, it would be necessary to prove that the meeting was *bona fide* a representative meeting, that the persons who signed did so not as individuals but as duly accredited representatives of churches. In this lies the *crux* of the whole of this section of the discussion. On the proof or disproof of this point depends the decision that must be given on the particular form of question now in hand. Fortunately it is a question which admits of fairly direct treatment.

"The meeting was convoked," says Mr Justice Ormsby, "in part at least by printed summonses addressed, it would appear, to various churches. . . . Now it is a general rule applicable alike to public companies, associations, clubs—and surely no less to religious bodies—that, when the shareholders in such company or the members of such association or body are to be summoned to transact important business, it should be previously and clearly notified to them what that business is. If the object of the meeting at Mulanthuruthu was to elect a metran, or to confirm the appointment of a metran already consecrated by the patriarch, we might reasonably expect that such matter would be explictly stated. But not a reference is made to the subject. The parishioners are exhorted to choose certain persons to speak before the synod, putting them in possession of their views, so that the matters that may be resolved upon may be accepted by you! No hint is given as to what these matters are, except that they are 'the spiritual affairs of our Church in general.' There is indeed a reference to 'disputes and schisms,' but as to what disputes or what schisms, no indication is vouchsafed us."

Of the issue and service of the notice of meeting on all the churches, there was no formal evidence whatever. "All that the evidence on record proves, supposing for a moment that it is beyond suspicion, is that some sort of order, or command, or message, was sent down to some of the churches. But even in the case of these churches, there is absolutely no evidence or next to none, that these 'notices' were duly promulgated in the various parishes, or that one parishioner in fifty knew anything about them." The record of the proceedings of the Synod at Mulanthuruthu, professes to be signed by the representatives of one hundred and two churches, but there were at least one hundred and seventy-five in the diocese, so that some seventy-three churches were not even professedly represented, and there is no proof on record that notice of the meeting was served on the parishioners of these seventy-three churches.

On the other side it is said that "to expect, in a

matter like this, proof of service of notices as we have in civil suits in courts, is to expect an impossibility. It could not be expected that the notices with the acknowledgment of service would be forthcoming. How, then, was the fact to be proved otherwise? It must be only by the evidence of witnesses who had service of notices on them, and who saw notices served on others." Perhaps, but it must be remembered that we are here dealing with what professes to be a regular synod, summoned under direct authority of the patriarch. Are we to suppose, whatever may be said about the inexperience or incapacity of the Syrians in the use of methods of precision, that both the patriarch and his numerous understrappers were incompetent to convene a synod and to conduct its business in such a manner that every item of the proceedings from beginning to end should be capable of verification? Why were printed notices used at all if not for evidential purposes? How much better Menezes managed his business at Diamper in 1599!

Again, 'deeds of consent' are mentioned; that is, commissions which should give express authority to those who held them to act within specified limits on behalf of those who granted them.

They were avowedly documents granted by congregations to delegates who should have authority to attend the Synod of Mulanthuruthu to deliberate and vote at its sittings on behalf of the said congregations. We may pass by the preliminary difficulty of framing 'deeds of consent' on 'notices' so vague. But whether they were properly framed or not, no copy was produced in court; and no verification of their contents was possible. They are said to have been collected and put into a box, and carried off to Mardin by the patriarch. Wherever the fault may lie, nothing effectual was done during the long years of the trial to fetch them back from Mardin and subject them to the scrutiny of the courts. If they could have helped the plaintiff's case, ways and means of fetching them back would have been found; for the plaintiff's case was the patriarch's. But not a single copy ever fell under the eye of the judges. In these circumstances how can it be maintained that the meeting at Mulanthuruthu was a representative meeting?

But we shall be told that some thirty witnesses "swear to having seen deeds of consent given by the people to the representatives that attended the meeting. These deeds of consent contained, *it is said,*[10] authority to the representatives to agree to the resolutions of the meeting on behalf of the people. The witnesses also swear to their signatures in the record. . . . It would be, under the circumstances, unreasonable to decline to hear the evidence of the witnesses who were brought to swear to the production of deeds of consent by the representatives. That is legal evidence of the fact that such deeds were given, *though not to their contents.*[10] All that we want here is that the men who attended the meeting were representatives. Even without the deeds of consent, if the men were competent to represent the community by their position in that community, it would quite answer the purpose." Does not this last sentence mark an extreme position; does it not betray a consciousness of the weakness of the reasoning that immediately precedes it?

At all events, all that has been said seems to me to leave untouched the conclusion arrived at by Mr Justice Ormsby, viz., that "without proof that (1) the persons whose names are appended to the record of the proceedings of the meeting at Mulanthuruthu did really sign, *and* (2) that they were duly authorised to sign, that record becomes absolutely worthless; and, without the record of that meeting's proceedings, there is no sufficient evidence to prove plaintiff's acceptance by the community."

Mark, nevertheless, how this doubtful document is further pressed into the service of the plaintiff's cause, to prove affirmatively his acceptance by the people. The Chief Justice and Mr Justice Sitarama Iyer contend that the question to be answered is, On which side are the majority of the Syrians to be ranked? They find that in addition to the one hundred and two churches represented at the so-called synod of Mulanthuruthu, there are nine more churches admitted by the appellant to contain only adherents of the respondent. "So, adding these nine to one hundred and two, we have clearly one hundred and eleven churches wholly recognising the respondent as their metropolitan." But this reasoning is vitiated by the fallacious assumption, that the men who signed the record at Mulanthuruthu were duly authorised by the churches which they professed to represent. Of this there has been no sufficient proof. In the High Court the same vitiating element appears in the same connection. Mr Justice Narayana Pillay says of twenty-seven churches, each represented by a single individual, that such representation "would be absolutely worthless, if the individual who has signed did so for him alone. But the plaintiff's case is that these individuals, as also the others who signed for the different churches, had written authority from the parishioners of their respective churches to represent them at the meeting." No doubt this is the plaintiff's case, but has he legally *proved* his case? The fact is that the meeting at Mulanthuruthu was a mere caucus, and not a proper synod at all; and the record of its proceedings, even supposing it to be genuine, cannot prove a majority on the side of the plaintiff at that date. It is tolerably certain that *now* Mar Dionysius Joseph has a majority on his side. It would be strange if the repeated decisions in his favour over such a long period of years did not tend to annex to the successful metran a larger following. But that he had at the institution of the suit in 1879 a majority on his side is extremely improbable.

The two Hindu judges of the Royal Court, however, possess marvellous resource. They maintain that the plaintiff had a majority in his favour ten years before the date of the institution of the suit. They seem to have had some misgivings after all about the validity of the proof of plaintiff's acceptance derived from the record of the Mulanthuruthu meeting, and therefore they change their ground. They explain that it is a mistake to suppose Mar Dionysius Joseph was accepted for the first time as metropolitan at Mulanthuruthu. This, they would have us believe, was not the case at all. He was so recognised long before this meeting, and what this meeting did was to ratify the acceptance made long previously.

This is a complete change of front. But let that pass. When did the community first acknowledge Mar Dionysius Joseph as metropolitan? The answer is that it was done as early as 1869; and the sole proof of this surprising discovery is to be found in the veracious utterances of Dionysius himself when he addressed his memorial to the Government of Madras. He then informed his Excellency in Council that "all the Syrian Christians have acknowledged, and do acknowledge him," as metropolitan; and, again in the same document, that "he has the solemn consciousness that almost all the Syrian Christians, as a matter of conscience, lean towards him as their present legally constituted superior and metropolitan."

Special pleading of this kind, made by a man in his own interest, is actually treated as proof of the alleged fact.

But the statements made by the plaintiff under this head were not and could not be true. However discontented the Syrian Christians might have been with Mar Athanasius Matthew in 1869 (and there is no evidence that they were discontented), they would not have dared to express it in any tangible form. They were by the royal proclamation liable to the pains and penalties by which the Sirkar enforces its orders. They were required to obey Mar Athanasius according to the custom of the see; and there is every reason to believe that they were at the date in question perfectly loyal to their metran. At all events, the self-interested pleadings of an ecclesiastic in his own suit can hardly be seriously treated as proof of disputed facts.

It appears to me, therefore, with all deference to the learned persons who have adjudicated otherwise, that the plaintiff failed in both divisions of the great issue to prove his case. Nevertheless Mar Dionysius Joseph sits to-day on the episcopal throne of Malankarai.

CHAPTER XXI.

THE HOPE OF THE FUTURE.

The native States of India as well as other parts of that ancient and famous land are engaged, consciously or unconsciously, in the experiment of assimilating a new civilisation. In proportion to the success of this experiment will the face of society change. Many old things will pass away, and many new things will take their place. The fresh graft on the stately old tree may be expected to develop fruit which in its maturity will be of priceless quality. Our system of education, our administration of justice, our railways, the diffusion of our literature, and the influence of Western ideas communicated in a thousand subtle ways, all tell powerfully on the mind and character, the feelings and manners of the people. These are the high road to position and influence and the chief means by which the people will become available, when political circumstances call for their aid to a larger extent than has hitherto been the case, in the administration of the country. The Brahmans have been from time immemorial the aristocracy, as well as the priesthood, but this is being changed. The idea of an aristocracy of intellect and character is by no means foreign to the aspirations of the best representatives of young India to-day.

Now the people of Malabar as a whole have taken advantage of their opportunities to as full an extent as their fellow-countrymen in other parts; and the native Christians have been conspicuous there as elsewhere for the eagerness and the success with which, in proportion to their numbers, they have availed themselves of the higher education and Western culture. In her young men, accordingly, the hope of the Syrian Church seems, humanly speaking, to lie. Many of these, stimulated partly by the better education and the more intelligent worship of the Protestant churches in their neighbourhood, have found their way to Madras to study there in the Christian and the Presidency Colleges, in the Medical College, and in the Colleges of Law and Engineering, for the higher degrees of the University. Let the minds of these young men be saturated with Biblical truth and spiritual ideas, let their hearts be possessed with intelligent faith, and it will soon be found that the old Syrian bottles will not hold the new wine. Their new spiritual life will demand a higher nourishment than the earthen vessels of the Jacobites can supply. Their character as seen and felt in their daily work, their family life, and their intercourse with their people will gradually tell on the community and may be the indirect means of effecting, more rapidly perhaps than we think, a reformation in Malankarai.

In this view, it is desirable that the people should take their Church affairs into their own hands and manage them without foreign intervention. Did they not throw off the authority of the Pope of Rome at the Coonen Cross in 1653? and why should they tolerate the usurped authority of a remote patriarch who has no intelligent sympathy with them, and little or no interest in the country beyond draining off money annually in the form of *Rasisa*, for which he gives nothing in return? No seminaries of learning, no preaching friars, or other agencies for the spiritual good of the Syrians of Malankarai are maintained by the patriarch.

"Hereditary bondsmen! know ye not,
Who would be free, themselves must strike the blow?"

There is one contingency to which the Syrians and their friends should not shut their eyes. Although there seems no reason to fear that this ancient Church will lapse into heathenism, or otherwise vanish from history in the same way as the sister Church on the Coromandel coast did, yet there is some danger of its being absorbed. With an English Protestant Mission on the one side, and a Roman Catholic Mission on the other, it will be difficult for the Syrian Christians to hold their ground apart. These stronger Churches will doubtless receive from time to time into their respective communions individual members of the Syrian Church; and if this disintegrating process goes on, if the weaker thus gives way to the stronger, if the Syrian Church be absorbed by the more vigorous organisations around her, history will probably interpret her fate as the penalty of intellectual stagnation and lack of faith.

Yet even in this event, the eye of hope, gazing further into the vista of the future, would fain discern the time when the deplorable sectarian differences which characterise our Western Christianity, and which have acquired a foothold to no small extent in India, shall be superseded by a freer and fuller growth of Christian doctrine and spiritual life; and when the Indian Church, reconciling all her sects in a common faith and a common purity, shall hold the unity of the spirit in the bond of peace, and shall in the most comprehensive sense be one. When such a time comes, when there will be one strong Indian Church, the absorption of any particular sect, however venerable, will be abundantly compensated by the ampler life and the larger hope of success in winning the whole of India to Christ, and in contributing the most effective share to the complete spiritual conquest of Asia.

APPENDIX

APPENDIX.

NOTES TO CHAPTER I.

1. See on Travancore, 'The Land of Charity,' by the Rev. Samuel Mateer, F.L.S.; London, John Snow & Co., 1871. Also by the same Author, 'Native Life in Travancore'; London, W. H. Allen & Co., 1883: and on Cochin, 'The Land of the Perumals,' by Francis Day, F.L.S.; Madras, 1863.

2. In addition to the foregoing works, see 'Mirabilia Descripta; or, The Wonders of the East,' by Friar Jordanus, translated and edited by Colonel Yule for the Hakluyt Society, 1863—p. 32: and Robertson Smith's 'Kinship and Marriage in Arabia'; Cambridge University Press, 1885—p. 122.

3. 'The Land of Charity,' pp. 169-175.

4. 'The Life of the Right Rev. Daniel Wilson, D.D.,' by the Rev. Josiah Bateman, M.A.; London, John Murray, 1860—chapter xiv.

NOTES TO CHAPTER II.

1. The list of the seven churches is as follows: *Cranganore*, *Quilon*, *Palur*, *Parur*, *South Pallipuram* or *Kokamungalum*, *Neranum*, *Nellakkul*, called also *Chael* or *Shail*.

2. See 'Lingerings of Light in a Dark Land,' by the Rev.

Thomas Whitehouse, M.A.; London, Wm. Brown & Co., 1873 —p. 18.

3. 'Christianity in China, Tartary, and Thibet,' by M. L'Abbé Huc; London, Longmans, 1857—vol. i. p. 25.

4. Cf. chapter ix., *infra*.

5. 'Decrees of the Synod of Diamper,' session viii., chapter ix., in Hough's 'History of Christianity in India,' vol. ii.

6. See, for example, a short paper by the late Bishop Fennelly of Madras in 'The Catholic Directory' for 1866, under December 21.

7. Catalogue No. 2 of Coins, by Edgar Thurston, Superintendent, Government Central Museum, Madras, 1888.

8. 'The Book of Ser Marco Polo,' iii. 18. It is needful to emphasise the fact that, though the story of King Alfred's sending alms to St Thomas is often adduced in proof or illustration of the belief that St Thomas's body lay in Southern India, it has really no bearing on that question. The 'Saxon Chronicle' simply states that, in the year 883, "Sighelm and Æthelstân conveyed to Rome the alms which the king had vowed (to send) thither, and also to India, to St Thomas and to St Bartholomew." The testimony of later chroniclers is quoted at great length by Sharon Turner in his 'History of the Anglo-Saxons,' vol. ii. pp. 146, 147; but it adds nothing to that of the contemporary writer, except this, that the ambassadors, on their return from India, "brought many foreign gems and aromatic liquors, the produce of the country." It is amusing to notice how difficult Gibbon found it—'Decline and Fall,' chapter xlvii.—to make up his great mind on this small matter. In the text, he talks of St Thomas's shrine, "perhaps in the neighbourhood of Madras," being devoutly visited by Alfred's ambassadors, but he ends a footnote on the subject with the words, "I almost suspect that the English ambassadors collected their cargo and legend [what legend?] in Egypt." It is doubtful whether they went by way of Egypt at all, the Red Sea being closed at the time against European

commerce and European travellers; but, by whatever route Alfred's ambassadors went, they did not go to visit a shrine; they went, as Freeman puts it, "all the way to India, with alms *for the Christians there*, called the Christians of St Thomas and St Bartholomew."—'Old English History'; London, Macmillan & Co., 1871—p. 132.

Notes to Chapter III.

1. See Rawlinson's 'Sixth Oriental Monarchy'; London, Longmans & Co., 1873—p. 87.
2. 'Ecclesiastical History,' i. 13.
3. 'Ante-Nicene Christian Library,' vol. xx. 'Syriac Documents'; Edinburgh, T. & T. Clark, 1871—p. 1.
4. Otherwise referred to in the 'Syriac Documents' as Addæus, or Addai.
5. Otherwise referred to as Aggai, Attai, Achai, Achi.
6. The story of Maris and his successors is told from Bar-Hebræus, Elias of Damascus, &c., in the 'Patriarchate of Antioch,' by the Rev. John Mason Neale, D.D.; London, Rivingtons, 1873.

Notes to Chapter IV.

The story of St Thomas's Indian apostleship as given in the 'Acts of Thomas,' may be read in 'The Ante-Nicene Christian Library,' vol. xvi.

A curious travesty of the 'Acts' was found in a Tamil manuscript now in the Mackenzie Collection. This manuscript is a translation from Latin by Nanapracasa Pillai, a native Christian, who was probably trained by the Jesuits at Pondicherry, in whose library he most likely found the Latin MS. It has been translated into English by the Rev. William Taylor of Madras. See the 'South India Christian Repository' (1837), vol. i. pp. 263-266. According to this travesty St Thomas first landed at the capital of the King of Malabar, then went to Mailapore, at that time ruled by *Candapa Raja* (meant to be the Tamil equivalent of *Gandapha-rasa* or Gondophares).

1. 'Introduction to the New Testament,' by George Salmon, D.D.; London, John Murray, 1885—p. 422; cf. pp. 431, 432.

2. 'History of the Origins of Christianity,' Book VII. chapter xxv.

3. Cf. Matthew xiii. 55; Mark vi. 3.

4. 'Mirabilia Descripta—The Wonders of the East,' by Friar Jordanus; translated and edited by Colonel Yule for the Hakluyt Society, 1863—p. 23, and cf. p. 192 of this volume.

5. Mygdonia is the name of a province in the north-east of Mesopotamia, adjoining Osrohene. This sister-in-law of Misdeus may, therefore, have been either a native of that province or otherwise connected with it by family ties.

6. See his paper on "Coins of Indian Buddhist Satraps with Greek Inscriptions," being No. 7 of 1854, 'Journal of the Asiatic Society of Bengal,' vol. xxiii. pp. 711, 712.

7. This monogram  is thought by Prinsep to be a combination of the *b*, *m*, and *n* of the old Sanscrit alphabet ('Journal, As. Soc. Bengal,' July 1838, p. 553). Professor H. H. Wilson quotes but does not approve this suggestion ('Ariana Antiqua,' p. 340), nor does he suggest any other explanation. Cunningham regards it as a pictorial representation of the compound name *gandaphor* = "sugar-cane crusher," from the circumstance that the outer channels for the cane-juice in a sugar-mill are chiselled in the form of this peculiar monogram.

The Gondophares coins on pages 52, 53 have been copied from Wilson's 'Ariana Antiqua.'

8. Taht-i-Bahi, situated 28 miles N.E. of Peshawur, is an isolated hill, 1771 feet above sea-level, or about 570 feet above the plain. The ruins of a Buddhist city on this hill have yielded many trophies to the archæological explorer. The name is derived from *Bahai*, which in the colloquial means reservoir, so that Taht-i-Bahi = seat of the reservoir. It appears

that, besides two other reservoirs higher up, there is one at the foot of the hill, where it joins the plain, concerning which the people have a tradition that it is connected with the Indus by an underground channel. Hence the name of the hill and the ruins. See 'Archæol. Surv. Ind. Reports,' 1872-73, vol. v. pp. 24, 58, 59.

9. See 'Jour. Roy. As. Soc.' (New Series), vol. vii., art. xviii. (Trübner & Co., 1875), pp. 376 *ss.* It is but fair to note that archæological experts are not agreed about the reading of the inscription on the Taht-i-Bahi stone, and perhaps the rendering given in the text, though the last, is not final.

10. Andropolis was the capital of the Nomos Andropolites. Whether its chief magistrate was entitled to the rank of *Basileus* we do not know. But even if he was not a king, our author would be sure to make him one, as it seems to have been a first principle with him that St Thomas should always have kings for the nursing fathers of his Church.

11. Mommsen's 'Provinces of the Roman Empire,' translated by Professor W. P. Dickson, D.D., LL.D.; London, Bentley & Son—vol. ii. pp. 13, 14.

12. See Colonel Yule's 'Marco Polo,' vol. ii. pp. 335, 336, where additional authorities on this point are quoted.

13. Ante-Nicene Christian Library: 'Works of Hippolytus,' vol. iv. p. 131.

14. The version of the story given in the Latin hymn—"In Festo Sancti Thomæ Apostoli, ad Vesperum"—is rather in favour of a locality, such as Carmana, on the borders of Iran and within the area of sun-worship:—

"Templum solis comminutum
Corruit cum idolo;
Ac metallum pretiosum
Solvitur in pulverem;
Rex illius civitatis
Fugit cum Carisio.

Tunc sacerdos idolorum
Furibundus astitit,

Gladio transverberavit
Sanctum Christi martyrem
Glorioso passionis
Laureatum sanguine."

The whole of this hymn—from the 'Mozarabic Breviary' edited by Cardinal Lorenzana in 1775—is quoted in 'S. Thomas, the Apostle of India,' by the Rev. Ch. Egbert Kennet, D.D.; Madras, Addison & Co., 1882.

15. The name Calamina, as an item of the primitive tradition, seems to have been transferred to the Coromandel coast, and applied to Mailapore ('Voyages and Travels' of Sir John Mandeville, chapter xvi.); and attempts have been made, by means of wild guesses in etymology, to show that the name grew on South Indian soil. (1) Tamil etymologies have been invented for Calamina. (*a*) Some hold that *Cal-ur-mina* and others that *Cal-mel-mina* was the original form of the word, the final *-mina* being, with doubtful legitimacy, affixed as a mere termination. The former word means *rock-city* and the latter *rock-upon*, and both suggestions assume that the rock of the Little Mount was the scene of St Thomas's martyrdom. (*b*) The Abbé Du Bois derived Calamina from *Calamin*, the Tamil name of a well-known fish on the Coromandel coast, thinking that a fishing village, where this particular fish was taken in abundance, might receive from that circumstance its name. [According to Russell, 'Indian Fishes,' 1803, the fish known at Madras as *Calamin* = *Scatophagus Argus*, Cuv. and Val., *Chætogon Argus*, Linn.] (2) A Syriac derivation has been attempted. We are told of a Syriac word *Galamath* = *rock-city* or *hill-town*, which some say is also the meaning of Mailapore. This Syriac name, we are assured, was given to Mailapore by the followers of St Thomas, and it is added by way of explanation that, in the mouths of people who did not use Syriac for their vernacular, *Galamath* became *Calamath*, and *Calamath* became *Calamina*.

Several other examples might be quoted. But enough.

Even supposing that these etymologies were linguistically legitimate, they one and all proceed on false assumptions. Etymologies must be tried at the bar of history, and if they cannot give a fair account of themselves there, they must be considered counterfeit. The etymologies in question all run in the very teeth of history.

16. It has indeed been maintained that the relics were removed from India to Edessa only as late as the year 394, and the 'Chronicle of Edessa' is quoted by Dr Kennet (p. 17), in support of the assertion. But what the 'Chronicle of Edessa' says under the year 394 is this: "They brought the coffin of Mar Thomas the apostle to his great temple in the days of Mar Cyrus, the bishop," which means, not that the relics of the apostle were brought to Edessa then for the first time, but that they were moved from one part of the city to another and deposited in a particular church.

Notes to Chapter V.

1. See Neale's 'Patriarchate of Alexandria'; London, Masters, 1841—p. 16.

2. Ib., p. 18.

3. Ante-Nicene Christian Library: 'Clement of Alexandria,' vol. i. p. 355.

4. 'Ecclesiastical History,' Book V. chapter x.

5. 'Liber de Viris Illustribus,' cap. xxxvi.

6. Ante-Nicene Christian Library: 'Clement of Alexandria,' vol. i. p. 399.

7. 'Letter to Magnus,' Book II. i.

8. 'Ecclesiastical History,' Second Century, Part I. chapter i. § 3.

9. As, for example, by Philostorgius; see chapter v., *infra*.

10. 'Church History'; London, Bohn, 1853, vol. i. p. 114.

11. 'The Indian Empire,' Trübner's Oriental Series (2d edition), pp. 234, 235.

12. For a discussion of the question, see chapter x. of the 'Introduction to the New Testament,' by George Salmon, D.D.; London, John Murray, 1885.

13. See Max Müller's 'Lectures on the Science of Language,' vol. i. lecture 8.

14. Ante-Nicene Christian Library: 'Works of Hippolytus,' vol. ii. p. 131.

15. Rawlinson's 'Sixth Oriental Monarchy,' p. 400.

16. See Alban Butler's 'Lives of the Saints,' St Bartholomew's Day.

17. "The statue by Marco Agrati in the Milan Cathedral, famous for its anatomical precision and its boastful inscription, *Non me Praxiteles sed Marcus pinxit Agratis.*"—Mrs Jameson's 'Sacred and Legendary Art'; London, Longmans, 1888—vol. i. p. 245.

Notes to Chapter VI.

1. Renan quoted by Huc, 'Christianity in China, Tartary, and Thibet'; London, Longmans, 1857—vol. i. p. 66.

2. Neale's 'History of the Holy Eastern Church,' General Introduction; London, Masters, 1850—vol. i. p. 125.

3. 'Ecclesiastical History,' ii. 9-14.

4. Max Müller's 'Chips from a German Workshop,' vol. i. pp. 162, 163.

5. Max Müller, ib.

Notes to Chapter VII.

1. 'History of Christianity in India,' Book I. chapter ii.

2. 'Christ and other Masters'; London, Macmillan & Co., 1875—Part II. chapter ii. p. 81; cf. Kurtz's 'History of the Christian Church' (1864), § 94, 4.

3. Book I. chapter ix.

4. Cf. Genesis xli. 38.

5. 'Apology to Constantius,' § 31.

6. It is possible that Theophilus may have been a Hindu, as from the earliest times there was much commerce between India (Proper) and the island of Socotra. But it seems more probable, as Socotra was included along with Arabia Felix and Abyssinia under the name India, that Theophilus was an Indian in the same sense as the Homeritæ.

7. So far Philostorgius. A few notes from other sources are added to complete the story.

8. See article on "The Ethiopian Church," by the Rev. Dr Reynolds, in Smith's 'Dictionary of Christian Biography.'

9. Muir's 'Life of Mahomet,' new edition; London, Smith, Elder & Co., 1878—Introduction, p. v. The story is also told by Gibbon, 'Decline and Fall,' chapter xlii.

10. Muir, ib.

NOTES TO CHAPTER VIII.

1. Hefele's 'History of the Councils of the Church,' Book IX. chapter iii.

2. 'The Church and the Eastern Empire,' by the Rev. H. F. Tozer, M.A.; London, Longmans, 1888—chapter v.

3. Kurtz's 'History of the Christian Church,' § 82, 3.

4. Etheridge's 'Syrian Churches'; London, Longmans, 1846—pp. 97, 98.

5. 'Nineveh and its Remains,' by A. H. Layard, D.C.L.; London, John Murray, 1849—vol. i. pp. 247, 248.

6. A list of the twenty-five metropolitans is given by Layard, ib., pp. 255, 256.

7. Neale's 'History of the Holy Eastern Church,' General Introduction, vol. i. p. 143. See also Gibbon's 'Decline and Fall,' chapter xlvii.; and, for an account of the inscription at Siganfu, see Huc's 'Christianity in China, &c.,' vol. i.; also 'Calcutta Review' for July 1889.

8. Neale, ib., pp. 151, 152.

Notes to Chapter IX.

1. "It is not necessary to dispute whether the seat of this bishopric was the modern Kalyán or Quilon (Coilam), as the coast from Bombay southwards to Quilon bore indefinitely the name Caliana."—Sir W. W. Hunter's 'Indian Empire,' p. 231.

2. Sir James Emerson Tennent says: "Between the sixth century and the arrival of the Portuguese in the sixteenth, we have but few accounts of the internal condition of the island, and no mention whatsoever of a Christian community."—'Christianity in Ceylon'; London, John Murray, 1850—p. 4.

3. See chapter xi., *infra*.

4. See 'The Manual of the Salem District,' published by order of the Madras Government, chapter i.

5. See an article on "Some Pahlavi Inscriptions in South India" in 'The Indian Antiquary,' vol. iii. (1874) pp. 308-316, by A. C. Burnell, Ph.D., of the Madras Civil Service.

6. We have thus three crosses:—

No.	Where situated.	Date of cross or inscription.
1	In the church on St Thomas's Mount, near Madras.	Seventh or eighth century.
2	In the old church at Cottayam, in North Travancore.	Do. do. do.
3	Do. do. do.	Not earlier than tenth century.

7. 2 Corinthians xiii. 14.

8. See the Decrees of the Synod of Diamper, chapter xiv., decree 14, as given by Michael Geddes in his 'History of the Church of Malabar,' or by Hough in his 'History of Christianity in India.'

9. Joshua xxii.

10. Book III. chapter xviii.

11. 'Cathay and the Way Thither,' by Colonel Yule; Hakluyt Society, 1886—vol. ii. p. 375.

12. 'East Africa and Malabar in the Sixteenth Century,' by Duarte Barbosa; Hakluyt Society—p. 175.

Notes to Chapter X.

1. A census was taken in 1857, when the number of Jews in the Cochin State was 1790. It is a pity that the numbers of the white and the black Jews cannot be had separately.

2. "It would be interesting to know by what steps the name fell into desuetude. Lagarde, who finds in 'Jehovah' the idea of a promise-keeper, supposes that the name fell into disuse in troublous times, when God no longer appeared to care for His people, and when men did not venture confidently to address Him as the fulfiller of His promises. But it seems more natural to suppose that reverence for 'this glorious and fearful name' (Deuteronomy xxviii. 58) engendered a fear to profane it by utterance. . . . In Palestine practice and theory on the point seem to have fluctuated considerably. One tradition tells us that even the priests ceased to utter the name three hundred years before the Christian era. The treatise 'Joma,' on the other hand, affirms that the high priest continued to pronounce the name distinctly on the day of expiation, and 'Berachoth,' ix. 5, even enjoins its use in ordinary salutations."—Professor Robertson Smith in the 'British and Foreign Evangelical Review,' January 1876.

3. See, for instance, Max Müller's 'Lectures on the Science of Language,' sixth edition, vol. i. pp. 230-234.

4. 'Grammar of the Dravidian Languages'; Trübner & Co., 1875—p. 91.

5. Buchanan's 'Christian Researches in Asia,' third edition, 1812—pp. 207, 208.

6. The authorities on the *sasanam* of the Jews of Cochin are the Rev. Dr H. Gundert, of the Basel Mission, in 'The Madras

Journal,' vol. xiii. Part I. pp. 115-146, and Part II. pp. 11-14; A. C. Burnell, Ph.D., in 'The Indian Antiquary,' vol. iii. pp. 333 *ss;* and 'The Manual of the Malabar District,' by William Logan, of the Madras Civil Service; Madras Government Press, 1887—vol. i. p. 208, and vol. ii. Appendix xii.

7. 'History of the Jews,' vol. iii. p. 97.

8. No proper census of Jews exists; but the following totals given in the ninth edition of the 'Encyclopædia Britannica' may be accepted as approximately correct: In Europe, 5,000,000; in Asia, 200,000; in Africa, 700,000; in America, 300,000; in Australia, 20,000: total, 6,220,000.

9. Logan's 'Malabar,' vol. i. pp. 275, 276.

10. 'The Land of the Perumals; or, Cochin Past and Present,' by Francis Day, F.L.S.—chapter viii.

Notes to Chapter XI.

My authorities here are mainly Gundert, Burnell, and Logan, cf. note 5 in chapter ix. and note 6 in chapter x. I am specially indebted to Logan, however, for the materials of this chapter.

1. As the Jewish *sasanam* is frequently referred to in connection with the two Christian *sasanams*, we shall set down the main facts concerning them in tabular form, as follows:—

Sasanam.	Granted to	Date of grant.	King that granted the Sasanam.
No. 1.	Jews.	*c.* 700 A.D.	Bhaskara Ravi Varma.
No. 2.	Syrian Christians.	774 "	Vira Raghava Chakravarti.
No. 3.	" "	*c.* 824 "	Sthanu Ravi Gupta.

2. Dr Burnell thought that Manigramam meant the village of Manes, and therefore believed its first occupants were Manichæans. But there seems to be no historical foundation for

this belief. The name Manigramam more probably means the village of gems.

3. During the period covered by the *sasanams* (700-824), Malayalam and Tamil, at least in their written form, were practically one language. But after the close of this period, Malayalam and the Malayalam-speaking peoples began to draw apart from Tamil and the peoples east of the Ghauts. Logan's 'Malabar,' vol. i. p. 274.

4. Ib., p. 184.

5. Ib., pp. 272, 274, and 275; cf. pp. 261, 262.

6. Ib., p. 187.

7. *Nayan*, Sans. = leader, soldier; pl. *Nayar*. But *Nayar* has come to be treated as if it were singular instead of plural.

8. Logan's 'Malabar,' vol. ii. p. 120.

9. Ib., vol. i. pp. 275, 276.

10. Ib., vol. i. p. 203.

11. *Knaye* Thomas, or Thomas *of Cana*, probably means Thomas *the merchant*. Cf. the use of the word *Canaanite* in Proverbs xxxi. 24 (R.V., margin), and Hosea xii. 7.

12. See Whitehouse's 'Lingerings of Light in a Dark Land,' pp. 303, 304.

Notes to Chapter XII.

1. See Tennent's 'Ceylon,' Part VII. chapter ii.; London, Longmans, 1860.

2. According to the Mohammedans, the Fourth Vedam is the Kuran, the other three being the Hindu, the Jewish, and the Christian.

3. Quoted by Logan, 'Malabar,' vol. i. p. 196.

4. The 'Keralolpatti' "relates how the Zamorin became the most famous of the Malayali rajahs. He seems to have adopted the high-sounding title of *Kunnalakkon*, or king of the hills (*kunnu*) and waves (*ala*). The Sanscrit form of this title *Samudri*, or as it is pronounced by Malayalis *Samutiri* or

Tamutiri (or vulgarly *Samuri* or *Tamuri*), is that by which the chief rajah of this house became known to Europeans as the Zamorin of Calicut."—Logan's 'Malabar,' vol. i. pp. 276, 277.

5. 'Madras Census Report' for 1881, vol. i. § 151.
6. Logan's 'Malabar,' vol. i. p. 108.
7. Ib., p. 295.
8. Hough's 'History,' Book I. chapter iv. § 11.

Notes to Chapter XIII.

1. 'Mirabilia Descripta; or, The Wonders of the East,' by Friar Jordanus; translated and edited by Colonel Yule, C.B., F.R.G.S., for the Hakluyt Society, 1863—pp. x-xii.
2. Ib., p. 23.
3. Ib., p. 24.
4. Ib., pp. 55, 56.
5. Ib., p. vii.—*Columbum* = Quilon; *Catalani* is, according to Colonel Yule, probably the genitive case of Jordanus's father's name.
6. Whitehouse's 'Lingerings of Light in a Dark Land,' p. 78.

Notes to Chapter XIV.

1. "A third of the property of all condemned heretics was confiscated to the use of the Holy Office, another third was assigned for the expenses of the trial, and the last third went to the Crown."—Milman's 'History of the Jews'; London, John Murray (fourth edition), 1886—vol. iii. p. 303.
2. "There were four inquisitions in the Portuguese dominions: in Portugal, those of Lisbon, Coimbra, and Evora; and, in the East Indies, that of Goa. These were all sovereign tribunals, without appeal in all matters within the extent of their respective jurisdictions. Besides these four tribunals,

there was a Grand Council of the Inquisition, in which the Inquisitor-General presided. This was the chief, and whatever was done in the others was reported there."—Dellon's 'Account of the Inquisition at Goa,' chapter xxiii.

3. In Spain and Portugal converted Jews and their descendants to the latest generations were called 'New Christians.' Cf. Milman's 'History of the Jews,' vol. iii. pp. 300-304. It would appear that many such must have immigrated into the Portuguese dominions in India. For, while it is well attested that the Syrian Christians were for a time brought under the jurisdiction of the Inquisition and suffered from its vigilant rigour, there is no evidence that the colony of Jews at Cochin or their Indian proselytes were influenced by Portuguese Christianity, or that they ever came, to any extent at least, within the clutches of the Inquisition.

4. The office of the Second Inquisitor was then vacant.

5. The quotations made in this chapter are from an anonymous translation of M. Dellon's book, published at Hull in 1812. Cf. Captain Marryat's 'Phantom Ship,' chaps. xxxvi., xxxvii., xl.

6. Buchanan's 'Christian Researches in Asia,' pp. 140-162.

7. See 'Calcutta Review,' No. 144 (1881), Art. "The Holy Inquisition at Goa," by E. Rehatsek.

Notes to Chapter XV.

1. Hough's 'History of Christianity in India,' vol. iii. pp. 5, 6.

2. 'Bibliotheca Orientalis' by J. S. Assemanus.

3. The 'Jornada' was translated into French by F. Jean Baptiste de Glen, and published under the title, 'Histoire Orientale,' in 1609. It was also translated into English by Michael Geddes, who was chaplain to the English factory at Lisbon, 1678-83. His 'History of the Church of Malabar,' which includes "the Acts and Decrees of the Synod," was

published, London, 1694. The proceedings of the Synod are reprinted from Geddes by Hough in the second volume of his 'History of Christianity in India,' from which my quotations are made.

4. See Hough's 'History,' for example, vol. ii. pp. 13-18, where the learned author sets down nineteen such particulars under the head of "doctrines and customs," to show how far the Syrian Church "agreed with the Reformed Churches of England, Scotland, and other nations, and in what respects she differed from the Church of Rome."

5. The elder, Matthias, died at Lisbon; the younger, Joseph, visited Rome and Venice, where the information obtained by conversation with him was incorporated in a small volume, and published under the title of 'The Travels of Joseph, the Indian.'

6. Buchanan's 'Christian Researches in Asia,' p. 131.

7. See Alford *in loco*.

8. It was the *Peschito* that the Syrians used, and these are precisely the New Testament books which are wanting in that version. So far, therefore, the statement of facts is correct. Unfortunately there are probably no other cases in which the statements can now be so satisfactorily verified.

9. Diamper, short for Udiamperur, is ten or twelve miles south-east of Cochin.

10. The Native Christians of Malabar were allowed to retain Syriac as their sacred language, and not compelled to adopt Latin; and Rome followed this policy wherever she managed to annex Christians of the Syrian rite to her fold.

11. The extant Nestorian liturgies are those of Nestorius, Addæus and Maris, and Theodore of Mopsuestia. Of three lost Nestorian liturgies the titles only have been preserved,—those of Narses, Barsumas, and Diodorus of Tarsus. One or more of these six may have been used in Malabar before 1599.

12. Hough's 'History,' vol. ii. p. 210.

Notes to Chapter XVI.

1. It is not possible to obtain from the census reports an exact classification. The number of Jacobite Syrians may be taken as approximately 330,000, and the number of Romo-Syrians as 110,000. The number of Protestant Syrians is comparatively small.

Notes to Chapter XVII.

The authorities consulted for Part I. are, 'The Humiliation of Christ,' by the Rev. Professor Bruce, D.D.; Edinburgh, T. & T. Clark, 1881 — chapter ii.: Tozer's 'The Church and the Eastern Empire,' chapter v.: Neale's 'History of the Holy Eastern Church,' General Introduction: Gibbon's 'Decline and Fall,' chapter xlvii. And for Part II., *Judgments* delivered in the Royal Court, or Court of Final Appeal, Travancore, by (1) the Chief Justice and Mr Justice Sitarama Iyer; (2) Mr Justice Ormsby: printed at the Keraladayom Press, Trivandrum, 1890.

1. The metrans or bishops of Malabar were chosen from the Pakalowmattam or Palamattam family, which, according to the Syrian legends, was selected for this distinction by St Thomas himself. The Anandaravan was that member of this family, who, according to their laws of inheritance, was, so to speak, heir-apparent to the Episcopal throne. This practice was undoubtedly very ancient, and it continued till about the middle of the first quarter of the present century, when the Palamattam family appear to have died out. The same practice is still observed by the Nestorians of Kurdistan, among whom the office of patriarch is hereditary, not elective.

2. For the sake of easy reference, a list of the native metrans of Malankarai, from the beginning of the Jacobite *régime*, is here given; with this *caveat*, however, that the dates are only such approximations as can be derived from the somewhat inconsistent materials available:—

Date of accession to office.	Name of metran.	By whom consecrated.	Date of death.	Remarks.
1653	Mar Thomas I.	Mar Gregorius (1665)	1685	Ruled 12 years before consecration.
1685	" " II.	Unknown; perhaps Gregorius.	1686	
1686	" " III.	Mar Ivanius.	1688	
1688	" " IV.	" "	1728	
1728	" " V.	Mar Thomas IV.	1765	
1765	" " VI.	" " V. (1761), and Foreign Prelates (1770).	1808	
1808	" " VII.	Mar Thomas VI.	1809	This metran and the next five following never directly or indirectly received consecration from the patriarch.
1809	" " VIII.	" " VII.	1816	
1816	" " IX.	" " VIII.	1817	
1817	Mar Pulikote Dionysius.	Philoxenos of Tholiyur.	1818	
1818	Mar Punnatharai Dionysius.	" "	1827	
1827	Mar Cheppat Dionysius.	" "	1852	
1852	Mar Athanasius Matthew.	Jacobite Patriarch of Antioch (1842).	1877	First native of Malabar consecrated by the patriarch.

Notes to Chapter XVIII.

On this subject Whitehouse's 'Lingerings of Light in a Dark Land,' chapter xiv., may be consulted.

1. Buchanan visited Malankarai in 1806, and was greatly touched by the condition of the Syrian Church. He resolved on three things: (1) To supply the churches with printed copies of the Syriac Scriptures, which in course of time he did. [It was

perhaps in consequence of this proposal that Mar Dionysius VI. gave to Buchanan an ancient copy of the Scriptures written in Estrangelo Syriac, which he afterwards presented to the University Library at Cambridge.] (2) To have the Scriptures and the Liturgy translated into the vernacular (Malayalam), of which work a beginning was successfully made under Buchanan's direction and at his expense. (3) To negotiate a union between the Syrian Church and the Church of England. The outcome of this thought will appear in the course of the present chapter.

See 'Memoirs of the Life and Writings of the Rev. Claudius Buchanan, D.D.,' by Dean Pearson (1834), Part II. chapters v. and vi., and Part III. Also Buchanan's 'Christian Researches in Asia' (1812), pp. 99-135.

2. See Le Bas' 'Life of Bishop Middleton'; London, Rivington, 1831—vol. ii. pp. 205, 206.

3. The Rev. Joseph Fenn retired on the failure of his health after nine years' absence from England. The Rev. Benjamin Bailey went on furlough in 1831, returned 1834, and finally left Travancore in 1850. He had still twenty years of work in him. He became a rural dean, and the rector of a quiet village in Shropshire. The Rev. Henry Baker went on furlough in 1833, and returned in due course to Travancore, where he worked at his post till his death in 1866.

4. A curious schism took place in the diocese of Malankarai during the episcopate of Mar Thomas VI., called also Dionysius the Great. One Kattumangat Ramban succeeded in persuading a foreign bishop (Mar Gregorius) to give him consecration. When this became known to the native bishop (Mar Thomas VI.), disputes arose which were referred to the Dutch Commodore for settlement. The decision was given against Mar Koorilos (Cyril), as the new bishop was styled. He accordingly fled beyond the limits of Malankarai, and procured land where he built churches and gradually drew away some of the Syrians. The name of the diocese is Tholiyur,

and the village, where the successors of Mar Koorilos, of whom Philoxenos was one, have resided, is called Anjoor.

5. 'Life of the Right Rev. Daniel Wilson, D.D.'; London, John Murray, 1860—chapter xiv.

6. Ib.

Notes to Chapter XIX.

1. Cf. 'Nestorians and their Rituals,' by the Rev. George Percy Badger; London, Masters, 1862—vol. i. p. 71.

2. See 'The Guardian' of 16th September 1874. Also same paper of the 23d *id.* for the patriarch's reply.

3. The seven dioceses were Quilon, Thumpone, Niranom, Cottayam, Arthat, Kantanad, and Ankamali, together with the churches surrounding them respectively. Cf. chapter ii. note 1.

4. See Paper on "The Syrian Christian Church," by the Rev. R. H. Maddox, in 'The Report of the Missionary Conference, South India and Ceylon,' 1879—vol. ii. p. 181.

5. Ib.

6. A new sect sprang up early in 1875 as a result of the extravagances which had marked the revival of religion there in 1873-74. They published in the Malayalam newspapers 'a divine proclamation' to the effect that "there remained only six years from May 1875 until the glorious coming of King Jesus of Nazareth on the fiery cloud." This Six Years Party numbered about 5000, including some 18 Syrian priests and about 300 of the adherents of the Church Missionary Society. The 'party' fell off in numbers long before the failure of its great prophecy; but, while it lasted, it indulged in wild extravagances and caused much anxiety.

Notes to Chapter XX.

1. The Courts, the periods during which this case was on their respective files, and the names of the judges are here mentioned: (1) The Zilla Court of Alleppy, or Court of First In-

stance, 1879-84: *Mr Justice Lafrenais,* and Mr Justice Krishna Menon. (2) The High Court of Travancore, or Court of First Appeal, 1884-86: Mr Justice Narayana Pillay, and *Mr Justice Arianayagom Pillay.* (3) The Royal Court of Travancore, or Court of Final Appeal, 1886-89: the Chief Justice, *Mr Justice Ormsby,* and Mr Justice Sitarama Iyer. The names of the Christian judges are printed in italics. The second of these three was a Roman Catholic.

2. This chapter is mainly a review of the judgments of (1) the Chief Justice and Mr Justice Sitarama Iyer; (2) Mr Justice Ormsby.

3. The properties consisted of (*a*) lands, the seminary, the Church, and other buildings valued at 72,700 fanams; (*b*) funded moneys, articles of furniture, and other moveable property, valued at 343,432¼ fanams; (*c*) mitres, crosses, staves, jewels, with vestments and other paraphernalia belonging to the Syrian metran as such, valued at 9300 fanams. The total value of the contested property was therefore 425,432¼ fanams, or about Rs. 60,776.

4. It was maintained in evidence by the defendant-appellant that a Syriac manuscript existed in the time of Mar Athanasius Matthew, which had unfortunately been stolen. It was said to contain "the history of the meeting of the Fathers of Malankarai to draw up canons." It was also described as having been "written and left behind by the primitive metrans of Malankarai," the writing having been "kept up by metrans after metrans from time to time." From what metran's time it began, or at what metran's time it ended, witness could not affirm. But "looking at those papers [*sic*] they appeared to be 1500 or 1400 years old. Those of the least age would be between 40 and 50 years old." Well may we ask incredulously, Is the defendant-appellant also among the experts? Nevertheless, the Chief Justice and Mr Justice Sitarama Iyer, who disbelieved the story of the theft, believed that some of the so-called papers were 1500 years old. They were willing

even to add to the great age of the manuscript; for they obligingly inform us that "the existence of a manuscript history of the Malankarai Syrian Church, almost from the second or third century, in the seminary in the possession of the appellant, and its antiquity and authenticity admit of no doubt. That such a record will satisfactorily and conclusively solve the question now under consideration equally admits of no doubt"!! —*Credat Judæus.*

5. The work on which the plaintiff most relied, and which seems to have been mainly followed by the two learned Hindu judges in the Royal Court, though considered inadmissible by Dr Ormsby, was a 'History of the Syrian Christians,' published in 1869, by Ittoop. It is written in Malayalam and has never been translated. It follows the lines of the local tradition.

6. "It may be objected that all this evidence is open to suspicion as the testimony of partisans. The objection is not without foundation. It may be said that all, or almost all, the evidence in this case is open to like objection. Indeed, having critically examined it, I entertain no doubt that a very great part of the oral evidence adduced on both sides is altogether worthless."—Ormsby, pp. 95, 96.

7. See Neale's 'Patriarchate of Antioch,' p. 119.

8. See Hefele, who gives the complete text of the twenty; and see Gibbon's note, chapter xlvii.

9. The fifteenth issue in the Court of First Instance runs: Is the first defendant a duly consecrated bishop or not? Mr Justice Krishna Menon replies: "The first defendant was undoubtedly consecrated by the late Athanasius and Koorilos of Anjoor, and his consecration may be held to be valid to a certain extent;" and after defining this *extent*, the learned judge concluded, "but the validity of the first defendant's consecration need not be decided in this case

10. The italics are mine.

INDEX.

PRINTED BY WILLIAM BLACKWOOD AND SONS.